Whitewashing the Movies

Whitewashing the Movies

Asian Erasure and White Subjectivity in U.S. Film Culture

DAVID C. OH

Rutgers University Press

New Brunswick, Camden, and Newark, New Jersey, and London

Library of Congress Cataloging-in-Publication Data

Names: Oh, David C., author.

Title: Whitewashing the movies: Asian erasure and white subjectivity in U.S. film culture / David C. Oh.

Description: New Brunswick: Rutgers University Press, [2021] | Includes bibliographical references and index.

Identifiers: LCCN 2020040334 | ISBN 9781978808621 (paperback) | ISBN 9781978808638 (hardcover) | ISBN 9781978808645 (epub) | ISBN 9781978808652 (mobi) | ISBN 9781978808669 (pdf)

Subjects: LCSH: Asian Americans in motion pictures. | Whites in motion pictures. | Ethnicity in motion pictures. | Motion pictures—United States—History—20th century. | Motion pictures—United States—History—21st century.

Classification: LCC PN1995.9.A78 O43 | DDC 791.43/6529957—dc23

LC record available at https://lccn.loc.gov/2020040334

A British Cataloging-in-Publication record for this book is available from the British Library.

This book is dedicated to my partner, Eunyoung, and my children, Noah and Aaron.

Contents

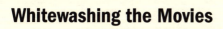

Whitewashing the Movies

Introduction

● ● ● ● ● ● ● ● ● ● ● ● ● ● ● ● ● ● ● ●

Matt Damon addresses *The Great Wall* whitewashing controversy: "I Take That Very Seriously."
—*People*

Whitewashing Controversy Still Haunts *Doctor Strange*
—*USA Today*

Sony Defends *Aloha* after White-Washing Criticism
—*Variety*

Ghost in the Shell's Whitewashing: Does Hollywood Have an Asian Problem?
—*The Guardian*

Netflix Whitewashed Its *Death Note* Remake, and That's Not Even the Only Reason It's Problematic
—*Cosmopolitan*

Attempting the Impossible: Why Does Western Cinema Whitewash Asian Stories?
—*The Guardian*

1

In the past few years, conversations about the underrepresentation of people of color in film have shifted to the reason for their invisibility—Whiteness[1]. More specifically, online activists have criticized films for whitewashing racial difference. The headlines above are one manifestation of the popular attention paid to White hypervisibility in the stories of racial others. Another is online activism, which has called for greater symbolic inclusion in Hollywood. This was most visible in #OscarsSoWhite, a Twitter hashtag created by April Reign, to publicly mock the Academy Awards' lack of nominees of color (Harris, 2017, February 20). Feeling left out of the perceived Black–White binary of #OscarsSoWhite, William Yu, a digital strategist created a new hashtag, #StarringJohnCho, a space for Yu to share photoshopped movie posters with John Cho as the male lead (Rogers, 2016, May 10). The purpose, though light-hearted in tone, was to challenge the racial alignment of the White leading man. Perhaps feeling empowered with grassroots cyberactivism, Asian American celebrities, such as Constance Wu, Daniel Dae Kim, BD Wong, Margaret Cho, Ming-Na Wen, and George Takei have used their platforms to criticize the whitewashing of Asian/American[2] characters and stories (Hess, 2016, May 25). Yet despite their activism and the increased racial sensitivity around the 2016 Academy Awards with #OscarsSoWhite, the Oscars featured a sight gag that used three Asian American children to represent PricewaterhouseCoopers' accountants (Hu and Pham, 2017; Lopez and Pham, 2017; Magnan-Park, 2018). In response, Sandra Oh, Ang Lee, George Takei, and other Academy members signed a letter that decried the use of Asian Americans as the butt of a racial joke (Hess, 2016, May 25).

Racist imagery that features Asian Americans and whitewashing, then, have come into the vernacular as a useful discursive device to challenge the symbolic erasure of people of color. As the actor BD Wong is reported to have said, "The term 'whitewashing' is new, and it's extremely useful" (Hess, 2016, May 25). Although the language may be new, the practice is not. In cinematic history, White actors have often taken Asian roles, notably dressed in Asian caricature, a practice called "yellowface" (Ono and Pham, 2009). Prominent examples include *The Good Earth* (1937), a Pearl Buck adaptation in which Luis Rainier won a Best Actress Academy Award, and *Broken Blossoms* (1919), a silent film starring Richard Barthelmess as Cheng Huan. This is the type of whitewashing criticism made about *Aloha* (2015), which starred Emma Stone as a mixed-race[3] Chinese, Hawaiian, White woman. Another common type of whitewashing is the replacing of Asian characters with White ones, a criticism made about *Dr. Strange* (2016) and *Death Note* (2017). Finally, whitewashing arguments have been made about movies that center White subjectivity in Asian worlds. *The Great Wall* (2016) was particularly pilloried for its insertion of Matt Damon, a popular White actor, in a Chinese–U.S. coproduction about

Chinese heroes that save the nation from monster attacks. *Ghost in the Shell* (2017), too, was criticized for starring Scarlett Johansson, a White actress, in what activists argued to be a Japanese character (Major Motoko Kusanagi) and for centering Whiteness in an imagined Asian fantasy world.

Despite the salience of whitewashing in the cultural terrain, the only scholars who have published work in this area at the time this book was penned is Nishime (2017b), who links whitewashing to yellowface as its historical precedent, such as in *Cloud Atlas* (2012); Magnan-Park (2018), who understands whitewashing as leukocentrism that commits "representational racial genocide" by whitening people of color (p. 135), such as in *Aloha*; Hu and Pham (2017), who argue that whitewashing involves processes of erasure and invisibility; and Lopez (2011), who argues that whitewashing is the erasing of Asian characters in ways that are narratively not obvious, such as in *21* (2008). As Hu and Pham (2017) make clear, invisibility has been central to the history of Asian Americans in cinema, and gaining visibility has been central to Asian American media activism. As such, understanding whitewashing as a process of erasure is consistent with the first of the aforementioned uses of whitewashing in popular discourse, and Lopez's (2011) argument fits the second—replacing Asian characters with White characters—although she delimits whitewashing only to cases in which the replacement is inconspicuous.

This raises questions about what should be understood as the "correct" definition of whitewashing. Does the conspicuousness matter? Is whitewashing specific to the replacement of the character or the actor? Can whitewashing be expansive enough to be used in cases in which there is not replacement but displacement? Before conceptualizing the term, it is helpful to deconstruct the word "whitewashing." Outside the application to racial representation, whitewashing most often refers to the whitening of a surface or the glossing over a transgression. Together, the definitions suggest that blight has been covered over with a white veneer. From the perspective of White normativity and White supremacy, the presence of the racial other is understood as the polluting agent that Whiteness covers. As R. G. Lee (1999) noted in his book about the construction of the "Oriental" as an alien presence in U.S. popular culture, Asian Americans have long been depicted as contaminating White society.

Because ideology is not divorced from its historical past, whitewashing can be understood as a historically continuous need to prevent the ideological spread of the Asian contaminant while telling exotic stories of White adventure and identity. It is within this context that I conceptualize whitewashing as a symbolic intervention of Whiteness that erases Asian/American subjectivity by replacing and displacing it with White subjectivity, thus rendering Asian/Americans as objects in their own stories.[4] I understand whitewashing as ideologically linked to a colonial impulse that has been cultivated within Western

European societies for centuries and that has made it to U.S. shores through immigration laws that favored European immigrants. Early European immigrants borrowed from these stories and created their own as they engaged in settler colonialism of the United States. Based in a Eurocentric, White-centric worldview, new stories formed and comingled with new waves of European immigrants, who brought their stories and their worldviews with them.

In their widely cited essay, Tuck and Yang (2012) name three different forms colonialism has taken: (1) external colonialism—the plundering of natural resources; (2) internal colonialism—the domination of marginalized, racially marked others; and (3) settler colonialism—a combination of external and internal colonialism. Like whitewashing, for these forms of colonialism to earn consent (at least in the West), the moral decay of White domination must be hidden. The invisibility works hegemonically because the oppression is unseen and is hidden behind a whitewashed veneer. When activists reveal the decay behind the surface, it is dismissed as radical hyperbole, or playing the "race card." Looking below the surface, whitewashing plunders the stories and histories of people of color, which has ideological resonance with the exploitative motivations of external colonialism. Like settler colonialism, whitewashing's displacement of people of color and replacement with White characters stakes symbolic territorial claims, moving people of color from the position of subject (sympathetic, relatable, and often heroic) to the position of object (despised, pitied, or relegated to being a helper). Whitewashing colonizes the imagination, taking from people of color to benefit White racial hegemony. I do not mean to overdetermine colonialism; rather, this is to say that although the era of high colonialism ended in the mid-twentieth century, investments in White supremacy have not been overturned and the stories have not been abandoned. Instead, there have been hegemonic adjustments that have resulted in more "genteel" forms of White racial hegemony in the West, including the United States, and neocolonial relations around the globe (Prashad, 2001, p. 38).

Then as now, the stories are not simply harmless representations; they have material consequences. As poststructural scholars have pointed out, discourse constructs social reality, and these worldviews, in turn, shape human relations. For instance, the stories of White benevolence hide modern forms of Western neocolonial exploitation and U.S. imperialism. Stories that erase racial others and replace them with White characters naturalize the racelessness that White people benefit from, and it centers White people in all parts of the world, despite their heritage ties to Europe, the second smallest continent by landmass. Ideologies of White benevolence, leadership, humanity, and superiority benefit White people in all corners of the world (Croucher, 2009), particularly as U.S. media have dominated global flows (Kraidy, 2005; Thussu, 2007). In the U.S. cultural industries, more specifically, White men dominate behind and in front of the camera (Smith, Choueiti, and Pieper, 2016). Yuen (2017) notes, "With history of exclusion and no legal protection, actors of color continue to face stunted opportunities in mainstream film and television" (p. 13). This is because C-suites in the entertainment industries have the least diversity in the U.S. corporate world, leading to a privileging of White-centered stories. In turn, the most influential agents are reluctant to hire actors of color (Yuen, 2017). Actors of color are consigned to a limited number of race-specific roles while White actors can play "raceless" roles as well as roles written about people of color. On the other hand, it is nearly impossible for actors of color to play White roles (Yuen, 2017). This is despite the fact that diverse production staffs and casts have frequently been box office successes (Yuen, 2017).

Returning to the three vernacular discourses of whitewashing mentioned earlier, the representations provide a frame in which meanings are produced. In the case of modern-day yellowface, it is an erasure that asserts that the physical presence of whiteness is more worthy, desirable, and sympathetic than Asian/Americans. Implicitly, it argues that the physical presence of Asianness is contemptuous and unworthy. Furthermore, yellowface as a mask asserts White representational and identity flexibility that allows Whiteness to be any other identity (Nishime, 2017b) while also denying not only that same flexibility to Asianness but also denying Asian/Americans their own identities. For instance, in *Cloud Atlas*, White actors play different racial identities so that audiences understand that the character is reborn into different bodies. What appears to have slipped the director's attention is that the same narrative goal could have been accomplished by replacing Jim Sturgess, the male lead, with an Asian American actor who can play White. This would have been counterrepresentational as it would grant Asianness the representational dexterity that White stories have long held. Similarly, *Dr. Strange* (2016) was criticized for whitewashing the role of "The Ancient One," reimagined as a Celtic woman in Tibet rather than a Tibetan mystic. The director, Scott Derrickson, famously claimed that he chose Tilda Swinton, a White woman, to play the role to avoid stereotypes of Asian mysticism (Lawler, 2016, November 7). Although the intention was laudable, his choice to whitewash to avoid stereotyped representations speaks to its familiarity. The filmmakers could, for instance, have chosen to have a Tibetan woman monk, who had learned ancient Celtic mysticism. This simple reversal would productively play with the stereotypes that the director said he wanted to avoid. Thus, the first form of whitewashing allows for White representational flexibility while denying the same to Asian/Americans.

The second form of whitewashing is perhaps the most direct example—the replacement of Asian/American stories and people with White characters, thus erasing Asianness entirely. Unlike yellowface, the signifiers of Asianness are replaced nearly entirely. Asianness is rendered invisible in stories that are usually based in some historically real event or real people. This is the fullest version of symbolic annihilation,[5] as stories about Asian/Americans become stories about interesting or sympathetic White people. The clearest and often cited example of this is *21* (Lopez, 2011). Seemingly embroiled in whitewashed representations, Jim Sturgess, an English actor, replaces the real-life Jeff Ma, an Asian American MIT student, who along with other Asian American students and an Asian American professor, John Chang, "cheat" Las Vegas casinos by counting cards (Headley, 2010, July 2). Whitewashed representations symbolically annihilate and deny Asian/Americans' existence by plundering stories that might demonstrate that Asian/Americans are interesting, with compelling, complex lives.

The final use of whitewashing refers to White characters who are centered in Asian stories and worlds. This is perhaps provocative to include in the book as no other scholar has understood this as whitewashing because it does not actively erase Asian/American subjectivities. There is no canonical text whose character was cast as White in the transition to the silver screen nor stories about Asian/Americans whose stories were reimagined as White. Thus, some critics would argue that centering Whiteness in Asian fictional worlds is not an erasure. I would argue, however, for its inclusion. Activists and critics' frustration with *The Great Wall* as whitewashed, I believe, is not inconsistent with whitewashing's erasure of Asianness, the centering of White subjectivity, and a colonial fantasy of White people as the defenders and saviors of people of color. This centering displaces Asian characters. Although there was no Asian character written out of a script, the script's reimagination of an Asian world led by a White savior figure displaces Asian heroism in favor of imagined White valor. To understand the audacity of this narrative trope, it may be helped with an imaginative reversal. For instance, a reversed, counterhegemonic story might feature a disenchanted Chinese soldier who travels across Europe and lands in the U.S. colonies during its Revolution against the British. There, the soldier gives up his former training to become, in a matter of months, the best musketeer in the Continental Army. He discovers his true, heroic purpose in the new lands with Betsy Ross, his lover, and George Washington, his loyal sidekick, as he leads his ragtag collection of colonists against the British forces.

The hypothetical example is meant to illustrate the "commonsense" but also the representational violence in the displacement of Asian/American leads with White characters. The direction of this displacement is reflective of a colonizing imagination of Asian/American cultures and subjectivities. It can symbolically hide Western-produced global inequalities by positioning the White figure as a sympathetic, even victimized, figure. A more plausible account might include the legacies of Western colonialism and military adventurism. For instance, *The Last Samurai* (2003) rehabilitated army captain Nathan Algren (Tom Cruise), whose personal reclamation symbolically marked the United States' moral recovery after its decimation of Native Americans and which glossed over the role of the United States' forced arms sales to Japan that initiated the Meiji Restoration and the later Japanese colonial empire.

Furthermore, in these worlds, it produces notions of White exceptionalism. Even in worlds in which White people are an outlier, they are the most spectacular in their demonstrations of heroism for a people that are not their own. Through their heroism, White characters are changed, often morally restored but certainly more self-actualized. Thus, Asian worlds exist for the sake of the White heroes to facilitate their growth. Asianness is the context, then, of White subjectivity. It is rendered hypervisible but unimportant except to the extent that it enriches White people. Asians affirm the White hero, almost invariably a man, or else they are relegated to the role of the "bad guy" (Tierney, 2006). In this third type of whitewashing, it is not a distaste for Asianness as is the case for the previous two types; rather, it makes Asianness acceptable only when it affirms Whiteness and the right of White people to assert their central, hypervisible place in Asian worlds.

Studying Whitewashing Matters

There is a long and well-established literature that argues that media are a major socializing institution that shapes understanding of the world (Hall, 2003; Kellner, 1995; Lippmann, 1927). Whitewashing as a particular form of media representation is important to study because as Shohat and Stam (1994) argue, not casting a community to represent itself is triply problematic; it implies that the community is unworthy of self-representation, incapable of self-representation, and unworthy of concern. As offended communities push back, there has been a coalescing interest around the recently developed lexicon. Yet despite the deployment of the term to resist White racial hegemony, whitewashing has been inadequately theorized (Nishime, 2017b). In fact, there are no recent books that address media representations of Whiteness (although there are several books on Whiteness as a racial standpoint or social construction). The most recent, notable book that addresses Whiteness and media is Dyer's *White* published in 1997. Another important book that specifically addresses Hollywood's construction of Asianness vis-à-vis the West is Marchetti's book *Romance and the "Yellow Peril": Race, Sex, and Discursive Strategies in Hollywood Fiction* published in 1993. The recent interest in whitewashing is a meaningful opportunity to revisit the question of mediated Whiteness in relationship to Asianness. Indeed, that is the purpose of this book. It blends Marchetti's interest in Hollywood's imagination of Asianness in relationship to a White self and Dyer's interest in understanding the construction of Whiteness within this historical, representational moment in which whitewashing has become a common filmic response to the White imagination and its relationship to Asianness.

In this historical moment in which the population is moving toward a more diverse nation and in which (racial) politics have become more divisive, Whiteness has become more visible (Nakayama, 2017). This is truer now with the emboldening of White racial politics since President Trump's campaign and eventual election. Understanding Whiteness is necessary to an antiracist project because its construction is what justifies systems of racial oppression and privilege, so to hope for a more just world requires understanding what is created as well as what is destroyed (Supriya, 1999). "As the concerns about race continue within the United States, it is important to expand the research on representations of Whites in film as a means to better understand race relations from different perspectives" (Banjo and Jennings, 2016, p. 19). To leave Whiteness invisible would mean only seeing the harms of racism without understanding the accrued privileges, and partial knowledge can only lead to partial change. Asianness, in particular, is a useful lens through which to see the construction of Whiteness because Asian/Americans represent new threats to White racial hegemony in the United States and the Western racial order across the world. As the Census reports, Asian Americans continue to be the fastest growing racial group in the country (Holland, 2016, June 23). With demographic shifts and the threat of antiracist movements, White people have become increasingly anxious and Whiteness is increasingly visible as they perceive themselves to be victims of multiculturalism (Gabriel, 1998; Gilroy, 2012; Johnson, 2017; Kennedy, 1996).

Outside the United States, China has increasingly been viewed as an outsized danger (Ono and Jiao, 2008). Its economic might, military ambitions, and political influence have raised the specter of a new "yellow peril" threat, which leads to an urgency to reify the Western global racial order. The discourse of threat has been particularly amplified during the Trump administration. Yet even so, the United States and other Western nations find their economic interests deeply entangled with China, thus producing an ambivalence rather than simple vilification. North Korea also figures deeply in the U.S. imagination as a foreign, cartoonish threat. Therefore, understanding whitewashing matters because it allows a productive opportunity to see Whiteness through its construction of the Asian other, and this, in turn, can lead to progressive social change that makes visible the White imagination of itself.

Because whitewashing is a relational project, the purpose of the book is threefold. The first is to understand White self-construction, the second is to deconstruct representations of the Asian other, and the third is to engage my scholarly imagination to apply cultural theory to imagine inclusive representation and its ideological implications. Like Yu's #StarringJohnCho hashtag, the goal is to imagine the lead as an Asian/American character and to determine whether casting changes alone would be a sufficient response. To theorize whitewashing, I draw primarily on the work on mediated representations of Whiteness, the White imagination of Asia/ns, cultural appropriation of the racial other, and symbolic annihilation. Returning to the conceptualization provided earlier of whitewashing as the intervention of Whiteness into the person and the world of the racial other in ways that center White subjectivity, I draw on the literature on whitewashing, postcolonialism, cultural appropriation, and symbolic annihilation to consider the three uses of whitewashing: (1) be(com)ing the other, (2) interjecting the White self into the story of the racial other, and (3) being centered in the world of the other.

Invisible Power of Whiteness

My own interests in Whiteness began as I questioned enduring representations of Asian America. To not interrogate Whiteness in that work would be a purposeful omission. It would be akin to feminist critique that does not deconstruct patriarchy or queer critique that does not challenge heteronormativity. In this way, to really understand racial marginalization means understanding racial privilege. At academic conferences, I have heard colleagues claim that it is no longer theoretically interesting to study Whiteness. The critique is anchored in good intentions, or at least I hope that it is, but it is too reductive. The criticism tends to be that it is already well known that Whiteness leads to problematic representations of Others and more heroic or sympathetic representations of self. This, of course, is true in broad strokes, but where it matters is the particular ways Whiteness adapts (Dyer, 1997). In its colonial past up to the latter part of the twentieth century, it was hypervisible as a grand organizing logic of White supremacy (Pieterse, 1992), and recently, it has shifted into more subtle "new racism" that locates racism only in individual racist bigotry, excusing and being blind to structural racism (Prashad, 2001). Whitewashing, then, is an expression of White representational strategies that reveal a particular way the discursive work of Whiteness operates.

I understand Whiteness to be a discursive strategy that benefits White supremacy (Nakayama and Krizek, 1995). As such, I should plainly argue that Whiteness is not a proxy for White people, but it is about a particular discursive strategy that normalizes White racial hegemony. This separation of bodies and discourses is not meant as an excuse because Whiteness has material and discursive advantages for White people and because Whiteness is furthered actively or in passive complicity by many White people (Sullivan, 2006); however, I make an intentional distinction because it would be intellectually and morally problematic to argue for racial determinism in which White people are assumed to only be hegemonic agents of Whiteness discourses. Although it is more likely White people are invested in Whiteness because of accrued benefits (Lipsitz, 1998; Sullivan, 2006), this is not necessarily the case as antiracist White people, that is, woke White folks to use the current vernacular,

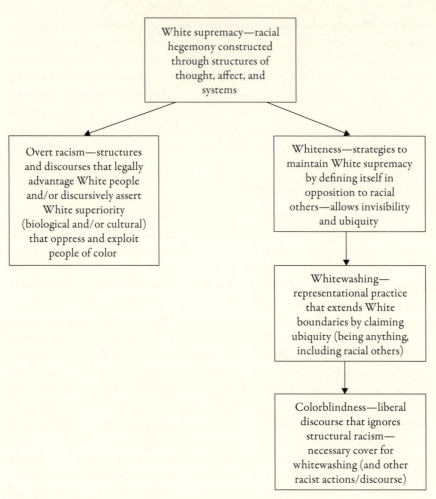

FIG. 1 White supremacy, whiteness, whitewashing, and color blindness

exist and are important allies in any movement for critical multiculturalism (see Shohat and Stam, 1994). Furthermore, people of color, including Asian Americans, are not exempt from advancing discourses of Whiteness.

The other necessary separation is between Whiteness and White supremacy (see figure 1). I understand White supremacy as a hegemonic system that oppresses people of color and advantages White people, providing greater access to and control over symbolic and material resources. While White supremacy is often referenced in terms of the harms caused to people of color, White supremacy's other manifestation is White privilege, the unearned advantages granted simply because of racial identification as White (McIntosh, 1988|2004). The goal for White supremacy is primarily, I believe, to secure greater access to material and symbolic racial privilege. Historically, White supremacy has been invested in the belief in White people's moral and intellectual superiority (Shohat and Stam, 1994). Distorting the story of Noah's sons and claiming divine providence, White supremacy justified colonialism and a hierarchical view of the world that naturalized the tyranny of colonial domination (Pieterse, 1992). Today, White supremacy is openly mocked as a relic of a historical past while at the same time tacitly supported as an organizing racial logic. It is important to acknowledge, however, that fears of shifting geopolitical power and U.S. racial composition has led to a more visible acceptance of White supremacy as demonstrated in President Trump's thinly veiled racism, the rise of the "alt-right," increased membership and activity in White supremacist and nationalist groups, and increased right-wing, nativist political movements in the United States, Australia, and Western Europe. That said, Whiteness still most often operates as a normative, invisible, and universal logic, particularly in its onscreen representation.

Whiteness is the discursive tool used to secure these advantages (Lipsitz, 1998), and it is to the mechanism through which this happens that I now turn. My understanding of Whiteness is deeply informed by Dyer's (1988, 1997) groundbreaking work on Whiteness in film and Nakayama and Krizek's (1995) foundational article on Whiteness in communication studies. Dyer's emphasis is on the seemingly paradoxical dual nature of Whiteness as everything and nothing, in particular, as he draws on metaphors of White as color and as light. It is everything insofar as White characters on screen can play any identity and fit into any cultural space. This, of course, is the central conceit of whitewashing that the audience does not find the presence of Whiteness to be peculiar or symbolically colonizing. The paradox of not seeing whitewashing's hypervisibility is exactly what secures Whiteness's invisibility. The presence of White characters in Asian worlds has to be accepted as normal regardless of how much narrative jiujitsu films must make to justify the presence of White people. At the same time, Whiteness is a nearly empty signifier, carrying no particular meaning and certainly not having in Western cinema, at least, a defined character. Although there are stereotypes of White ethnic or other subgroups, there are very few, if any, well-known stereotypes that embody the whole of White people as a racial category. This paradox is necessary for Whiteness to function as it does because it must mean nothing in order to be anything, and by being anything, it is nothing in particular. In contrast, people of color are consigned specific, restricting stereotypes that are applicable regardless of where they are in the world. For example, despite the size and diversity of communities across Asia and the Asian diasporic communities around the globe, we are understood as embodying the same racial stereotypes.

Nakayama and Krizek (1995) advance the argument by claiming that this dual nature is a strategic rhetoric. Borrowing de Certeau's (1984|2011) distinction between strategy and tactics, they argue that the discursive work of

Whiteness normalizes itself as universal while remaining invisible, allowing it to go uninterrogated. Whiteness claims the majority while conflating itself with national belonging; White is U.S. American, and White is the majority. In this way, White people who use Whiteness rhetoric refuse racial self-labeling, viewing it as only a state of being rather than a discursive formation. Whiteness refuses to be marked directly but only indirectly as *not* being or *not* having the perceived characteristics of people of color. Although Nakayama and Krizek's (1995) work was not focused on representation, their conclusions have guided media studies research within a communication framework as the strategies that produce Whiteness in everyday discourse finds expression in popular culture. In an adaptation by Projansky and Ono (1999), they claim that strategic whiteness is "a history of modifications to renegotiate the centrality of white power and authority" (p. 152). They point out that Whiteness is self-protective and responsive to discursive challenges (Projansky and Ono, 1999). All the while, the goal, as several media scholars have noted, is for Whiteness to function as an invisible norm (Butterworth, 2007; Chidester, 2008; Dubrofsky, 2013; Shome, 1996). As I have argued elsewhere, maintaining the project of Whiteness requires well-known stereotypes of racial Others in order for the invisible norm to be hidden yet perceptible (Oh, 2012). Whiteness displaces race on people of color, overdetermining their difference while also exhibiting mastery over them, to secure the benefits of invisibility that create White privilege (Kennedy, 1996).

As Said (1978) observed three decades ago in his foundational work on Orientalism, the Oriental Other is constructed as an ahistorical, negative identity that constructs a positive self in contrast. Similarly, people of color within and outside the borders of the United States, including Asians and Asian Americans, are Othered to project a positive White self. Indeed, the distinction between Asian and Asian American is often blended in the White imagination, leading Palumbo-Liu (1999) to popularize the use of "Asian/American" to linguistically capture the lack of differentiation. When relevant, I will also use the term to refer to the racial construction of Asians and Asian Americans as lacking meaningful difference within White racial logics. Racist representations of Asian/Americans work as controlling images to construct White normality (Chan, 2009; Hamamoto, 1994) because without those defined at the margins, it would be more difficult to center Whiteness (Shome, 1996). For this purpose, Asian/Americans and Black Americans are represented as binary opposites—hyperfeminine and hypermasculine, robotic and primal (Oh, 2012). Thus, Whiteness always has a constitutive, relational quality. This is usually difficult to see, however, as Whiteness has successfully shifted much of the progressive dialogue about race toward disadvantages faced by people of color and much of the conservative dialogue toward "American" disadvantage, in both cases hiding Whiteness. The former replaces responsibility with sympathy, and the latter conflates nation and race, implicitly reifying the dream of a White America. Even liberal racial discourse has shifted primarily from proactive racial justice toward neutral "colorblind race talk" (Bonilla-Silva, 2006, p. 54), the effect of which, intentional or not, is to roll back antiracist gains (Ono, 2010).

The idea of color-blind racism is sometimes also called postracialism or postracism. Though postracialism is more commonly used, I suppose, to blunt the critique of discourses about the end of racism, I prefer postracism because it avoids the tendency to talk around racism (DiAngelo, 2011; Frankenberg, 1993). Postracism more clearly signals that in the current historical moment, many are invested in believing that race no longer matters in shaping people's life outcomes because racism, at least systemic racism, has been relegated to the past (Enck-Wanzer, 2011; LeBlanc, 2018; Milazzo, 2015). The more common use of postracialism to describe this condition ironically sidesteps explicit discussions of racism just as it calls into question some White people's defensive avoidance of discussions of racism. Of course, the common way to sidestep discussions of race is to proclaim color blindness as a nonracist ideal and to argue that color-consciousness is racist, even if it is antiracist in purpose (Omi and Winant, 1994).

Mediated representations of color blindness hide the specificity of White identities (Drew, 2011) and presents a White perspective to audiences without acknowledging it as such (LeBlanc, 2018; Thornton, 2011). Films such as *The Blind Side* (2009) hide systemic racism by presenting racism as an individual-level problem that is solvable through White benevolence and Black deference (Bineham, 2015). More typically, sports films that feature racial discrimination center and lionize White coaches and other figures as necessary in the struggle for integration and civil rights (Schultz, 2014). Films about interracial friendships, particularly with Black friends, show that racial difference is not an obstacle to camaraderie and closeness. Their light repartee demonstrates how little race matters, while at the same time situating the Black friend as a side-kick, thus demonstrating the superiority and heroism of his White friend (Artz, 1998; Thornton, 2011). In stories of White teachers in "urban" schools, such as *Freedom Writers* (2007), the message that students of color can accomplish amazing work with the right (White) direction appears progressive because it argues against biological inferiority, yet at the same time, it argues for cultural pathology in communities of color (Hughey, 2010). As such, color blindness in film "imagines racism as a discrete, finished phenomenon and diverts collective consciousness from its persistence and from its permutations into new and nefarious forms" (Schultz, 2014, p. 211). It evades moral responsibility while holding onto control and representation, perpetuating racism while disavowing its existence (Yuen, 2017).

For whitewashing to work, it requires color blindness as a strategic rhetoric of Whiteness. It is necessary to foreclose narrative openings; otherwise, White leads' replacement of Asian/American bodies and their presence in Asian worlds is more open to interrogation and ridicule. These representational moves are unsubtle and symbolically destructive as they erase Asian subjectivity. To function, then, requires powerful ideological cover. This is the work of color blindness. As a discourse, color blindness asserts that the representation is not racist but that it is racist for an audience to be color-conscious enough to question White involvement in Asian stories and White replacement of Asian/American characters. As ideological cover, color blindness, despite its discourse of liberal racial acceptance, allows more openly color-aware, "ironic" racist jokes and representations, a phenomenon that has been dubbed "hipster racism" (Dubrofsky and Wood, 2014, p. 285) This, in turn, secures Whiteness's invisible norm by positioning it in opposition to clearly constructed racial Others. Because color blindness reifies White racial logics, White leads cannot simply exist in these worlds, they must advance a discourse of White importance—heroes, victims, and romantic leads. Whitewashing, then, argues that White people are not only a part of Asian worlds but that their presence is normal, necessary, relatable, and most sympathetic. As a strategic representational practice, whitewashing animates and extends the boundaries of Whiteness by claiming any and all racial difference. It uses liberal postracism to advance illiberal desires to symbolically plunder and gain representational territory.

White Imagination of Self

In the days of colonialism and the formations of settler colonies like the United States, South Africa, and Australia, Whiteness is hypervisible. Whiteness was forcefully argued to be more morally righteous, civilized, and intelligent, even as White colonizers committed barbaric atrocities to fuel desires for colonial expansion, enslavement, exploitation, and theft (Crofts Wiley, 2004). In contemporary times, Whiteness is rarely argued in explicit terms except during times of counterhegemonic crisis and challenge (Gabriel, 1998; Lipsitz, 1998). White male resentment, in particular, was dramatized in the film *Falling Down* (1993), and White hegemonic masculinity has been recently reasserted in *The Expendables*'s callback to the hypermasculinity and White backlash of the 1980s. As Kutufam and I (2014) argued about the movie *300* (2006), White masculinity presented itself as the last bulwark against a tide of racial difference in an existential war to preserve the West. The notion of White victimhood, of course, also finds recent political expression in the racial backlash to multiculturalism and the Obama presidency with the rise of the Tea Party (Enck-Wanzer, 2011) and especially with alt-right movements that blur White supremacy, White nationalism, and neo-Nazism, which fear Black and Brown bodies as contaminants to the White body politic (Hughey, 2010; Watts, 2017).

This fear of contamination by racial Others has long justified White supremacist discourse and policy (Dyer, 1997; R. G. Lee, 1999; Omi and Winant, 1994). These retching convulsions of Whiteness, while salient in politics, are thus far the exception more than the rule in commercially popular cinema.

This is not to say that ideologies of Whiteness are dramatically different in Hollywood; rather, its expressions are not so overtly revealed. There is quite a large body of research that has taken on the antiracist project of making visible Whiteness's invisibility by pointing to the ideological construction of self. As Dyer (1997) explains: "The ideal of whiteness makes a strong appeal. It flatters white people by associating them with (what they define as) the best in human beauty and virtue" (p. 80). Through representations of people of color at home and in the Global South as morally inferior and primitive, Whiteness is constructed in opposition as superior (Pieterse, 1992; Said, 1978; Shohat and Stam, 1994). It equates itself with moral goodness (Benshoff and Griffin, 2004; Chidester, 2008; Dyer, 1997; hooks, 1992), providing a paternal helping hand to people of color who are represented as unable to help themselves (Balaji, 2011; Bineham, 2015). It imagines itself as fair and honorable (Dyer, 1997), humane and philanthropic (Balaji, 2011), and rational and disciplined (Dyer, 1988; Giroux, 1997). The latter is a dualistic articulation of the West as the mind and the East as the body (Shohat and Stam, 1994). That dualism works as Whiteness is often conflated with the West (Frankenberg, 1993), and with the United States, Whiteness is often conflated with national belonging and identity (Entman and Rojecki, 2000; Johnson, 2017). This has been both a discursive formation that links patriotism to Whiteness (Giroux, 1997; Lipsitz, 1998) and a structure that has been codified in law (Omi and Winant, 1994).

In addition to its construction of superiority, Whiteness has understood itself sympathetically. White people are represented as worthy of sympathy and identification, whereas people of color are dehumanized and deprived of agency (Rada and Wulfemeyer, 2004). White men are represented as "White knights" who rescue and transform their lovers from the filmic oppression of their own men and the cruelty of their own culture (Marchetti, 1993). This was the central theme of *The World of Suzie Wong* (1960), a story of a U.S. traveler on a journey for self-discovery, who falls in love with a bar girl with a heart of gold—a single mother and implied prostitute (Marchetti, 1993). White characters are sympathetic for their liberal humanity, and they are sympathetic as victims, a representation that belies White global domination. Indeed, early colonial stories of the "dark continent" featured adventurous stories of White imprisonment by savages (Pieterse, 1992). The backlash films discussed earlier also feature the West and Whiteness under threat, requiring a muscular White response. Indeed, the images of victimhood provide moral justification for continued domination and the protection of White interests (Gabriel, 1998; Johnson, 2017).

This finds gendered expression as White masculinity, in particular, is represented as most desirable (Espiritu, 2004; Oh and Banjo, 2012). Based in notions of medieval chivalry and rationality (Richards, 1999), White masculine heroes are brave, strong, determined, and patriotic (Higate and Hopton, 2005). While they are represented as protectors of Western civilization (Oh and Kutufam, 2014), White women (Frankenberg, 1993), and White families (Lipsitz, 1998), White men are imagined to live according to the demands of noblesse oblige by rescuing people of color from themselves (Dyer, 1988), cinematically fulfilling a quintessential colonial discourse (Coloma, 2012). Like stories of White adventurism in Africa, stories of White men in Asia consistently return to the theme of White paternal protection (Espiritu, 2004; Kang, 2002; Locke, 2009; Marchetti, 1993; Nakayama, 1994; Sun, 2003; Tierney, 2006). The trope has been so persistent that it now veers on the edge of self-satire. In addition to the stories of White heroes saving Asian/American women (Espiritu, 2004; Marchetti, 1993; Nakayama, 1994), filmic White men often must learn ethnically specific practices, such as martial arts, in a limited period of time to defeat the enemy and complete his heroic mission, a trope Tierney (2006) refers to as supraethnic viability.

White antiracist films deprive people of color of their agency to create change and, instead, depends on the White hero to demonstrate his goodness (McFarlane, 2015). This changes the historical imagination by centering good White people, thereby assuaging guilt and maintaining faith in the morality of Whiteness. Antiracist sports films such as *Glory Road* (2006) distort the historical record and "imagines racism as a discrete, finished phenomenon and diverts collective consciousness from its persistence and permutations in new and nefarious forms" (Schultz, 2014, p. 211), and *The Blind Side* (2009) argues that racist boundaries can be surmounted through the interpersonal help of benevolent White people (Bineham, 2015). In *The Blind Side*, Michael Oher (Quinton Aaron) is rescued by Leigh Anne Tuohy (Sandra Bullock), a White mother, who stands up to the social judgment of her socialite friends and the poverty that shackles Oher's opportunities. In *The Help* (2011), another film featuring a White antiracist heroine, Skeeter (Emma Stone) reveals through her work at the *Jackson Journal* and book, Black maids' stories of racial abuse faced in their jobs and the women's microacts of resistance. As such, the stories of antiracist White women heroes also erase the agency of people of color (McFarlane, 2015) and only differ in the kinds of gendered help that is given, that is, men's leadership and bravery versus women's nurturance and support. This is also true in other White hero films featuring women, such as *Dangerous Minds* (1995) and *Freedom Writers* (2007). Both films assume that the inner cities are marked with chaos and dysfunction but that with the right White teachers, students of color can find the inspiration and discipline needed to escape their condition (Giroux, 1997; Hughey, 2010). It demeans adults of color while centering

White women's morality. Historically, White women had taken it upon themselves to act as a civilizing force in colonialism (Dyer, 1997; Turner, 1999). They were argued to be necessary in preventing White men from succumbing to the carnal temptations from women of color, and they "saved" women of color by assimilating them into the colonial project (Syed and Ali, 2011). White women act as moral agents to discipline women of color into heteronormativity and feminine respectability (Coloma, 2012). In turn, colonial subjects internalized White patriarchal discourses of White women as the most beautiful and most chaste (Dyer, 1997). Even now, the politics of desire still favor White women as desired objects, imagining them as more morally chaste (Lester and Goggin, 2005) and worthy of protection (Watts, 2005).

Whitewashing's representational work, then, is indebted to and in service of White notions of self. As whitewashing centers White subjectivity, it is positioned within filmic texts for the purpose of amplifying notions of White moral virtue, civilization, heroism, protection from racial Others, and rescue. Indeed, while popular cultural texts already center Whiteness, whitewashing does this aggressively to the extent that it erases Asian subjectivity in the process. This suggests that whitewashing is a representational practice that fits somewhere between the postracist White hero and the overtly racist hero in White backlash stories. Although whitewashing does not fear the racial Other quite as much as the backlash films do, it dares the viewer to not see Whiteness. The collective failure to do so secures its normative center. As such, whitewashing is akin to the children's story *The Emperor's New Clothes*. Whitewashing is an ostentatious act that requires collective complicity and an inability to see its obvious racist plundering and territorial incursion.

White Consumption of the Other

As defined, whitewashing means be(com)ing the Asian Other through erasing Asian/American subjectivity and claiming it to advantage White subjectivity. This specific argument does not yet exist in the literature, so I am pulling together related strands. First, becoming the Other means consuming and appropriating the Other. The appropriation literature differs, however, because it addresses how exotic difference amplifies White pleasure or agency but not the replacement of the Other in the process. Appropriation is about the power to borrow and stake claim. It is a colonialist impulse to mark territory and to extract resources for the colonizer's own pleasure. However, this does not mean becoming the Other or necessarily erasing the Other. The point is to understand the purpose of whitewashing's becoming or taking the place of the Asian other as a form of symbolic annihilation in addition to hypervisible White consumption of the Other.

The representational practice of "yellowface" in which White actors play Asian characters, usually through grotesque makeup and prosthetics, comes closest to modern-day whitewashing. Indeed, it can be understood as a precursor to whitewashed representations of the day (Nishime, 2017b). Ono and Pham (2009) argue that yellowface maintains White domination because it allows White actors to engage in identity play but denies the reverse for Asian Americans. Yellowface implies that Asian Americans are not capable enough to play themselves on screen (Ono and Pham, 2009). This is why Asian characters who populated film and television such as the evil Fu Manchu and the wise detective Charlie Chan were all played by White men (Chan, 2009). Furthermore, White men were necessary for love scenes to be deemed acceptable by law and by audiences' standards (Espiritu, 2004; Marchetti, 1993). This filmic practice goes at least as far back as D. W. Griffith's *Broken Blossoms* (1919) (Marchetti, 1993), and its theatrical practice stretches further to performances of *The Mikado* (1885) (J. Lee, 2010) and *Madame Butterfly* (1898) in the late nineteenth century (Yoshihara, 2002). The difference today is that mimicry usually takes the form of whitewashing, which stretches but does not puncture the veneer of color blindness and employs a more acceptable racism instead. It avoids caricatured, uncomfortable racial transformations, favoring on-screen images that adopt a performed embodiment of Asianness or a multiracial Asian character who simply "looks White." Regarding the latter, White actors have been featured in film as "Eurasians" since the mid-twentieth century, such as in *Love Is a Many-Splendored Thing* (1955) (Marchetti, 1993). Although mixed-race representation has the potential for progressive imagination, these casting choices are made primarily to tell exotic stories while employing bankable White stars. Mixed-race actors playing themselves and Asian American actors playing mixed-race characters is almost nonexistent, which points to the conservative limits of these casting decisions.

Appropriation, similarly, might be understood as a form of cultural borrowing that asserts power over the Asian Other. Having the ability to consume an Other's cultural authenticity for White voyeuristic pleasure requires no commitment from White performers or audiences, but it does clarify who is consumed and who is consuming (Yousman, 2003). Appropriation also allows White people to claim expertise about Asia (Yoshihara, 2002), and as Said (1978) argues, the West has long felt that it can speak for the Orient but not vice versa. Although some may claim that their interest is actually appreciation, a reasonable standard is whether performances of Asianness elevate the actors or U.S. cultural industries by using the culture of the Other or whether they elevate Asian culture in order that it be admired and understood with more complexity (Oh, 2017). Is it an elevation of the self or an elevation of another? Whitewashing, through its centering of Whiteness, in its very practice, then, cannot appreciate but rather appropriates and mimics.

Cultural appropriation is usually understood as a way to spice up White lives or to exert agency against restrictive structures, which has the by-product of dominating Asian people. As a spice, White people are able to add "exotic" flavor to their lives without traversing their boundaries or changing their world-views (hooks, 1992). Hamamoto (2000) writes, "Asiaphilia is a deceptively benign ideological construct that naturalizes and justifies the systematic appropriation of cultural property and expressive forms created by Yellow people" (p. 12). Appropriation often is masked as praise (Matlow, 2007), with tourist-like voyeurism often confused for appreciation and liking (Lipsitz, 1998). Using the rhetoric of postracism, it is often argued to be cross-cultural learning that is universally available but is, in fact, unidirectional in representational practice (Tierney, 2006). White people are represented as not only appropriating and succeeding over Asians in their own practices, they are legitimated on screen by locals who support and are rescued by them (Tierney, 2006).

For White performers, their forays into difference can be removed and worn at will to add variety and to gain acclaim. For instance, White women performers of *Madame Butterfly* were widely lauded for playing a character that was understood to be so foreign to White womanhood that performing in the titular role demonstrated exceptional acting acumen (Yoshihara, 2004). The desire for transracial play also manifests as a common representational trope in which White travelers, particularly to Japan, embark on a journey of self-discovery (Blouin, 2011; Phillips, 1999). Escaping hardships in the West, White travelers go to the land of the rising sun, an exotic playground in which they are lost in the spectacle of exotic difference (Morley and Robins, 1995). Because of their racial and cultural isolation, White characters in films such as *Lost in Translation* (2003) cannot turn outward for connection and thus turn inward to find an anchor for their existential drift (Oh and Wong Lowe, 2016). In these cases, culture is not appropriated; it is objectified to benefit White subjectivity. Indeed, in stories of Asian–White encounter, Asians are often mere vehicles for White redemption (Prendergast, 2007).

Despite the setting of the stories in Japan and in other Asian nations (East Asia, primarily), the centering of White subjectivity and the erasure of Asian subjectivity can be understood as symbolic annihilation. Asian/American subjectivities are positioned as unimportant except to the extent Whiteness is defined or is benefited in its relationship with Asia or Asian America. Asian/Americans are made peripheral and deemed useful to the extent that they serve as vehicles for the reification of White desirability. The message is that those who are underrepresented do not matter (Klein and Shiffman, 2009), which prevents opportunities for interracial connection (Shim, 1998) and even for the development of self-respect among Asian Americans (Oh, 2018). This denies Asian/Americans' subjectivity as humanizing representations and meaningful stories of Asian/Americans' lives are withheld. This may not matter much for Asians who live outside of the United States, but for Asian Americans, it creates psychic harm as Asian Americans internalize the belief that their mistreatment is deserved (Yamato, 2004). Although most White producers and directors almost certainly do not do whitewash as an explicit strategy of Asian/American symbolic annihilation, it would be too generous to take the claim at face value. This is because the centering of White stories in ways that reify Whiteness's strategic rhetoric necessarily means marking and denying subjectivity to Asian/Americans. Whiteness's gains do not happen in a representational vacuum; they happen through their referential construction of an inferior other and a superior self.

Studying Whitewashing

The goal of the book is to understand representations of whitewashing but to also engage my scholarly imagination to subjectify Asian/American lives. To do so, I draw on the ethos of Afrofuturism to imagine a different world in which systemic oppression against people did not exist and in which Black lives are centered. Similarly, I imagine stories with the White leads replaced by Asian/Americans. The project is not the same, however. Afrofuturism is a desire for new narratives about the future that is intertwined with Black identity and technology that empowers Black agency (Nelson, 2002). It imagines parallel historical possibilities that project into the future, "characterized as a program for recovering the histories of counterfutures created in a century hostile to Afro-diasporic projection and as a space within which the critical work of manufacturing tools capable of intervention within the current political dispensation may be undertaken" (Eshun, 2003, p. 301). It is a powerful literary project to imagine "[Black] future selves liberated from their symbolic annihilation in history and the racist history of the past few centuries" (Womack, 2013, p. 18). In Chicanx and Latinx literature, there has also been a similar reimagining, except that the interest is not in projecting an alternative vision of the future but an insertion into their histories to foreground their narratives and lives (Pérez, 2009; Sandoval, 2008). In a similar vein, this project imagines Asian/Americans in their stories and worlds—it imaginatively corrects the representational problem of whitewashing.

There are important differences, however. Unlike the scholarship on Afrofuturism, I am not studying texts that are already counterhegemonic reimaginings. Rather, with the exception of the one chapter on Chinese American films about Chinese cities, my project engages squarely with the dominant cultural industries in the United States, whether alone or in coproduction with Chinese producers. As such, the goal is not to say what Asian Americans have presented as alternative futures based on alternative histories but to use the scholarly imagination to envision the ideological work of Asian/American representation. Indeed, I am not imagining new stories based on Asian/American characters but simply how the existing meanings in the films would change merely through different casting choices. It is the old analytical trick of transposition. To help see what is present, it helps to imagine other bodies in those representations. It provides contrast. In this case, it is not only to understand the specificity of Whiteness but to understand the specificity of that which is erased—Asian/American subjectivity.

Valuing the subjectivity of the marginalized is what connects Afrofuturism and resistive Latinx and Chicanx scholars. Afrofuturism looks ahead with an imagined past, Latinx feminist literature looks back to the past to make visible the formerly invisible to understand the present, and Asian American imagination strives to be recognized in the present moment. For Asian/Americans, the future is a fraught space as Asianness is already overdetermined as the cyborg (Bui, 2020; Oh, 2016). Asianness, especially Japaneseness, is presented as a postmodern near future dystopia, a soulless place of automatons and lost humanity (Blouin, 2011; Morley and Robins, 1995). In contrast, the historical past is also fetishized in the Western imagination. Asia is valued for what it was while being devalued for what it is. Perhaps it is for this reason that as an Asian American scholar, my interests are in the present. It also brings Asian American studies into the realm of scholarly imagination, considering different representational possibilities.

Therefore, I am positing two primary questions: (1) how does whitewashing subjectify White leads through the objectification of Asian/American culture, people, and spaces; and (2) how would the representational work of the movies be changed if the stories centered Asian/American actors in lead roles? To research the aforementioned questions, my interests are in recent filmic representations of whitewashing. This book is not an attempt to track the historical movement of whitewashing but rather to understand it in a specific conjuncture in which people of color, particularly Black American activists, have argued forcefully that their lives matter in interactions with police and on screen. As is often the case with social movements in the United States, Black American activism has opened spaces for Asian Americans and other marginalized groups to step into these rhetorical openings to argue that their lives should also be valued. In addition, the current conjuncture is a moment in which postracism has become the "genteel racism of the new millennium" (Prashad, 2001, p. 38). For this reason, I analyze films released over the last decade, since 2008.[6] This leaves out popular films criticized for their whitewashing, such as *The Last Samurai* (2003) and *Kill Bill: Vol. 1* (2003).

To choose films, I used a purposive sampling strategy. My intention is to examine White subjectivity in Asian/American worlds because it is in these cases that whitewashing is most visible. For this reason, I did not include *21* (2008). Although it was widely criticized for deviating from the real-life story of Asian American students and a professor and because it is not set in or against Asian/American people or places, there is little to analyze except to point to the symbolic annihilation of the specifically Asian American story. This is, of course, the general challenge of studying absences in representation. As such, I focused only on films in which whitewashing was central to the story. For instance, although Tilda Swinton's casting choice as the Ancient One in *Doctor Strange* (2016) generated resistance for its whitewashing in a tent-pole superhero franchise, the movie was excluded because Swinton's role is secondary.

I started with movies that have been widely criticized for their whitewashed stories, including *Aloha* and *The Great Wall*. From there, I searched the American Film Institute's catalog of films and found that recent films fit six thematic categories: (1) interracial romance with White men and Asian/American women, (2) interracial romance with White China experts and fish-out-of-water Asian Americans, (3) White male heroism in fantasy stories, (4) White male heroism and satirical humor in North Korea, (5) White survival from Southeast Asian dangers, (6) whitewashing in anime, and (7) whitewashing international coproductions of White heroism. While the themes have some relation to genre, the fit is not a neat one-to-one correspondence. Rather, the different themes allow the study of whitewashing in different contexts. The different types of whitewashed stories position Whiteness differently and further shape the form Whiteness takes. First, romance provides a lens into the function of the politics of desire in centering White subjectivity as desirable romantic and sexual figures. It also provides insight into the removal of Asian/Americans from a common human desire—romantic love and sexual desire. Second, action films are important because of the simplification of narratives of good and evil. They provide a framework to tell stories of White heroism and to provide symbolic redemption for the White male character specifically, and as allegories that erase harms caused by White colonialism, slavery, and military adventurism. Third, disaster films are revealing because they position the White family as the most sympathetic. This representational strategy erases the harms caused to filmically unworthy victims. Fourth, anime allows an understanding of how transnational flows interact with the project of whitewashing. Because the stories' origins are Japanese, the centering of White heroes happens within narrative worlds that are tied to the values and signs of the originals, demonstrating how these different symbolic worlds and ideological interests are navigated. Similarly, studying coproductions demonstrates how Whiteness functions in an environment of uneven globalization. China as a rising global hegemon is able to assert its own stories but in an uneasy ideological negotiation that is still dominated by the West. It thus provides a lens into understanding how Chinese assertions of self-identity are resisted by the Hollywood filmic imperative to center White subjectivities in Asia.

After identifying the themes and films, the analysis was grounded in a communication-centered approach to cultural studies. What this means is that the analysis assumes that representation is linked to larger ideological meaning that benefits multiple, interlocking hegemonies and that the ideological work is continuous, requiring constant renewal, and made up of contradiction and complexity. Its communication-centered approach means that my primary interests are in the production of social meaning. Thus, the analysis is motivated toward understanding how representation works to reify Whiteness as a historically constituted hegemonic construction. I am less interested in the aesthetic qualities of genre or production except to the extent that they provide insight into cultural ideology. Centrally, the book is a paradigmatic analysis because of its interests in understanding oppositions and the creation of meaning (Berger, 2016). I am interested in meanings for the White lead(s) as well as the Asian character(s), and I am interested in the meanings for an imagined Asian lead. As Ono and Pham (2009) note, yellowface representations would be very different if played by Asian Americans. Indeed, desire for the Asian/American other challenges the social order (R. G. Lee, 1999).

Structure of the Book

The introduction sets forth the importance of the work, the conceptualization of whitewashing, the relevant literature and theoretical framework, and a summary of the chapters. It draws on studies of Whiteness in media, Asian/American representation in media, symbolic erasure, and cultural appropriation. It also briefly describes the methodological choices that guided the selection of films.

Chapter 1 examines *Aloha* (2015), a film that was widely criticized for whitewashing the multiracial Hawaiian-Chinese-Swedish character Alison Ng with the casting of Emma Stone. In addition, I consider the White male protagonist, played by Bradley Cooper, who fits conventional stories of White male redemption in exotic lands. Set in Hawai'i, the movie exoticizes Pacific Islander identities while symbolically erasing them on screen.

Chapter 2 studies *Shanghai Calling* (2012) and *Already Tomorrow in Hong Kong* (2015), both romances that feature Asian Americans, who struggle to make their way in China until they meet White China experts and residents with whom they fall in love. The films transfer Asian American foreignness in the United States to their foreignness in Asia while granting Whiteness a position of bicultural superiority, yet the films present a counterrepresentation in which Asian Americans, not White Americans, are the ones who find themselves lost in Asia.

Chapter 3 examines the construction of the White (multiracial) male (anti-)hero and fantastical historical visions of Japan. Analyzing *47 Ronin* (2013), the chapter examines the heroic journey of a White English-Japanese "half-breed" to become Japanese despite being socially oppressed and isolated for his mixed race and supernatural difference. It examines a White fantasy of racial difference in which White men are oppressed and in which acceptance occurs through individual, extraordinary effort. At the same time, the film constructs White biological difference as a sign of racial superiority. It situates the White anti-hero within the White savior trope in opposition to mythical dragon women and the yellow peril.

Chapter 4 focuses on *The Interview* (2014), which features White men infiltrating and assassinating North Korean leader Kim Jong Un. Kim is a unique figure in the U.S. popular imagination because he is constructed as singularly evil and mockable, and the lack of ambiguity creates space for satire that justifies simplistic notions of the United States' militaristic antagonism with North Korea.

Chapter 5 examines heroism of a different sort as White men and, to a lesser extent, White women survive the horrors of a massive tsunami in Indonesia and a military coup in Thailand. *No Escape* (2015) and *The Impossible* (2012) present further opportunities to explore the centering of White experience that erases the victims, survivors, and heroes in their own nations, and in the case of *No Escape*, a film that recasts the real-life Spanish couple upon which the movie is based with Ewan McGregor and Naomi Watts, two White British actors. The whitewashing in these films eliminates the possibility of Asian self-sufficiency, audience identification, and heroism, and instead elevates Whiteness in opposition.

Chapter 6 is centered on filmic adaptations of popular animes. In particular, it focuses on *Ghost in the Shell* (2017) and *Dragonball Evolution* (2009). Both films were widely criticized for their casting of White actors in iconic roles. The chapter examines how the Japaneseness of the source material is retained to reference the originating texts while centering Whiteness through the erasure of manga and anime heroes.

Chapter 7 examines transnational production with a focus on Chinese films that have been coproduced with Hollywood studios, including *The Great Wall* (2016), *Outcast* (2014), and *Enter the Warriors Gate* (2017). Studying the films reveals not only the ways the Western imagination continues in the movies despite shared Chinese production but also how coproductions create a more ambivalent representational terrain that insists on the symbolic presence of Asian subjectivity and heroism, particularly with more creative control.

The conclusion draws major conclusions together to form a new theoretical understanding of whitewashing, noting that Asian/American casting in the roles alone would only function ideologically as a partial corrective. Instead, the chapter ends with suggestions for more socially just production and future directions for scholarship.

1

Whitewashing Romance in Hawai'i

• •

Aloha

Of the films criticized for whitewashing during the past few years, *Aloha* (2015) was especially singled out for its casting of Emma Stone as Allison Ng. Despite director Cameron Crowe's (2015a) claim that the Allison Ng character was inspired by a real life mixed race White, Hawai'ian, and Chinese person, the casting choice was understood as fitting a pattern of whitewashing. The controversy was often credited as one of the primary reasons for the film's poor box office returns (Smith, 2015). Indeed, despite having an estimated $40 million budget and starring consistent box office draws Emma Stone and Bradley Cooper, *Aloha* only recuperated $20 million (Smith, 2015). In a column on *The Daily Beast* website, Yamato (2015) argued that the representation was especially egregious because only 40 percent of Hawai'ians are White, whereas all *Aloha*'s major leads are White (the film also features Rachel McAdams, John Krasinski, Bill Murray, and Alec Baldwin). Indeed, the cover image of a *New York Times* slideshow on the history of whitewashing in Hollywood featured *Aloha* as its cover image ("Whitewashing," n.d.), and an *IndieWire* article included *Aloha* in its list of the twenty-five worst cases of whitewashing (Sharf, n.d.). This prompted an apology by Crowe (2015a), who wrote on his blog, "I have heard your words and your disappointment, and I offer you a heart-felt apology to all who felt this was an odd or misguided casting choice." Emma Stone also claimed that the controversy was an opportunity for social awareness. In an interview, she said: "'I've learned on a macro level about the insane history of whitewashing in Hollywood and how prevalent the problem truly is. It's ignited a conversation that's very important" (Smith, 2015, n.p.).

The representation fits a long pattern of filmic portrayals and White men's journeys toward responsible patriarchy through romances with multiracial Hawai'ian women (Konzett, 2017). In *Aloha*, the story centers on the redemption of Brian Gilcrest (Bradley Cooper), who is dealing with his own moral purgatory after leaving the military to become a private defense contractor. His redemption comes through his homecoming to Hawai'i and his relationship with three women: Tracy Woodside (Rachel McAdams), his ex-fiancée; Grace Woodside (Danielle Rose Russell), his biological daughter with Tracy; and Allison Ng, a fighter pilot and Brian's handler. Brian's ambivalent return to his childhood roots is because of a mission to secure a blessing for a pedestrian gate and to allow a powerful defense contractor, Carson Welch, to use lands for a joint venture between private military enterprise, Global One, and the U.S. Air Force. His job sets up the central moral conflict for Brian—to choose the goodness of the U.S. military and the Hawai'ian spirit or the moral depravity and wealth of Carson's private defense corporation. Complicating matters, his personal past sets up a parallel moral conflict—to embrace a future relationship with Allison and her faith in "the sky," spirits, and mana or to break apart a family to rekindle his past relationship with Tracy. I argue that Brian's redemption narrative acts as a metaphor for the redemption of the U.S. military in its neocolonial relationship with Hawai'ianness. Because Allison's mixed-race body embodies both traditional Hawai'ianness and future-oriented (White) Americanness, their romance symbolically joins the military as a benevolent masculine force to value Hawai'i and bring it into the future. Thus, *Aloha*'s Whiteness functions to advance discourses of neocolonial benevolence.

This chapter will examine the whitewashed representation of Allison Ng, who fits the first type of whitewashed character described in the introduction, the erasure of a mixed-race actress with the replacement of a White actress. I heed Nishime's (2017b) argument that it is problematic to argue against Stone's casting simply because she appears White as there are mixed-race Hawai'ians who do appear White. She argues instead that the criticism should be about the lack of opportunities for mixed-race Hawai'ians for the roles. I largely agree, although I would add that Stone's casting is problematic not as a singular representation but as constitutive of a pattern of representation that imagines the morally good mixed-race character as White in appearance. This also works with the larger system of racial meaning in the United States and its filmic imagination. If it were the case that mixed-race Hawai'ians were regularly cast in their own roles, then the Stone casting would simply be a novel anomaly. Also, if Stone's White appearance mattered in the narrative, then it would be justifiable. This is not true in either case, pointing to larger patterns of Hawai'ian erasure.

It is also worthwhile to analyze the representation of Brian Gilcrest because of the ways it fits larger patterns of White, heterosexual male representation in films about Hawai'i. Like the third type of whitewashing, he is set in an "exotic" world. However, unlike films like *The Last Samurai* (2003), Brian's world is largely White—the defense contractor, the U.S. military, the Woodside family, and his romance with Allison, who audiences would likely understand as White based on their intertextual knowledge of Emma Stone, one of the most well-known contemporary actresses. That *Aloha* centers Whiteness to the near exclusion of indigenous Hawai'ians is an erasure that should be considered, particularly as it masks the harms of the U.S. military's neocolonial presence.

Finally, as a conceit of the book, the chapter concludes by imagining Allison Ng and Brian Gilcrest, two whitewashed characters, as played by a visibly mixed-race Hawai'ian and Brian Gilcrest as indigenous Hawai'ian. This reimagining does not change the narrative but considers the ways connotative meanings change as a result of the transposition of non-White bodies. It is not simply an optimistic turn but a recognition that there is complexity in the transformation. Given the same narrative, it will create representational opportunities that challenge structure as well as reinforce existing ones.

Whitewashing Allison Ng

Before discussing the literature on Hollywood's racial representations of Hawai'i, it is necessary to clarify that I do not refer to *Aloha* as whitewashed simply because Stone presents as White as there are multiracial Asian Americans who do. There is no reason to doubt director Crowe's account of meeting a multiracial Hawai'ian redhead (Crowe, 2015a). Thus, it is not this single representation that is problematic but rather the pattern of Hawai'ian representation in which multiracial Hawai'ian women characters are played by White actresses in stories of White male maturation and redemption (Fojas, 2018; Konzett, 2017). As Konzett (2017) argues, "It is not surprising that in present films set in Hawai'i, white actors such as George Clooney (*The Descendants*) and Emma Stone (*Aloha*) can be effortlessly cast as Hawaiian or part Hawaiian, allowing them to go native, since no Hawaiian identifiers are necessary in a seemingly white-dominated on-screen Hawaii" (p. 210). Indeed, this has historically been a common strategy for representing sympathetic people of color on screen. For Hawai'ian representation, this dates as far back as D. W. Griffith's *The Idol Dancer* (1920), which featured a White man in love with a French-Polynesian heroine (Konzett, 2017). Another prominent example is the casting of Joan Blackman, a White actress, to play Maile Duval, a biracial French and Hawai'ian woman in the 1961 film *Blue Hawaii* (Konzett, 2017; Taylor,

2015). Similarly, in films set in Asia, Marchetti (1993) noted that White women have played Eurasian women in films such as *Love Is a Many-Splendored Thing* (1955). Mixed-race characters, then, are a vehicle through which Hollywood tells "exotic" stories and imagines a colorblind raceless utopia, all while using White actresses (Beltrán and Fojas, 2008), thereby having Hawai'anness without Hawai'ian people.

Thus, the whitewashed casting of Emma Stone fits a long pattern of mixed-race representation in romances set in Hawai'i. Indeed, Crowe could have chosen actual mixed-race Hawai'ian actresses such as Alui'i Cravalho, Shannyn Sossaman, Nicole Scherzinger, or Kelly Hu. Although the Allison Ng character is shown frequently explaining her mixed-race background, there is not a narrative reason for her character to present as White. It is not consequential to the romance, to her military career, or to her connection to Hawai'i. The choice, then, appears to fit what I describe as the first type of whitewashing, be(com)ing the other. In *Aloha*, her character experiences little development or growth, so she does not become Hawai'ian but rather simply embodies Hawai'ianness, thereby erasing indigenous Hawai'ian experience and a more common phenotypical expression of multiracial Hawai'i. As such, her role in the film is to be the object through which Brian finds redemption, choosing the spiritual purification of Hawai'i expressed by and embodied in Allison.

In multiple scenes, *Aloha* legitimates Allison as primitively Hawai'ian in her spiritual beliefs, which is positioned without comment alongside her occupation as a fighter pilot of the hypermodern F-22 Raptor and her interests in space exploration and science. Her belief in the primordial spirits and myths of Hawai'i are necessary for it to be clear that Brian's redemption is not just carried out through heterosexual romance but also through his connection to Hawai'ianness, which gets reduced to the primordial. This imagining of exotic Hawai'i as premodern fits the colonizing imagination of Hawai'i intermingled with the commodification of Hawai'i as a tourist destination (Fojas, 2014; Konzett, 2017; Taylor, 2015). Although *Aloha* avoids the exoticizing gaze that transforms the native population into naive, happy inhabitants or, worse yet, subhuman cannibals (Arvin, 2018; Palencia, 2015), it still emphasizes the "exotic, primitive, and mythical Hawaii and the South Seas" (Konzett, 2017). The earliest indication of Allison's faith in spirits comes during a disagreement as Brian and Allison are walking toward Dennis "Bumpy" Kanahale's (played by himself) camp. Their dispute is interrupted as a light mist rolls into a lush forest, connecting to common images of Hawai'ian paradise (Konzett, 2017; Palencia, 2015). When Brian asks what the mist is, Allison replies: "I'm tempted to say *menehune*. Like Hawai'ian leprechauns." This draws them into laughter with one another. As the rain wipes away his cynicism, he nods his head and replies, "There is a lot of mana up here." This illustrates that the belief in the spiritual is made more possible because of their connection to a Hawai'ian paradise uninterrupted by modernity, that her faith is justified, and that she is a true believer, which becomes closely tied to authentic Hawai'ianness.

Her Hawai'ianness is further clarified during their negotiations with Bumpy at a communal dinner. When Bumpy expresses skepticism and his protection of the sacred sky, "the shelter above us all," Brian brusquely describes the terms of a possible deal. Bumpy responds by telling Brian to eat and leave as a veiled threat, demonstrating his wariness of Brian, despite their childhood friendship. To help the negotiations, Allison strongly denies the possibilities of weapons in space, saying: "King, I believe in our land and our myths and our traditions and more than anything, I believe in the sky. This is not the military of old, Bumpy. This is the new. And, you have my word as a member of the 15th Airlift of the United States Air Force Space Command that we will not put weapons above these sacred islands. You can trust me." That her claim convinces Bumpy draws together and validates three interlinking strands: Allison's visible presentation (and extratextual knowledge of Emma Stone) as White; the U.S. military presence in Hawai'i; and authentic Hawai'ian concerns as rooted in myths and primordial beliefs, belying the contemporary political concerns of the real-life Bumpy Kanahele's anticolonial, independence movement. Instead, the film suggests that indigenous Hawai'ians' primary concern is about whether the U.S. military acts as good stewards of Hawai'ian lands, skies, and oceans. This fits with prior popular depictions of nativist movements, which provides superficial inclusion to either represent indigenous Hawai'ians' concerns as sympathetic yet unrealistic (Konzett, 2017) or as narrative devices to present challenges to the White hero (Fojas, 2018). Both are true in the depiction of Bumpy's village and the anticolonial movement they represent.

As Allison and Brian exchange farewell greetings, Bumpy provides a gift of the independence flag because they are *ohana* (family), overdetermining Brian and Allison's authenticity as Hawai'ians. He further explains that he senses the couple's plentiful mana, particularly with Allison. Thus, to validate Allison, especially, as Hawai'ian, the film slips into tropes of indigenous Hawai'ians as primordial and especially in tune with their land, replicating representations of Native Americans (Taylor, 2015). In the next sequence, to further cement Allison as an embodiment of Hawai'ianness, the film shifts to Allison and Brian's drive back to their hotel, where she is flabbergasted that Brian still believes that the deal was a simple transaction and that the discussions of myths and the sky are simply metaphors. Their argument is interrupted, however, when they hear drumbeats ahead on the road. She commands him to stop the car and to look down, expressing awe and fear of the "night warriors of Waimanalo." The moment situates the filmmaker's position that the traditions and spiritual presence of Hawai'i are meaningful and ultimately redemptive. It also positions Allison as the legitimate bearer of redemptive possibilities for the morally compromised White hero. Thus, in a moment of filmic irony, the colonizing logic of Whiteness positions a visibly White woman with the power to redeem a White man by becoming a portal to access authentic Hawai'ianness. The white-washing of Allison Ng did not only function to provide a commercial oppor-tunity to include a bankable star but to also claim authentic Hawai'ianness for White Americans.

Thus, it is not inherently progressive to recognize on screen the presence of mixed-race Americans (Nishime, 2014). "Hollywood traditions of whiteness also continue to serve as potent frames of understanding, even in films and other media texts that foreground mixed race actors and/or a multicultural aesthetic" (Beltrán and Fojas, 2008, p. 11). In the case of *Aloha*, Emma Stone's inclusion replicates the arc of historical representation in which White actresses play mixed-race Hawai'ian heroines, who are objectified for the benefit of the White hero. Crowe says in his documentary *Making of Aloha*, which is included as a special feature on the DVD, that his original plan was to write a screen-play that centered around Allison Ng. He said: "Filming it, I realized it's really about the journey of Gilcrest. In earlier versions of the script, it was very much about the career of Emma's character, and Gilcrest was kind of, in a way, the spine of the story" (Crowe, 2015c). If true, his more progressive, initial inten-tions yielded to common filmic tropes about mixed race Hawai'ians and dom-inant casting patterns.

The White Hero's Redemption

While it is the Allison Ng character that is criticized for being whitewashed, *Aloha* also follows common tropes in its converging depiction of Hawai'i, Whiteness, and the U.S. military. In a brief description of the film's represen-tational problems in the conclusion of Konzett's (2017) book *Hollywood's Hawaii: Race, Nation, and War*, she briefly points out the superficial, incho-ate attention to indigenous concerns, the problematic casting of Emma Stone, and the misleading representation of the U.S. military as the protector of Hawai'ian interests. Her criticisms fit with Hollywood's racial framework that centers Whiteness to the near exclusion of indigenous Hawai'ians or the mixed-race population on the islands, that advances a colonialist view of the U.S. military presence as a beneficial force, and that reinforces primordial portray-als of Hawai'i. To add another critique, *Aloha*'s journey of a reluctant White hero redeemed in the paradise of Hawai'i is a formulaic trope of White mas-culinity in Asian worlds and in Hawai'i specifically. Arguably, the Brian Gil-crest story is the more problematic whitewashed representation as it further reinforces the subjective value of White men's stories and redemption through the exotic Other while also acting as apologia for the U.S. military, which is portrayed as a benevolent presence, though momentarily misled by the conflu-ence of capitalist greed and political weakness in Washington, DC. As such, it advances a progressive message that warns against neoliberal privatization of the military and space but that services the settler colonial interests of the United States and the geopolitical control of its network of military bases.

It also avoids some problems of earlier racist depictions of Hawai'i that represent indigenous Hawai'ians as violent and abusive in contrast to the moral goodness and civility of White masculinity, and it avoids representing White men as victims of racial discrimination (Fojas, 2018). For uncritical viewers, the sympathetic portrayals of indigenous Hawai'ians and the valorization of traditional myths and beliefs may read as "positive" racial representations. This relative improvement in representation disguises the problematic coupling of White masculinity, the U.S. military, and temporality such that they slip beneath detection with only the egregiousness of the whitewashed Allison Ng character noticed. What I argue is that the redemption story of Brian acts as a metaphor for the redemption of the U.S. military in its role in the domination and destruction of the islands that situates the future in the hands of the colonialist nation-state and the past in the interests of indigenous Hawai'ians.

Although it is beyond the scope of this project to provide a detailed historical account, it is necessary to very briefly detour to describe U.S. control over Hawai'i. In short, the United States illegally confiscated nearly two million acres after supporting an illegal coup d'état by White businessmen in 1893 (Goodyear-Ka'ōpua and Kuwada, 2018). Ever since, decolonial movements have resisted U.S. occupation, seeing it as an extension of the original violence of the coup (Goodyear-Ka'ōpua and Kuwada, 2018). As Brown (2014) notes, there is *aina*, mourning the land, because of the U.S. military's ecological devastation in the use of the islands for live fire exercises, the desecration of grave sites that are intentionally unmarked as a way of returning mana to the soil, and the conglomerates that take over lands and extricate resources. "Native Hawaiians do not only mourn the loss of our land, we also mourn the loss of our identity that is tied to the loss of land—the loss of our sovereignty" (Brown, 2014, p. 391). Despite the anguish of U.S. imperialism over Hawai'i (Palencia, 2015), its existence as a state hides the settler colonialism that continues (Arvin, 2018). In its place, the "United States sees itself no longer as a colonial oppressor or imperialist power but rather as a global protector of its democratic freedoms and capitalist practices" (Konzett, 2017, p. 75).

With this history, it can be expected that the film industry would craft narratives that fit colonialist interests that mingle with dominant racial ideologies when set in Hawai'i. As Konzett (2017) argues, film functions to shore up U.S. racial and cultural hierarchy as well as its geopolitical interests. In the case of Hawai'i, Hollywood presents annexation and the administration of the state as benevolent rule, often through a romantic narrative that is "intertwined with military affairs" (Konzett, 2017, p. 138). According to Fojas (2014), "empire demands a story, and stories demand protagonists, objects, and spaces" (p. 191).

These stories are most frequently centered around a White man's efforts to prove his value in an exotic backdrop (Fojas, 2018). They are "escapist fantasy and white melodrama, negating any historical accountability of the United States toward its quasi-colony of Hawaii" (Konzett, 2017, p. 217). Through the White man's adventure, the "benevolent spirit of Hawaiian island life" transforms either the immature or jaded man into a responsible paternal figure (Konzett, 2017, p. 196). While doing so, the films erase indigenous Hawai'ians who do not feature as central characters in stories about their homeland (Fojas, 2018; Taylor, 2015). As Konzett (2017) reminds readers, Whiteness is most empowered but not normal in Hawai'i. However, films about the islands feature a "bleached-out identity of Hawaii, allowing white Americans a quasi-native position in the film and making Hawaii appear as a natural extension of the United States" (Konzett, 2017, p. 144). Thus, White masculinity and U.S. imperialism become closely linked in representations of Hawai'i.

Aloha makes this connection by paralleling the redemption of Brian with the redemption of the U.S. military. Thus, Brian's journey to paternal responsibility is a metaphor for the U.S. military's relationship to indigenous Hawai'ians. Just as Brian's central moral dilemma is caused because he has left the military to become a private defense contractor for Carson Welch, the military is depicted as unintentionally threatening global peace by also partnering with Carson Welch's private defense corporation. Furthermore, Brian's heroism restores his estranged relationship with General Dixon, who is angry with Brian. Although the reasons are not directly stated, the implication is that it is because of Brian's abandonment of the military. Thus, the connection between White masculinity and the U.S. military is narratively explicit. All three of Brian's redemption subplots (with Allison, Tracy, and Grace) make this connection, but it is his redemption vis-à-vis Allison in which this is most important and where the temporal notion of the future and the sky become linked to the U.S. military presence.

It should be noted that Allison is represented as a rising star in the Air Force Space Command and as a mixed-race Hawai'ian, embodying the type of racial/colonial utopia that films about Hawai'i often imagine (Nishime, 2014). She represents the dichotomy between sky and land that are linked to the future and the past. The sky and space are where the U.S. Space Command is positioned as belonging—the launch of the satellite, its flights across the sky, Allison's piloting of an F-22 fighter jet, Brian's scientific work on sound induction in space, and the missions that Woody pilots. Thus, the sky is positioned with the United States and modernity. On the other hand, the land is positioned as Hawai'ian, particularly traditional beliefs in mana, the indigenous movement to regain control over land, and the blessings of the pedestrian gate. Temporally, the land, then, is located in the past. To the extent that these are also raced marks indigenous Hawai'ians in the past, linking to romanticized notions of primordial Hawai'i (Taylor, 2015) and the U.S. military as White, both through the metaphor of Brian and the visual domination of White people in all of the important military roles in the film. General Dixon is played by Alec Baldwin, Woody is played by John Krasinski, Captain Lacy is played by Danny McBride, and Allison Ng is played by Emma Stone. There are no indigenous Hawai'ian service members noticed even as background extras, and Black servicemen are depicted only occasionally in minor roles. This racialized, temporal imagination is consistent with neocolonial representations of Hawai'i (and Asia, more generally), overdetermining the future and hope as White (Konzett, 2017).

Multiple scenes construct the sky as figuratively important. The film opens with a montage that splices together traditional images of Hawai'i, historical moments in the U.S. control of Hawai'i, and images of the U.S. space program. Eventually, the historical footage gives way to character-generated imagery of a satellite rotating in space. The movie also closes with ending credits set against the background of a starry, night sky. The bookmarked images of space and the historical progression in the montage point to the future of Hawai'i as located in space. The film overdetermines this temporal, spatial relation with explicit dialogue. When Allison tries to break through Brian's rough demeanor the night before their meeting with Bumpy, she says she'd like a drink to talk about "the sky, the future, everything." In Allison's earlier conversation with Bumpy, she claims that the military is not "the military of old" but rather the "new." This not only serves as colonial ideology but also connects the skies with the present and the future as the point about the military happens in the context of protecting the skies and the meaningfulness of the sky as shelter for all people. Finally, and most explicitly, during Allison and Brian's drive back from Bumpy's village and before the encounter with the night warriors of Waimanalo, she tries to break through Brian's cynicism by questioning his lack of faith, saying: "Tell me you don't believe in the sky. You think it's just air up there. It's the future. It's the pull of the unknowable. It's the answer to every question." Thus, there are multiple associations that are important in this mediated syllogism—the future as the military, the future as hope, the military as White. Together, they point to colonial control in which the future of Hawai'i is under White control, a future of possibility and hope when constructed through a colonial imagination. As such, it justifies White colonial control (Konzett, 2017) that is made palatable by the sympathetic redemption of the White male hero (Fojas, 2018).

What *Aloha* does, then, is to rehabilitate the White hero, thereby rehabilitating the military's settler colonial presence. This is whitewashing both in the common definition of the word, which is to conceal faults, as well as whitewashing that sets the White protagonist in an "exotic" world and makes him its hero and protector. In *Aloha*, this comes through Brian's decision to sabotage

Carson Welch's nuclear satellite that launches from Hawai'i. Leading up to this moment, the film establishes that Brian is morally corrupted because of his involvement with Global One, Carson Welch's company, in Kabul, Afghanistan. Although the circumstances of his work are not described in the film, he is shown in a flashback as unwilling to take cover and resigned to death when he spots a falling rocket. He survives but is crippled with damage to his leg and foot. Learning about his past, Allison responds with a reference to his childhood interest in space, saying, "You lost your iridium flares," suggesting that his work as self-described "soul-crushing mercenaries" had stolen his future. He responds, "Tonight was kind of the first night I was truly happy I lived." The shared moment of vulnerability is shown as creating an opening for his personal redemption, but if the film ended here, then it would not also mean a redemption of the colonizing military presence.

As such, the film presents an obstacle to their relationship—Allison's discovery that Carson is planning to send a nuclear payload onto the satellite and that Brian is aware and complicit. This jeopardizes their relationship and his heterosexual redemption with a mixed race woman. After a montage in which Allison is shown running joyfully across a field and into neighborhoods near the base, she comes upon the Woodside household, where she discovers Mitchell, who is editing his home video footage of Carson's rockets. Realizing the nefarious nature of the launch, she finds Captain Lacy, who is watching his infant child while his wife participates in outdoor aerobics with other military spouses. He tells her that collaboration with private defense contractors is the "new military," undercutting her promise to Bumpy and momentarily revealing her naïveté for trusting Brian and for having faith in the military. At this point, the message of the film appears to be firmly anti-imperialist and anti-neoliberal. However, this possibility is narratively foreclosed when like Brian, the military is redeemed as a hopeful sign of the future and protector of Hawai'i.

This sets up an irreconcilable conflict. Before Brian's confession and the couple's shared sexual intimacy, he is shown as receiving codes and specifications for the satellite, revealing that he had been hiding the information from Allison. Through this earlier scene and the saccharine montage of their date and his considerate preparations for a second lunch date, Brian is represented as navigating dual, conflicting interests that beckon the moral ambivalence of his character. However, this is upended during their date when Allison accuses him of knowing about the launch and, subsequently, storming out of the restaurant. Momentarily leveled by the accusation, Brian chases after her, telling her that he will not provide a recommendation of her work. She responds by saying that she defended him against her colleagues' concerns but that he has "sold his soul so many times, no one's buying anymore."

This creates a rift in the relationship that is only rejoined when Bob Largent (Bill Camp) picks them up at the ritual blessing of the pedestrian gate, claiming that Carson has called for their help to launch the satellites earlier than scheduled because of a Chinese hack.[1] In a makeshift control center located in the back of a food warehouse, Brian deftly neutralizes the Chinese threat through his superior coding skills, which allows for the successful satellite launch. The scene allows for two moments of heroism. The first is as an underdog equipped solely with a single laptop, fighting against a mobilized Chinese cyberinvasion. The second is his own sabotage of the satellite. Narratively, then, if the destruction of the satellite is the purpose of the story, the Chinese threat is unnecessary to move the story forward. Its only purpose is to demonstrate Brian's superior skill and to present China as a yellow peril threat. This is, of course, a common trope in film to feature a superior White hero who overcomes long odds against Asian foes (Ono and Pham, 2009).

The narratively important act of heroism is, instead, his second, which is his own sabotage of the satellite. This is motivated by his realization that the satellite launch has emotionally devastated Allison. Unlike the other characters in the control room, who are congratulating one another and Brian for the successful launch, Allison is seated on the steps of the control room. Overwhelmed by the weight of the broken promise and the violation of the skies, Allison watches while only able to draw shallow breaths. Noticing Allison for the first time since working to launch the satellite, Brian's self-satisfaction fades, looking down and to the side as he feels guilty for his role in the harm caused to Allison/Hawai'i. This is the moment that he secretly plots to destroy the satellite, which fulfills the Lono and Pele myth that Mitchell (Jaeden Martell), his ex-lover's son, had foreseen. As Pele is described in the film as the "fire goddess" who has created the islands, Allison is further linked to the land and to primordial Hawai'i while Brian is linked to Lono, the god of mischief, and with the future.

This scene, too, secures Brian's redemption but still represents the U.S. military as suspect. Indeed, General Dixon is first represented as angry that Brian has led to the dissolution of the contract with Carson, leading to what he describes as a setback of a decade's work. When Brian explains that the satellite contained a nuclear payload, Dixon dismisses it, claiming that it was simply a telecommunications satellite that would have served a humanitarian purpose, thus showing the general as well-intentioned even if naive. He also tells Brian that he will face lengthy investigations in Congress and then warns him against establishing contact with Allison. Configuring the military as a father figure through the control of "our girl," the military is further established as linked to White masculinity. After a brief scene showing Allison climbing into the cockpit of an F-22 and Brian having a heart-to-heart conversation about chasing after Allison, the scene cuts back to Colonel Lacy, General Dixon, and the defense contractor Bob Largent, all out of uniform in Hawai'ian shirts. This signifies the unofficial nature of the men's conversation, where Lacy shares that

Brian is a hero and where he is informed that Carson is going to be arrested. Cutting to a disheveled Carson in a flowing white shirt and bare feet, standing on a sand bar, laughing and raising his arms to the sky, he is arrested, thus completing the redemption of Brian and of the military. As Dixon says, "This is what we get for letting civilians into space." As Konzett (2017) notes, the film works to reproduce U.S. geopolitical interests that are intermingled with racial hierarchy in stories that soften the image of settler colonialism.

Though less significant, Brian is also redeemed through his relationship with the women in the Woodside family—his ex-fiancée and his biological daughter. The film establishes in an early scene that Tracy has unresolved feelings for Brian that are exacerbated by her emotional distance from her husband, John, a.k.a. "Woody." In the first scene when coffins are removed from a military transport plane, the camera crosscuts between Brian and Tracy, who notice each other across the runway of Hickam Field, a military airport. Brian breathes deeply when he notices her, while Tracy is shot looking wistfully into the distance while wind flows through her hair. With the extreme close-up of the actors and the somber tone created by the sound of "Taps" for the fallen soldier, it creates a mood of tragic loss. The mood is broken as Captain Lacy introduces Brian to various figures before Tracy interrupts to say that she's been worried and has tried to call five times. She notes that Woody, her husband, did not inform her that Brian was arriving, saying with exasperation, "He never tells me anything." Thus, the film sets in motion the moral dilemma that Brian faces—take advantage of her estranged marriage and break up her family or uphold the sanctity of her marriage while moving away from the past and into his new future.

After he is introduced to her children, Grace and Mitchell, Tracy invites Brian to dinner, being met with Woody's silent and Brian's reluctant agreement. At the Woodside's home, Brian notices that Tracy has folded a photograph of them together so that only her image shows in a small picture frame. This suggests that Tracy has left room in her life for Brian, even as it is hidden away. When the two have a moment together in the kitchen, Tracy confides that she is stressed because of Woody's confidential missions and his inability to communicate before rehashing old times in which she asks if he can forget the girl who ran naked across an airfield on a dare after a Cure concert. He mentions later that he cannot remember why they broke up, which leads to an ex-lover's quarrel about his unwillingness to commit to the relationship. She concludes by saying, "Hey, I really loved you."

Shortly after, Woody walks into the tense aftermath of their conversation and grabs a beer from the refrigerator. Woody leans against the refrigerator and stares intently. Then, he moves toward Gilcrest and pats him on the shoulder before pointing and smiling. Tracy is further frustrated by his silence, but Gilcrest reveals that Woody has communicated quite a bit as Gilcrest reads his nonverbal signs as a welcome to his home, knowledge of Brian and Tracy's prior relationship, Woody's physical strength, and perception of Gilcrest as a nonthreat. In this moment, Brian is depicted as making a first gesture toward bridging the gap in the Woodside household rather than driving a wedge between it. Later in the film, the family is shown as further ripped apart when Woody leaves the home to live alone after fighting with Tracy. As he leaves, he destroys the Santa Claus decoration on his front lawn, and the family separates. Later, Woody seeks reconciliation through a letter that Tracy shares with Brian. Acting as a healer, Brian helps to restore the relationship by putting himself down, saying that he does not have Woody's "romantic gene." He encourages her to forgive and embrace Woody by saying, "He's your guy." The security of the family is gained when Woody returns home and embraces Brian twice after a subtitled moment of nonverbal communication in which Woody expresses to Brian his desire to keep his family together and when Woody learns that Brian did not have sex with Tracy but with Allison.

At this moment, the film forecloses the possibility of familial ruin, replacing it with a "happy ending" for the family as Brian's moral choice reflects again the theme of the past and the future in which Brian turns away from his past relationship with Tracy to a future sexual relationship with Allison, thus protecting the family. The protection of the White family can be understood as the nation-state's protective role in maintaining the White family (Gabriel, 1998; Oh and Kutufam, 2014). If this representation happened alone, this reading may be understood as a stretch, but because the film clearly establishes the relationship between Brian, Whiteness, and the U.S. military in a colonial narrative of the future of Hawai'i, and the continued metaphor of past and future, his intervention in the family must also be interpreted through a colonial imagination of the place of the White family in Hawai'i. This is furthered in the narrative conclusion to the film, which is not a happy future with Allison but a happy future as Grace's biological father.

Before the satellite launch and Brian's redemptive choices, Brian is shown in his room, packing as he prepares to depart Hawai'i. Tracy shares that after years of keeping it a secret, she needs to have a straightforward conversation to reveal that he is Grace's father. Although the film's lingering wide shot suggests that the confirmation of his parentage weighs heavily on him, it is not until the final scene in the movie that his last act of redemption is complete. The film cuts to Brian, standing next to a sports utility vehicle, watching Grace from a distance as she practices hula with other girls in a brightly lit dance studio. From there, he approaches the window carefully, watching Grace dance. As he does, she notices Brian and expresses a confused but knowing look. After laughing nervously a bit, she rushes out of the studio in bare feet, hugs Brian, and returns to the studio. The movie ends as it cuts to her flowing arms and the final credits. Thus, although the love story between Allison and Brian drives the film, it is his paternal restoration that is filmically most consequential. Because the film does not establish the importance of this moment for Brian or Grace, this might be understood as an unusual choice to conclude the film except when Brian's redemption/the military's redemption can take the form of the benevolent patriarch. As Konzett (2017) argues, films about Hawai'i provide colonial rationale for U.S. settler colonialism. As such, the military also becomes the father, the benevolent patriarch, to its daughter, Hawai'i. That this metaphorical relationship becomes embodied in Grace rather than Mitchell is unsurprising as Hawai'i has often been feminized in the colonial imagination.

Politics of Inclusion: Imagining Hawai'ians in Hawai'i

In an intellectually playful mode, I turn toward the project of reimagination. If the cultural imaginary can be colonized for the purposes of dominant interests, then it seems that a necessary tool to deconstruct this hegemonic complicity is through reimagination that sees the whitewashed characters as visibly mixed-race Asian, Hawai'ian, and White for Allison Ng and indigenous Hawai'ian for Brian Gilcrest. While mixed-race actresses might sometimes pass as White, situated knowledge of their multiple heritages allow the viewer to more easily see Hawai'ianness in the actress. In this case, I think of actresses listed earlier such as Alu'i Cravalho, Shannyn Sossaman, Nicole Scherzinger, or Kelly Hu for Allison Ng. For Brian Gilcrest, I draw on Pacific Islander actors such as Mark Dacascos, Jason Momoa, or Uli Latukefu. Within the narrative framework of *Aloha*, the purpose is to understand whether different casting choices would have mattered. Even if the stories would have been the same, would their counterracial inclusion read against the grain even if the story is the same? In what ways does this challenge and in what ways does this reinforce in similar or different ways U.S. racial and geopolitical hegemonies? To answer the question, I will consider both Allison and Brian's function in the film's narrative and also their relationships with key characters in the movie. I do not swap them simultaneously but rather in turn as each transposition creates ripples with other characters.

Imagining Allison Ng as a phenotypically more common mixed-race Hawai'ian creates progressive, connotative meaning, but it also reinforces existing tropes of indigenous women's role in White men's redemption. Casting a mixed-race actress would complicate Hollywood's history of sympathetic mixed-race representation as visibly White. For the Allison Ng character, its progressive meanings would primarily be located in the character's occupation as a military officer and fighter pilot. The casting choice is already gender progressive as fighter pilots are most often the domain of men in Hollywood war movies (e.g., *Top Gun* [1986] and *Red Tails* [2012]). Other than movies about the Tuskegee Airmen of World War II, it is also rare to represent pilots of color.

Despite the U.S. military's well-known racial diversity, fighter pilots' on-screen homogeneity positions White masculinity as exemplary of stylized, high-risk aerial action. Although this is contained somewhat by only showing Allison piloting a propeller plane (with the exception of her seated in preparation to fly an F-22 but not shown in the air), having a pilot of color visibly match her character's claims to multiracial heritage would challenge the appropriation of patriotism/Americanness as a conservative (White) value (Lipsitz, 1998; Oh and Kutufam, 2014).

As a visibly mixed-race Hawai'ian character, she would also more strongly reinforce the myth of Hawai'i as a multiracial utopia (Nishime, 2014). By virtue of her mixed-race identity, the character would problematically act as a cultural model of mixed-race identity that approximates racelessness, and it would suggest the U.S. military is the institution through which this progressive multiracialism exists. This reinforces the colonizing image of the military as a postracial institution (Konzett, 2017). This would mean multiracialism as a cover for U.S. military–related settler colonialism would be more powerfully argued through the filmic text. Because the two different aspects of her racial heritage are positioned differently—White with the military and the future and Hawai'ian with the primordial (Chinese is ignored), she would more clearly establish a visual connection between Hawai'ianness and premodern beliefs and traditions, a common, romantic trope of indigenous Hawai'ians in film (Taylor, 2015). Because of the problematic, colonizing gaze of *Aloha*, simple casting differences would not be sufficient in subverting problematic messages and would more clearly reinforce problematic representations of mixed-race Hawai'ians than Emma Stone's casting, which allows the viewer to slip between understanding Ng as White and as Hawai'ian, and which easily conjures contemporary discourses about White women's cultural appropriation to produce readily available negotiated readings.

Casting Brian Gilcrest as an indigenous Hawai'ian man would, on the other hand, be a more powerful counterrepresentational move. It changes the dominant representation in cinema, which tells the stories of White men and which represents White men as worthiest of sympathy and interest. In *Aloha,* as an indigenous Hawai'ian man, the story, even if unchanged, would have a strong subtext of recovering identity rather than simply the moral malaise of greed and bad choices. His work for Global One would not only be about abandoning the military but about abandoning his Hawai'ian heritage. His early cynicism would produce more powerful messages about the anguish of denying identity such that his eventual restored faith would be more meaningful. As the film establishes the link between the U.S. military as the future and Hawai'i as the past, an indigenous Hawai'ian Brian would somewhat invert the temporality. For instance, Brian's future would be linked to Hawai'i and his abandonment of his military and mercenary past would be linked to the past. Although the film would still situate that past as linked to primordial beliefs, it would in some ways resemble decolonial movements that legitimate indigenous practices and traditions. In this way, his fulfillment of Mitchell's vision that Brian is Lono would no longer have solely figurative meaning but would be actualized in his body and person.

Because Whiteness is also a racially relational project, it is helpful to also consider countercasting in relationship to other characters on screen. For Allison Ng, the only significant relationship she has is with Brian. Imagining a visibly mixed-race Allison in a relationship with Brian would have little counterrepresentational potential that is specific to their relationship. For instance, although the history of mixed-race women as vehicles for White male redemption tends to cast White women in the roles, there is a long history of casting Asian/American actresses as romantic vehicles for White men's redemption in Asia. Perhaps most famous of these is mixed-race Nancy Kwan's (she played a monoracial Chinese woman) titular role in *The World of Suzie Wong* (1960). Specific to *Aloha*, the character would further embody the colonial imagination of Hawai'i as a feminized space for White men's moral redemption and maturation.

Casting Brian as indigenous Hawai'ian alongside Emma Stone as Allison would subvert the politics of desire seen in U.S. cinema. There are no films of which I am aware in which a Hawai'ian or Pacific Islander is cast as a romantic lead with a White actress. There are films and televisual texts where the actor is Polynesian and is in a relationship with a White woman, but their specific racial identity and/or heritage is left ambiguous. For instance, Dwayne "The Rock" Johnson is famously part-Samoan, but this is erased in his film work. Instead, he plays into "multiracial chic," a representational strategy used since the 1990s (Park, 2008, p. 184). Cliff Curtis, who has Maori heritage, also played opposite a White woman in *Fear the Walking Dead* (2015—). By highlighting Brian as a Hawai'ian character, it would challenge White masculinity by presenting other masculinities as romantically and sexually desirable. The nature of the relationship would also change as it would be a White-presenting woman restoring the identity and morality of a Hawai'ian man. She would no longer serve as the vehicle for redemption through Hawai'ianness because she would not be positioned as possessing special knowledge through exotic difference. Rather, she would act to help him value his own identity. While this, too, could be understood as problematic, particularly for its gendered representation of the woman who inspires a heterosexual man's redemption, this configuration would challenge structures of filmic interracial romance.

As an indigenous Hawai'ian man, Brian's interactions with the Woodsides would provide counterrepresentational meaning, too. His previous relationship with Tracy would center Brian as an object of multiple women's attraction, thus challenging White masculinity as the desired ideal. More interesting, perhaps, is his relationship with Grace. Having an indigenous Hawai'ian man play Grace's biological father would be a more progressive use of the mixed-race representation with a White actress. This is because unlike Allison, whose parents are off-camera, Grace's Hawai'ian father and White mother would be clearly visible and represented as sympathetic characters. Grace's interest in hula and the secret of her parentage would be more revealing as it would be more than a family secret but signal hidden heritages and the complexity of mixed-race expression. Finally, as Brian is integrated into the Woodside family, it would create a more powerful symbol of interracial connection, familial bonds, and unity. Although this might be argued to be an assimilative message of Hawai'ians blending into a metaphorical White family, I would argue that the counterrepresentational potential is salient because Brian would not enter as an infantilized dependent, a construct of the colonial imagination, but as a coequal parent and a father figure, thus challenging the feminized view of Hawai'i and the paternal view of the United States in the colonial imagination.

Conclusion

Whitewashing in *Aloha* reinforces and extends Whiteness through its claims of cross-racial authenticity and its settler-colonial discursive project. By physically marking Hawai'anness through the casting of Emma Stone as multiethnic and mixed-race Allison Ng, Whiteness claims Hawai'anness as a visible identity, constituting symbolic colonialism. That it does so by presenting Hawai'anness as premodern with Ng's beliefs in spirits and myths is further problematic as it relegates native Hawai'anness to the past, opening space for a White settler-colonial present and future. Thus, the film not only claims Whiteness's ability to be all things but it also constructs Hawai'i as a premodern other to present the White U.S. self as a normal, modern self. Brian's redemption as a White man who had sold out his Hawai'ian roots fulfills the prophecy as the Hawai'ian god of mischief that saves the Hawai'ian people. This not only presents a White savior narrative of White masculinity but constructs the U.S. military's settler-colonial presence as legitimate as his redemption is aligned with the redemption of the U.S. military. These representational moves, then, are more than just problematic casting choices. They are problematic narrative moves that benefit White racial hegemony by attempting to representationally secure White control while making Whiteness invisible in the process.

2

White China Experts,
Asian American Twinkies

• • • • • • • • • • • • • • • • • • • •

Shanghai Calling and *Already Tomorrow in Hong Kong*

In their feature length directorial debuts, two Chinese American filmmakers, Daniel Hsia and Emily Ting, both deal with Chinese American–White American romances in *Shanghai Calling* (2012) and *Already Tomorrow in Hong Kong* (2015), respectively. In both of the films, they feature fish-out-of-water narratives of Chinese Americans who are unfamiliar with and, to varying degrees, dissatisfied with being in Chinese cities, Shanghai and Hong Kong. Instead of a local familiarizing the leads with their new surroundings, they meet White American China experts, who help them adjust and appreciate the cities. Both directors ground their stories in personal experience with the Chinese American leads representing the directors' gender/race/ethnic identities. In an interview with the Asia Society, Hsia claims that his screenplay developed after seeing a friend, Vance Wagner (whose race is not established), move to China and become more fluent in Chinese than Hsia is (Hui, 2012). Ting, on the other hand, draws from direct, personal experience. In the director's commentary, she shares a story of meeting a White American in Hong Kong and sharing a night of conversation and romance, which became the seed of *Already Tomorrow in Hong Kong* (hereafter, *Already Tomorrow*) (Ting, 2015b).

Hsia's protagonist is played by Daniel Henney, a biracial Korean-White actor who first established televisual fame in the Korean television series *My Lovely*

Samsoon (2005) and has since played roles in Korean and U.S. television and film. Opposite Henney is Eliza Coupe, a White American actress who plays recurring roles on U.S. television. To represent Ting's experience as a Chinese American woman, she cast Jamie Chung, a Korean American actress to play Ruby, and real-life husband Bryan Greenburg, a White Jewish American actor, to play Josh. Thus, both films are distinctively U.S. American romances, featuring Chinese and White Americans falling in love. As independent films made by Chinese American directors, they also subvert common representational tropes and occasionally voice counterhegemonic discourses. At the same time, their reliance on the White American China expert perhaps also points to an unintentional whitewashing. Whether intentional or not, the representational implications bolster Whiteness, making them a productive pair to study.

In *Shanghai Calling*, Hsia claims in an interview with shanghaiist.com that he hoped to turn around the "tired cliché" of a White man traveling to Asia and having a relationship with an exotic Chinese woman, who "falls hopelessly in love with him as if she's been sitting around her whole life waiting for him to come along" (Tan, 2018, n.p.). The goal was to expose assumptions about China and the United States in which China becomes the receiving nation for budding professionals (Hui, 2012). With these representational goals in mind, Hsia's film was financed primarily by Chinese interests. The film centers on Sam, an ambitious lawyer, who reluctantly moves to Shanghai on the promise of making partner after establishing a Shanghai branch office to do business with Marcus Groff (Alan Ruck). Wide-eyed and arrogant, the first person Sam meets on his arrival is Amanda, a relocation specialist who helps him find a new home. Over time, she becomes romantically involved with Sam, helping him to learn more about China and to become a better man, who is guided by human connections rather than greed. In the end, Sam is faced with a moral dilemma—to unethically take advantage of a Chinese businessman for the sake of his White U.S. bosses or to act ethically and forgo his promising career. Sam chooses the latter, starts his own firm, and stays in Shanghai to build a life with Amanda.

Always Tomorrow is an homage to Richard Linklater's film *Before Sunrise* (1995), reimagining the film with a White American and a Chinese American expat's chance encounter in Hong Kong (Wong, n.d.). Taking place over two nights separated by a year, the story begins when Bryan offers to walk with Ruby, who is lost on her way to meet friends. They emotionally connect on their walk, but the night ends abruptly at a bar when Ruby learns that Bryan has a Chinese girlfriend. A year later, they have a chance encounter on a ferry, which leads to another night together. Although they are both in long-standing relationships, their time together causes them to question their relationships and to consider a future together. Across both movies, it is inescapable that the

White American foreign resident, aka expat, is represented as more culturally knowledgeable than Chinese Americans. Their Whiteness provides special purchase to be able to embody Chineseness, a feature made possible through Whiteness's representational flexibility. At the same time, the films challenge White supremacy, reflecting ambivalent ideological discourses situated in the directors' identities as Chinese/Asian Americans. To understand why Chinese American directors would represent their stories in this way, I start with a brief review of Asian American self-representation in cinema. Then, I describe how the films represent White Americans as cultural experts that teach and integrate Chinese Americans into Hong Kong and Shanghai. To understand how this whitewashed trope exists in Asian American cinema, I argue that it requires positioning these narratives within discourses of postracism, but these discourses are ambivalently presented because of the directors' standpoints as Chinese Americans.

Asian American Self-Representation

There has been a relative dearth of literature about Asian American cinema since the early 2000s (Hu, 2017), so this chapter draws on the earlier literature on Asian American representation published in the 1990s and early 2000s to understand *Shanghai Calling* and *Already Tomorrow in Hong Kong* as independent Asian American cinema that is transnational in sentiment and, in the case of the former, in capital and distribution. The transnationalism of Asian American cinema has specific connections to the San Francisco International Asian American Film Festival's shift to embrace the popular and critical rise of international Asian cinema at major film festivals (Okada, 2015). This is exemplified in films such as Director Bong Joon Ho's *Okja* (2017) and Jon Chu's *Crazy Rich Asians* (2018). In the case of *Shanghai Calling*, the U.S.–Chinese joint venture is also consistent with increasing numbers of coproductions that center Chinese places (DeBoer, 2014).

This shift stands in contrast with the explicit U.S. centrism of early Asian American cinema (Okada, 2015). Asian American films of the 1960s and 1970s were produced with the intention of creating counterhegemonic representation (Hamamoto, 2000a) and, thus, centered around identity as a tactic of social survival (Hamamoto, 2000a). As Ono and Pham (2009) have argued, Asian American media have the potential to decolonize dominant narratives and inscribe new images in the cultural imaginary, yet this potential is only partially realized. Though writing about Asian American print media, Ono and Sloop (1995) claimed that Asian American media form a pastiche of various discourses—dominant and resistive. As they argue, this is characteristic of vernacular discourse. Similarly, Hamamoto (2000b) argues Asian American cinema filmmakers have internalized the politics of desire seen in the visual culture of dominant media. This should be expected, as Asian American filmmakers live within and articulate meanings in their films that exist in the U.S. cultural terrain. As such, Asian American cinema has never simply countered or conformed to U.S. racial hegemony; Asian American filmmakers disidentify but do not counteridentify with it (Feng, 2002). In other words, like any vernacular discourse, they resist and challenge dominant U.S. culture within that cultural terrain, but they do not overturn or reject it in its entirety.

While early Asian American filmmakers emphasized ideology over form, contemporary filmmakers are more interested in artistic experimentation (Hellenbrand, 2008; Okada, 2015). Whether because of this or as a result of it, Asian American filmmakers such as Justin Lin, the director of *Better Luck Tomorrow* (2002) and several films in the *Fast and the Furious* franchise, and Jon M. Chu, the director of *Crazy Rich Asians*, are bringing their Asian American cinema heritage to mass market film. As such, it is possible that Asian American filmmakers will move closer to dominant racial logics as popularity is often predicated on White tastes. This has been true in online spaces for Asian American YouTube stars such as KevJumba and Ryan Higa (Guo and Lee, 2013; Saul, 2010). So far, there has been no research of which I am aware that explores Asian American cinematic portrayals of transnational "return." However, there is early research on autobiographical documentaries of Chinese American return that points to the subjects' identification and disidentification with their homeland (Feng, 2002).

The whitewashing of the films' love interests, then, points to this ambivalence, particularly as the Chinese American directors, Hsia and Ting, reflect their own simultaneous discomfort with and love of U.S. cinema and its conventions. Given Asian American cinema's transnational turn, it should be expected that there are opportunities for counterhegemonic challenge but that it is also limited by the culturally bounded standpoints of Chinese/Asian American life. Next, I describe the films' whitewashed China experts and the hegemonic and resistive potential this representation creates.

Whitewashed China Experts and Chinese American Twinkies

For Ting, her inspiration for the interracial story was rooted in a reimagination of her own heterosexual experience with a White resident. For Hsia, however, he mentions in a "Behind the Scenes" DVD special feature that he intentionally wanted to challenge audience expectations. "Thematically, I think *Shanghai Calling* is about the world turning on its head. Sam, for instance, looks like he belongs in China, looks like he should speak Chinese and understand China, but he doesn't. Whereas Amanda looks like she doesn't belong, but she speaks Chinese and does understand how things work in Shanghai" (Hsia, 2012b). The shifting of audience expectations is reflective of a counterrepresentational impulse seen in Asian American cinema (Okada, 2015). While their work reflects Asian American cinema's transnational turn and its move toward form, both still reflect Asian American cinema's interest in identity (Hellenbrand, 2008; Okada, 2015). Like the documentary filmmakers in Feng's (2002) study, both Ting and Hsia engaged in autobiographical subject matter—their transnational relationships to China.

Whether it was because of representational authenticity or counterrepresentational intentions, both directors chose to not only include a White love interest but to transform that person into a China expert. Although that representational move subverts Chinese American ethnoracial essentialism by countering the stereotype of the forever foreigner (Hamamoto, 1994; Lee, 1999; Ono and Pham, 2009), its imagination is limited to Whiteness. In other words, it is not coincidental that White characters were imagined as having the ability to act as cultural ambassadors for the Chinese American returnee. A privilege of Whiteness's invisibility is its ability to become any identity (Dyer, 1997; Gabriel, 1998; Oh, 2017; Tierney, 2006). As such, the whitewashing of the characters functions to partially reify the symbolic colonization of Whiteness to possess any culture. As Chinese American directors, however, they move away from standard constructions of Asianness by featuring White Americans who possess contemporary cultural knowledge and language rather than premodern traditions and knowledge or hypermodern future technologies. Indeed, desirable Whiteness is constructed as the cultural insider-outsider, a person who knows the culture and language but who maintains their Americanness. While doing so, the films justify the White characters' inclusion by drawing on postracist notions of color blindness. Thus, the directors demonstrate an ambivalent vision—a limited challenge that is constrained by their articulation in the U.S. ideological terrain.

The clearest demonstration of the White China expert in both *Shanghai Calling* and *Already Tomorrow* is Josh and Amanda's superior fluency. In contrast, Ruby and Sam are unable to speak their heritage language. In *Already Tomorrow*, this is most apparent in a scene at Dave Custom Tailors in the historic Chungking Mansion. When the tailor greets Ruby at the door in Cantonese, Ruby scrunches her face and raises her eyebrows as she says, "Um. Sorry. I, I'm here to pick up a suit." At this point in the film, Ruby has lived in Hong Kong but is unable to understand simple greetings or express her reason for coming to the store. The film overdetermines her U.S. Americanness by constructing her as linguistically inept. When she is informed that "Suit not ready" and to come back the following week, Josh helps Ruby by speaking in Cantonese. After a brief exchange that is not subtitled, thus emphasizing the foreignness of the exchange, Josh has earned Ruby a 15 percent discount and a promise to have the suit ready by the weekend. In astonishment, Ruby says, "what?" with a breathy expression of pleasant surprise. Cutting to the street, Ruby says:

"What was that? I didn't know you could speak Cantonese so well." In their following conversation, she indicates that she finds his ability to speak Cantonese "weird" because she does not speak "any" Chinese. What is also important to note is that his Chinese fluency is so superior that he is able to gain better than expected results.

Similarly, in *Shanghai Calling*, Amanda is represented as a fluent Chinese speaker while Sam's inability to speak Chinese leads to humorous moments that challenge U.S. centrism. After Sam settles into his new apartment, he steps out of a shower and is shocked to see a middle-aged Chinese woman standing in his apartment. After she speaks Chinese to him, he throws up his arms and says: "I got nothing. I don't speak Chinese. Who are you?" When she speaks to him again in Chinese, his face is expressionless to demonstrate that he still does not understand. Moments later, the scene shifts to Sam on a busy street. Surrounded by high-rise apartments, he is unable to make sense of his map and is unable to navigate the strangeness of his surroundings. He gives up by hailing a taxi, but the taxi driver gestures while refusing to take him to the address. Sam insists, however, claiming that he understands how taxi scams work since he is a savvy New Yorker. The driver, resigned to his stubborn passenger, starts the fare and drives about ten feet before stopping, gesturing to the sign on the building that matches Sam's business card.

In contrast, Amanda has excellent command of Mandarin Chinese. When they arrive at a swanky restaurant, the hostess speaks directly to Sam and asks how many are in the party. Despite Amanda's response, the hostess looks again at Sam and asks whether they would like to be seated indoors or outdoors. Amanda replies again. Once they are seated, Amanda is given an English-language menu while Sam is given a Chinese-language one. When he wonders why, she says, "Because I obviously don't speak Chinese, and you obviously do." He replies: "Right. I've got to learn this stuff." Immediately following this exchange, he asks how Amanda has become "such an expert on China." She, then, provides extensive credentials—studying in college, studying abroad at Beijing University." Although she is shown speaking Chinese only once more throughout the film, this scene makes her expertise unambiguous.

Perhaps because of Chinese funding and because of sexist tropes of men as heroes, Hsia provides an explanation for Amanda's superior linguistic ability, and her fluency in Mandarin does not become a necessary skill to rescue Sam. It is instead presented to argue that the caliber of White expat is becoming more educated and professional, and by extension, that Shanghai is becoming a more desirable site for migration. While both directors' apparent intention is to progressively challenge notions of U.S.-mediated stereotypes of Asian American foreignness by overdetermining Ruby and Sam as culturally and linguistically monocultural U.S. Americans, their inversion is only a limited challenge. It successfully subverts the stereotype of Asian American foreignness, but it does so by reifying Whiteness as able to become any culture or language while essentializing Chinese Americans as bound by their (U.S.) culture. To make the point clearer, both directors could have chosen characters of color, such as Black Americans or Latinx Americans to play opposite Ruby and Sam. It is specifically White Americans who are represented as China experts, however.

In addition to White characters' linguistic fluency, they are presented as more fully Chinese. Ruby and Sam both bristle at, mock, or find mysterious wisdom in Hong Kong and Shanghai, while Amanda and Josh successfully navigate these spaces like locals and are so accustomed to cultural differences that they are not noticed. In *Already Tomorrow*, for instance, Ruby mocks a sign at a crab restaurant that she and Sam visit because it misspells crab as "Fresh Live Crap." In Ting's director's commentary (2015b), she notes that she also found these English misspellings to be a humorous part of the terrain of Hong Kong. In contrast, Josh does not laugh but brushes it off, saying, "Don't worry about that." The film continues this point at the restaurant when a couple sits next to them on unoccupied plastic stools at their round, outdoor table. After a bit of awkward silence from Ruby and Josh, she says, "That's another thing I can't seem to get used to." Not understanding what she is referring to until she subtly gestures toward the strangers at the table, he replies, "You get to a place where you don't even notice." Likewise, *Shanghai Calling* relies on a similar gag when Sam meets a private investigator with the moniker Awesome Wang (Le Geng). At a dinner meeting, six patrons join their table until they are literally rubbing elbows. The comedic gag concludes when a middle-aged man with a buzz cut sits between Sam and Awesome, while loudly slurping noodles. Awesome is undisturbed, but Sam is uncomfortable with the violation of his private space. Thus, the films both portray Chinese Americans as foreigners, and the White China expert as culturally assimilated.

In both films, the White romantic counterpart is presented as having expert, local knowledge. In *Shanghai Calling*, Amanda's expertise is demonstrated through her work as a relocation specialist for expats. She has local expertise in the Shanghai real estate market and can navigate these spaces fluently. She is also represented with knowledge of cultural idioms. When Sam encourages Amanda during a moment of self-doubt, he tells her that his mother says that some people are like ducks because they make things look easy but that below the surface they work very hard. Amanda, then, lets him know that this saying is Chinese in origin. Although her expertise is clearly centered in her education and training, in *Already Tomorrow*, Josh's expertise is manifest more frequently during casual strolls through the city. Indeed, the conceit of the movie is centered on their chance encounter and Josh's role as an informal tour guide, taking Ruby to many of Hong Kong's most iconic destinations. In an early scene, he remarks, "I should write a guide book." When Ruby asks Josh to have a drink at Lan Kwai Fong, a popular tourist destination, he replies,

"These are cheesy tourist places," and responds, "Let's get out of the depths of hell." He then takes her to a hip bar.

In the film's second act, which occurs a year later, Josh still knows Hong Kong much better than Ruby, who still gets lost. Indeed, he has to correct her when she walks in the wrong direction. Also, when she plans to go to Chungking Mansion to pick up a suit from the tailor's store, he informs her that Kowloon is "sketchy," saying that he would accompany her, thus demonstrating local knowledge that she does not possess. Later in the evening, he teaches her how to negotiate when they visit Hong Kong's famous night market, saying: "You have to work on your negotiating skills. When they say like 125, that really means like 10." After Josh is able to negotiate a desired price after walking away a few other times before, Ruby shouts in joy, raises one arm in the air, jumps up and down in excitement and gives Josh a high-five. Her excitement and earlier dialogue demonstrate that the successful negotiation is novel for her but common for Josh.

Both films spend substantial energy to demonstrate that it is the White American partner who is the cosmopolitan China expert. They not only possess greater cultural knowledge and integration but correct the provincialism and U.S. centrism of their Chinese American counterparts. It is important to note that this is not an accident of representation. Any cultural production draws on the discourses available in the cultural terrain to create meaning (Hall, 1997), and Whiteness is advantaged by its paradoxical hyperpresence and invisibility in U.S. racial formations. Furthermore, White Americans occupy the space of the globally mobile expat in the U.S. imagination and perhaps even in the Chinese imagination. It is perhaps for this reason that *Shanghai Calling* features only one nameless Black woman without speaking lines, who passes across the frame as a potential love interest for Sam's friend, Brad (Sean Gallagher). In *Already Tomorrow*, the only characters who are not Chinese or White are South Asian merchants and patrons in Kowloon, a place that Josh had described as dangerous for a young woman. Thus, the inclusion of the White China expert reinforces messages of Whiteness's ability to possess and be anything, and, ironically, the films, which mean to overturn the image of Chinese Americans as U.S. foreigners, present them as Chinese foreigners. While the nations have changed, the essentializing quality of foreignness has not.

Postracist Universalism

For these racialized representational moves to work, both films rely on postracist universalism to rationalize the hypervisibility of the White American expert and the Chinese American culturally naïf. To do so, the film relies on universalist narratives. The universalist narratives at times engage in color blindness—the premise that race is not noticed. in other cases, they ignore systemic disparities in racial experience, such as Ruby's ability to speak English as similarly weird as Josh's ability to speak Cantonese. This universalism is argued to be postracist, as it suggests that the social realities of systemic racism have been relegated to the past (Ono, 2010). It assumes a similarity of experience, which implies that antiracist critique is akin to whining. As this book argues, postracism is necessary to provide ideological cover for whitewashing, so it is unsurprising that postracism is manifest in these films, despite being written and directed by Chinese American filmmakers.

Indeed, postracism has been the most prevalent racial belief in the United States (Prashad, 2001), particularly for liberal-minded U.S. Americans. As such, these representations are created from this symbolic space in which the directors inhabit. By establishing universalism, the films construct White Americans' contested expertise and Chinese Americans' ignorance as natural because of universal human nature. This is predicated, however, on the universalist, postracist idea that White expertise in China is natural, just as Chinese American expertise in the United States is natural. However, this hides that the White American's expertise is gained relatively quickly and that there is expertise in both spaces—the United States and China. Thus, the films put the directors in discursive traps as they require the rationalization of the White China expert to create audience identification and sympathy with them. The postracist arguments themselves also create their own problematic discourses about Whiteness and Chineseness/Asianness.

The first universalist representation equates the racialized experiences of White and Chinese Americans. In *Already Tomorrow*, the film preempts possible criticisms of White men's "yellow fever" in multiple ways, the first of which is to represent and equate Josh's dating history of Chinese women with Ruby's dating history of White men. The film's conflict is situated in their uncertainty about whether they break off their long-standing relationships with their partners for the promise of romance. Josh is in a multiyear relationship with a Chinese woman, and Ruby is engaged to marry a Jewish American man. The film positions them as mirror opposites, so that her dating history of "coincidental" relationships with mostly White men is presented as similar to his dating history of Chinese women. That is, it creates a parallel argument in which they occupy opposite but similar roles.

This universalist representation is premised on two problematic ideas, however. First, it implies that the United States is a White nation just as Hong Kong is a predominantly Chinese nation. More problematically, it ignores the sexualization of Asian women in the White imagination as submissive sex objects, the desexualization of Chinese men, and the desirability of White masculinity (Espiritu, 2004; Marchetti, 1993; Oh, 2016; Ono and Pham, 2009; Shim, 1998). The trope is so common that White men–Asian women couples are seen in U.S. media much more frequently than Asian men–Asian women couples. The hegemonic politics of desire are ignored in favor of a claim of coincidental dating. The film furthers this construction of racial parallelism with the revelation that Josh's girlfriend's parents disapprove of her dating a White foreigner. This constructs White people as victims of anti-White racism, with the implication that Ruby's experiences of anti-Asian racism are simply about majoritarian prejudices against outsiders. The film, then, represents anti-White racism in Hong Kong as equivalent to anti-Asian racism in the United States. Indeed, the film pushes the argument further when Josh states that his parents approve of his Chinese girlfriend. In this case, White racial hegemony is further resolved as it is presented as more progressive than Chinese attitudes against miscegenation. This, of course, hides a long history of de jure antimiscegenation against the Chinese that existed in the United States but that did not exist in Hong Kong (Chang, 2003).

Shanghai Calling similarly works to present racialized experiences as equivalent. It displays much more awareness of interracial dissimilarity, however, perhaps because of the director's inclusion of an Asian American man as a love interest. As Espiritu (2004) notes, this disrupts hegemonic gendering of Asianness, so Sam's interracial romance becomes explicitly raced for counterhegemonic purposes. The point at which racially parallel experiences find expression is in Sam's connection with Amanda's daughter, Katie. When the audience is first introduced to Katie, Amanda is frustrated and worried that Katie has grown reserved and refuses to speak in English. Sam tells her that he will share a secret with her if she tells him the purpose of her shovel that she is holding. After whispering in her ear, she giggles and says, "I'm digging a hole to America." This inverts the old joke about "digging a hole to China," presenting the United States as the faraway place on the opposite side of the globe. Thus, this revelation links Katie and Sam's experience as foreign outsiders. Later, upon Amanda's probing at an expat bar, Sam reveals that he told Katie that the only Chinese word he knows is *fang pi*, which means "fart." He told her that he wanted her to know that she is not the only "weirdo." He then relates his own desires in the United States to fit in, which is why he rejected learning Chinese, just as he says this is why Katie refuses to speak in English. It should be pointed out, however, that while Sam is represented as unable to speak in Chinese, Katie is fluent in English; she simply refuses to use it. Thus, the film argues that their experiences are similar while also furthering the notion that Whiteness can be fully Chinese and fully U.S. American.

The second way the films argue for postracism is through the message of color blindness. Violations of color blindness are filmically rebuked, advancing the message that noticing race is itself problematic. As mentioned previously in *Shanghai Calling*, the waitstaff notice Amanda's Whiteness and do not speak to her or provide her with a Chinese-language menu. The film does not represent this as a logical or routinized practice based on experiences with other White Americans. Rather, because it sympathetically presents Amanda's perspective, the audience is meant to identify with her and view her (mis)treatment as problematic. This is amplified in a later scene when Amanda joins a conference call upon Sam's invitation. Fang Fang (Zhu Zhu), Sam's assistant, whispers to Sam, saying: "You shouldn't bring a guest to a meeting. It's unprofessional." When she serves tea to Amanda, Fang Fang smiles and speaks in Mandarin, with the subtitles reading, "These thick-headed foreigners don't understand anything." Amanda replies in Mandarin, saying: "Thank you. This tea smells delightful." Because of the identification with Amanda and Sam and because of the pleasure in seeing the tables turned when the "thick-headed foreigner" demonstrates her understanding, *Shanghai Calling* argues against stereotyping foreigners as culturally and linguistically ignorant. Indeed, this flipping of expectations is, as previously mentioned, the premise of Hsia's film.

Already Tomorrow operates similarly, forcefully making its point in what Ting claims has become the most controversial scene in the movie. In the scene, Ruby and Josh sit in the back of a bus with Ruby noticing an elder White man get onboard with a young Chinese woman. Josh tells Ruby not to be judgmental, saying that the couple could simply be co-workers, but then the young woman is shown seductively running her fingers through the hairs on the back of the man's head near the scruff of his neck. Although the film reveals her suspicions to be correct, she is later rebuked for having them. Ruby reveals that she harbors her own insecurities because of her relationship history. He teases her for being "one of those Asian girls who only date White guys." She replies: "I do not only date White guys. Like, the majority have been White, but it's not on purpose. It's totally coincidental." He replies that he is the "White guy with the Asian fetish." He tells her that in Hong Kong, it is East meets West, so she should get used to interracial couples. Because she agrees that she has to be open-minded, the film forecloses readings that interrogate the White man and Asian woman couple as problematic. The argument of the film reduces the pattern of filmic representation and off-screen couplings to individual-level, interpersonal decisions rather than ones that are also performed within the hegemonic politics of desire, with White masculinity transformed as most desirable not only in the U.S. cultural terrain (Lester and Goggin, 2005) but across parts of Asia, where global hegemonies have also privileged White masculinity as a cosmopolitan ideal (Ahn, 2015; Kim, 2006). As such, the film advances the politics of postracism and the notion that racial difference and historical racism do not matter in romantic desire.

Ting is well aware of the racial problematics of this representation, which is why she explains in an interview that she included the scene despite knowing the potential pushback. "The bus scene where Ruby and Josh discuss Asian girl/white guy coupling is a controversial one. Some who read the script cautioned me against it, but I felt it was really important for me to address it. I think I channeled a lot of my own viewpoints in that scene. I do find myself being judgmental every time I see an older white man with a younger Asian woman. But yet, I'm perpetuating the stereotype myself by dating a white guy" (Wong, n.d.). In the director's commentary, she claimed that she received hate mail and angry Internet reactions immediately after the trailer's release. She justifies the representation by alluding to *The World of Suzie Wong* (1960) by claiming that it is not an "Asian hooker with the, you know, White savior" (Ting, 2015b). The point, then, is that she attempts to representationally preempt critique from whom she imagines as her audience, likely savvy Asian Americans who are sensitized to gendered racialization. Thus, Ruby becomes a stand-in for the critical Asian American audience member, and her acceptance of individuals' romantic decisions is meant as an object lesson for Asian American critics. To punch back at her racially sensitized critics, Ting relies on postracist color blindness that rebukes racial awareness in romantic life as morally flawed, that is, judgmental.

Ambivalent Resistance: Disrupting Whiteness

Despite the films' use of dominant discourses of postracism that justify the inclusion of the supra-ethnic White lead, the films are still Asian American independent films that continue legacy questions of identity and representation that challenge hegemonic portrayals in U.S. media (Okada, 2015). Both films, then, are marked by their ambivalence, expressing both White racial hegemony and Chinese American counterhegemony. This is clearest in the choice of destinations—Shanghai and Hong Kong. As Ting frequently mentions in her DVD commentary (2015b), she intended to make Hong Kong a "third character" such as in Richard Linklater's treatment of Paris in *Before Sunrise*. As such, she argues that Hong Kong is on par with the romantic cities of Europe. In the special behind-the-scenes feature, Ting claims that the film is a "Love Letter to Hong Kong." As she notes, "We really shot the hell out of Hong Kong" (Ting, 2015c). Through the couple's visit to most landmark destinations and its use of montage, the film works almost as a travelogue to present Hong Kong as an attractive place that is suitable for romance to flourish.

Similarly, Hsia had an intentional goal of representing Shanghai as a modern city that attracts the best people from around the globe as an international magnet in the flows of global movement and opportunity. The film's opening montage of the city and its opening narration make this clear, saying: "Shanghai is very attractive to foreign businessmen. Hundreds of thousands of Americans now live and work in Shanghai." The argument that Shanghai is a globally important city is further reinforced when Donald (Bill Paxton), the mayor of Americatown who represents the old guard of White expats, loses in an election to Esther Wu (Kara Wang), a former Rhodes Scholar and executive at Climb Motors. As she says in her defiant introduction, "Shanghai isn't a hardship post for outcasts anymore." The subplot of Donald's election loss has no function toward driving the narrative forward, so its counterideological purpose becomes stark in contrast. Crystallizing the point, Sam chooses to stay in Shanghai to start his own law firm rather than return to New York City.

Both films also produce counterhegemonic challenges to U.S. media stereotypes of Asian Americans as perpetual foreigners (Ono and Pham, 2009) and to White exceptionalism as expats. Sam and Ruby are both represented as fish out of water in China, disrupting essentialized Chineseness. In addition, *Shanghai Calling* inverts the notion of foreignness by applying it to White expats (other than Amanda) with the prominent position Americatown takes in the narrative. As Amanda explains, "It's kind of like Chinatown over there just the other way around." Although its inclusion engages in postracial universalism, this inversion works counterhegemonically by pointing out the exoticness of White Americans in China and by making familiar Chinatowns in the United States. This functions counterhegemonically because of the prominent place Whiteness takes as the racial norm (Dyer, 1988; Nakayama and Krizek, 1995). Thus, even though the films engage in universalism, by pointing out that Whiteness can be visible and non-normative (like Chineseness), the weight of the comparison is largely counterhegemonic because of the salience of its presentation.

White people's privileged place in Asia is also questioned in both of the films as the language of expats is itself questioned. In *Already Tomorrow*, Ruby questions Josh, asking him why he gets to be called an "expat" while her grandparents were considered an "immigrant." She points out that a White investment banker in Hong Kong is called an "expat" but Chinese restaurant workers in Arcadia, California, are "immigrants." His response, that he had not thought of it from her perspective, presents the question as appropriate and truthful. In *Shanghai Calling*, on the other hand, it is Amanda who makes the same point. When Sam complains about his inability to adjust, she equates her life in China to his parents, saying, "We Americans like to call ourselves expats, but the fact of the matter is we're immigrants." Although the moments are fleeting, highlighting the different, unmentioned connotations in the labels lays bare White racial hegemony. White migrants have the power to name themselves abroad, and White residents have the power to name migrants that come onto their shores.

While these challenges are strikingly similar, *Shanghai Calling* diverges into further counterhegemonic challenge. Perhaps because of its non–U.S. funding structure, it uses a counterhegemonic coupling, an Asian American man with a White American woman. Countering the asexual representations of Asian American men that have dominated the silver screen, *Shanghai Calling*'s conventional story line within the romantic comedy genre represents Sam as a flawed but charismatic character who possesses sexual energy and romantic value. In contrast, White men in the film are confined to minor roles and occasionally featured as sexually deviant.

Although filmic portrayals of White men with Asian women is a standard trope, the reverse is rarely the case (Marchetti, 1993). When included as sympathetic figures, Asian/American men characters have been played by White actors in yellowface. In these representations, the men are often feminized and represented as fragile, such as in *Broken Blossoms* (1919). Although Sam is not a hypermasculine character, he matches expectations for masculinity that are often seen in romantic comedies, such as being rough around the edges but maturing through his heterosexual relationship with a woman. His work ambition and wealth also masculinize Sam as he fits normative standards of gendered masculinity (Kimmel, 2006). His masculinity also finds physical expression as *Shanghai Calling* sexualizes Sam for the voyeuristic gaze of the camera as it lingers on his lean, defined body after he emerges from a shower to be covered only by a towel. Furthermore, the actor Daniel Henney is relatively tall at 188 centimeters (six feet two inches). Through these intentional narrative and casting choices, the film represents Henney as the most normatively masculine character.

Shanghai Calling not only represents Sam as the most desirable male figure; it also questions White masculinity and its distorted relationship to China. Donald, the old guard of the expat community, is represented as friendly and influential but as irrelevant with the well-educated, Chinese American returnee, Esther Wu. His relationship to China as a privileged outsider is questioned as his racial difference is represented as no longer sufficient in maintaining status. Marcus's relationship with China is through his embrace of traditional arts and business investments. Marcus is presented as a sympathetic figure who has embraced his tenure in Shanghai with his appreciation and practice of calligraphy, his enjoyment of tea, and his traditional wardrobe that locals no longer wear, but this is presented as a superficial liberal veneer as he is also willing to break the law to bankrupt his Chinese competitors, revealing the hypocrisy of White people who love China for its traditional past while hurting Chinese people in the present. He embodies the White foreigner, who appropriates Chinese traditional culture while acting with imperial privilege. It is reminiscent of the colonial traveler who delighted in the products of traditional culture but who was disgusted by the sight and presence of actual Chinese people (Clifford, 2001).

Perhaps the clearest contrasts with Sam are the sexually licentious White men. Sam's friend Brad, for instance, self-identifies as unattractive to women. During a party when they first meet, Brad and Sam discuss Brad's dating problems.

BRAD: "Hey, is this seat taken? I thought my girl problems were supposed to be over, right?"

SAM: "Don't be so hard on yourself, man. We all have our dry spells."

BRAD: "You don't get it, dude. My whole life has been a dry spell. That's why I moved here. But just before I showed up, word finally got around that English teachers only came here to get laid."

Brad is not only represented as physically less attractive; he embodies a common insult directed toward White English teachers in East Asia, the "sexpat." Furthermore, Amanda is introduced to White expats, who all demonstrate sexual deviance. The first, an Englishman, ogles Chinese women who walk by and flirts with them despite being introduced to Amanda. She sarcastically comments, "That's totally acceptable." In a later scene, she meets a Frenchman for a date. He tells her that he promised his wife that he would not cheat with a Chinese woman, so to keep his promise, he is proposing a sexual relationship with Amanda instead. Amanda storms away from this date frustrated by the quality of men she meets. In the next scene, she says to her best friend with whom she is getting a foot massage that she is "done with expat guys" because they have an Asian fetish, or, as her friend continues, "they're turkey vultures because they hover around to pick up the discarded white meat." Thus, *Shanghai Calling* counters the usual representations of White men as the most sexually and romantically desirable (Espiritu, 2004; Hamamoto, 1994).

Chinese American Chinese Insider

Although the imagination of Asian American subjectivity is always an attempt to decolonize the mind and picture representation that is liberated from Whiteness, the attempt to do this in Asian American cinema is not new to the genre. A hallmark feature of Asian American cinema has been its interest in identity politics that assert our own value as an intervention in the ideological struggle over racial meaning (Hamamoto, 2000a). Because *Always Tomorrow* and *Shanghai Calling* are already Asian American films produced independently of the major studios, this imagination of Asian American subjectivity is less about remedying and more about imagining Asian American subjectivity if both of the romantic leads in each of the films are Chinese American. Having Asian American characters in these roles allows the possibility of seeing global lives connected to both Asia and the United States, representing Asian Americans as cosmopolitan figures (Shimizu, 2017).

Most obviously, this representation would move toward a romantic coupling that privileges Asian American men and women. While Chinese couples are, of course, the most ubiquitous in actual Chinese cities—Hong Kong and Shanghai—and in Chinese media, this common couple is nearly invisible in the U.S.-mediated terrain (Espiritu, 2004). Because the films, especially *Already Tomorrow*, are meant for consumption across the North American independent film circuit, the imagined audience can be understood as U.S. American. This would be a particularly powerful shift in *Already Tomorrow* because of the common representation of White American men with Asian American women in U.S. films. It is important to note that this is not the racialized, misogynistic argument that Asian American women should date and marry only Asian American men. Rather, it is to say that if structures can be understood as a pattern of behavior, thought, and representation (Croteau, Hoynes, and Milan, 2012), then the structured, hegemonic representation is the White man's possession of the Asian woman (Kang, 2002). Thus, any coupling that exists outside this representational matrix can be understood as counterhegemonic, such as Asian American women and Black American men, Asian American men and Black American women, Asian American women and Latinx American men, and so on. This is, then, a critique of structure, not an argument for racial purity.

Seeing two Asian Americans fall in love, then, acts powerfully to humanize Asian Americans' love, passion, and romance. For many Asian Americans, this has been the powerful appeal of recent films such as *Crazy Rich Asians* (2018) and *Always Be My Maybe* (2019), which were both released after the start of analysis for the book. Returning to *Already Tomorrow*, the film establishes that Ruby's previous dating history has primarily been with White men, which is explained as an accident of circumstances rather than intention. The choice of a Chinese American man would, however, produce different connotations. She would still reject explicitly the argument that her choices have been shaped by the politics of representation, which have positioned White men as the most desirable, but the subtext of the passionate night with a coethnic American man would be that there is something unique and magical in this interaction. For Josh, it would represent his attraction to Ruby as connected to his desire for shared lived experience in his romantic attraction. It would present Chinese Americanness as particular and not equivalent to or fully realized in the metaphor of a Chinese American–Chinese romance. While the films already argue for Chinese American difference as U.S. American, Josh's romantic interests would work with the more complicated discourses in Asian American communities about differences between the immigrant generation and American Born Chinese (ABC). It would avoid simple notions of Chinese Americans as fully U.S. American by pointing to a range of Chinese American experience.

Similarly, in *Shanghai Calling*, Sam replies affirmatively when Brad questions whether he has only dated White women. Although the film does not challenge this choice, indeed it appears to affirm it with his relationship with Amanda; the opposite would be true if Amanda were imagined as a Chinese

American woman. Sam's past relationships were not meaningful enough to change his ambitions, which were a consequence of both falling for Amanda and living in Shanghai. Thus, the original narrative claims that he did not find the right White American woman; a changed narrative would suggest that he found love because of a Chinese American woman. Ideologically, this would contest the culturally prevalent idea that White women embody idealized, desirable femininity (Lester and Goggin, 2005; Oh, 2018b). The recent hits *The Big Sick* (2017) and the Netflix show *Master of None* (2015) feature Asian American men's romantic lives and White women opposite Indian American men.

At the same time, White expat men's failed courtship of Amanda would resound with racial meaning. The representation of their behavior as disgusting would not only be represented as White expat men's character flaws but racist ones. Ogling Chinese women while in a conversation with a Chinese American Amanda or propositioning a sexual affair upon meeting would represent White men as treating Amanda as a disposable object of racialized sexual attraction. Her choice to date Sam instead would signify the importance of their specific, shared experience as Chinese Americans.

This imagined representational replacement is ideologically fraught, however. It would read as an endorsement of essentializing notions of ethnic/racial desire. That is, Sam would find humanity through a relationship with a Chinese American woman, a dating relationship he has never previously experienced, and Ruby would find romantic passion with a Chinese American man. However, this would be somewhat mitigated in *Already Tomorrow* through the conversation on the bus about being able to connect about shared experiences. Josh states that even without a language barrier, there is a "cultural barrier" with television shows and music that are a part of their childhoods. This is followed by Josh and Ruby both riffing on impersonations of the "The Soup Nazi," a well-known figure on the television show *Seinfeld*. As such, it would disrupt the notion of ethnic similarity and replace it with cultural similarity as necessary in a relationship, but that reading of cultural similarity would also likely still extend to the ethnic.

Shifts in representation would also create complicated meanings about Amanda's family. Because her daughter presents as visibly White, it would create unanswered questions about her relationship with her daughter, that is, adopted or biracial while physically presenting as White. With the story of her daughter's desire to fit in and her connection to Sam, this would lead to questions about the nature of that connection. Although the film presents a simple narrative of parallel difference, a White American wanting to fit in China and a Chinese American wanting to fit in the United States, the audience's extra-textual knowledge that the actor Daniel Henney, who plays Sam, is mixed race—Korean and White—would lead to a semiotic rupture that is not resolved in the film. Is their connection based on their shared difference as biracial

White/Asian American? Visually, it would also disrupt the common view of White American adults as humanitarians who adopt children of color, especially girls from Asia, by visually representing a Chinese American single mother raising a White American daughter.

Amanda, as Chinese American, would also be revealing in the scenes that establish that she is treated as an outsider who cannot speak English because of her racial difference. Although the scene in the restaurant would no longer make sense, the scene in the boardroom when Fang Fang speaks about the outsider's presence as unprofessional would be imbued with new meaning. In the original, it is Amanda's Whiteness that has her treated as an ignorant Other. In a reimagined casting, it would be Amanda's U.S. Americanness that would lead to her poor treatment. This would shed light on the ways Asian American returnees feel caught in a liminal space in their homelands (Cho, 2012). She would be treated as an outsider for her perceived inability to perform Chineseness rather than her racial difference. This points to the types of nuanced meanings about identity that are found in Asian American cinema but while centering it on transnational experiences rather than the strongly U.S.-centric treatment in much Asian American cinema (Okada, 2015).

In *Already Tomorrow*, if Josh were imagined as a Chinese American man, the movie, at its center, would include two Chinese Americans with different connections and knowledge to their "homeland." Ruby's surprise that Josh speaks fluent Cantonese would be reinterpreted to not be about her racial/national expectations that White people cannot speak Cantonese but rather that second-generation Chinese Americans ordinarily struggle with their "mother tongue." Again, this would highlight intraethnic conversations that are not well represented in U.S. or other media. Because the scene is written to be specific to racial/national difference, however, it would not make sense as it is currently performed. Furthermore, Ruby's mocking treatment of "Chinglish" and other cultural practices and Josh's corrections would be read as coethnics recalibrating their partner's view of their shared heritage culture and space rather than Whites' superior cultural knowledge. Josh and Ruby would be engaged in a discursive negotiation about Chinese Americanness and how they perform their liminal identities. The film would no longer be arguing for cosmopolitanism but rather specific disciplining of Chinese and other Asian Americans who internalize Western superiority when returning to their homelands. While in some ways a liberatory discourse that challenges Western logics, it would replace those logics with normative understandings of appropriate Chineseness.

Finally, *Already Tomorrow* would challenge model minority discourses. As a Chinese American, Josh's elite education and work in multinational finance could be understood as an enactment of the model minority. However, his decision to forgo his lucrative career to be a novelist would produce new meanings that reject the model minority. He has chosen personal fulfillment as an author rather than money and familial expectations as a banker. This would demonstrate his U.S. American connections to individualism and personal fulfillment rather than filial piety, marking the character as shaped indelibly by his U.S. American lived experience.

Conclusion

It is somewhat suspect to label *Already Tomorrow* and *Shanghai Calling* whitewashed, particularly as they prominently feature Chinese American characters. Thus, the films' inclusion is not because they are whitewashed as a whole but rather because they whitewash specific lead characters. In this case, they meet the criterion of inserting White characters in Asian spaces. What is interesting is that in both cases, the White American is the China expert. This is likely unintentional, but the films' representations problematically advance Whiteness, as the White China expert is so expert in knowledge about Chinese language and culture that s/he trains the Chinese American to appreciate her/his own cultural heritage. As Tierney (2006) has argued, White martial artists in Asian-centered films demonstrate what he calls the "supra-ethnic viability" of Whiteness on film when they outmaster the natives (p. 609). However, because the films are produced by Asian American directors, they still retain a clear counterhegemonic impulse, thus working ambivalently, a feature of Asian American cinema (Hellenbrand, 2008; Okada, 2015).

Before concluding, it is worth noting that the films also engage in what might be understood as Korea-washing. That is, the Chinese American directors of the two movies both chose Korean Americans to play the two leads of their respective films. While Asian American actors have long argued that their specific ethnic backgrounds should not matter in the roles they play, this might become a question if it is largely Korean and Chinese Americans who are playing prominent roles across films. Currently, Korean American actors comprise several of the most well-known Asian American faces in Hollywood—Steven Yeun, John Cho, Randall Park, Margaret Cho, Sandra Oh, Ken Jeong, Sung Kang, Daniel Dae Kim, Bobby Kim, Will Yun Lee, Grace Park, and Ki Hong Lee. Along with Chinese American actors such as Daniel Wu, Constance Wu, Henry Golding, and Lucy Liu, the vast majority of major roles for Asian Americans are played by Korean and Chinese Americans. In another prominent case, Awkwafina (Nora Lum) is both Korean and Chinese American. If these casting choices persist, it would be reasonable to argue that this is a form of intraethnic erasure.

3

White Grievance, Heroism, and Postracist, Mixed-Race Inclusion in *47 Ronin*

● ●

Perhaps because of *47 Ronin*'s (2013) spectacular box office failure, there have been several articles written to retrospectively deconstruct its flaws. Historian Alex von Tunzelmann (2014) seized on the film's racialized meanings, referring to the film as a "pompous, witless mash-up of western orientalist fantasies" (n.p.). Alluding to the film's whitewashed perspective, Katey Rich (2013), a *Vanity Fair* editor, points to the film's insertion of Keanu Reeves, saying that there is "just maybe a nagging sense that it's not a great idea to again cast a *white guy* as the star of a movie about Japanese warriors [emphasis added]" (n.p.). Ironically, the original cut of the film did not feature Reeves to the satisfaction of Universal Studios, which ordered reshoots, including the addition of a romantic storyline (Shaw and Waxman, 2012). Because the centering of a love story is a representational practice usually denied to Asian/American men actors (Espiritu, 2004; Hamamoto, 2000b; Ono and Pham, 2009), the reshoots furthered the film's problematic insertion of visibly White masculinity and the narrative tropes of White male adventurism and identity exploration in a fantasized Japan (Blouin, 2011). Because of its problematic inclusion of Whiteness in an archetypal Japanese story of heroic masculine sacrifice, a number of websites and blogs listed *47 Ronin* as an egregious example of whitewashing.

Notably, Racebending.com, a blog that was started to challenge the white-washed casting news of *The Last Airbender* (2010), also noted the whitewash-ing of *47 Ronin*. Unlike the other sources, its author, Marissa Lee, does not erase Reeves's mixed-race difference in her criticism.

> The fact that the character and actor are part white is precisely why he was welcomed into the American-targeted script. They had 47 Japanese characters from the original tale to pick from for the main character—forty seven!—and still felt they had to create a brand new lead. If the film genuinely wanted to focus on the pain experienced by Japanese people of mixed descent, why not cast award-winning actor Tadanobu Asano—an actual Japanese person of mixed descent—in the role of the heroic Kai rather than as the villain? Presumably, exploring hapa or hafu identity was not why Keanu was crammed into the story. Kai's "outcast" status is presented as an injustice, but the character *is* an outcast in more ways than one. He's the Hollywood self-insertive fantasy. (Lee, 2013)

Lee points to the importance of not reading Reeves as simply White but, at the same time, not ignoring his reading as White, a common reduction of his racial complexity (Nishime, 2014; J. Park, 2008). J. Park (2008) writes that Keanu Reeves, like Vin Diesel, is coded White while having traces of exotic racial dif-ference. His "virtual race," an ornamental racial and ethnic identity that can be worn and removed depending on the role, provides similar privileges as Whiteness (p. 182). She writes, "More easily than monoracial people of color, multiracial folks can be regarded as symbolically white because they already contain visible traces of whiteness, which hint at the invisible, historically fetishized biological property of white blood" (J. Park, 2008, p. 199). The instructive point is that any criticism of the film should consider both his mixed-race difference and his reading as a White man. Thus, the central question of this chapter asks how *47 Ronin* navigates Reeves's mixed-race complexity while inserting Reeves as an oppressed antihero in a White sav-ior narrative.

Written by Chris Morgan and Hossein Amini and directed by Carl Rinsch, *47 Ronin* is a mythological, samurai tale of two men's journeys, Oishi (Hiroyuki Sanada) and Kai (Keanu Reeves) that is based on the legend of the "Ako Inci-dent." Rejected as a "half-breed,[1]" Kai's journey is for the acceptance of his coun-trymen and the rescue of Mika (Ko Shibasaki), the daughter of Lord Asano (Min Tanaka). Oishi's journey, on the other hand, is a mission to avenge the treachery of Lord Kira (Tadanobu Asano) and the "witch" (Rinko Kikuchi) against Lord Asano. In the film, the forty-seven *ronin* [2] avenge Lord Asano, who is the victim of a plot by Lord Kira (Tadanobu Asano) and his helper, a powerful "witch." I argue that despite *47 Ronin*'s (2013) progressive openings because of its story of a mixed-race antihero, it is a paradoxical antiracist White grievance and White savior film that imagines anti-White racism and the overcoming of it as happening through passive Asian acceptance and White heroism in the mixed-race man.

To organize the chapter, I untangle the complications created with the narrative centering of the mixed-race protagonist as both a progressive challenge and as a reification of Whiteness in a film that appears to paradoxically embody both tropes of the antiracist White savior and White grievance. To conclude, I reimagine Kai as played by a mixed-ethnicity Japanese actor, such as Tamayama Tetsuji, a half-Japanese, half-Korean actor. The reason for reimagining the character as Korean Japanese rather than mixed race is because Kai is already played by a mixed-race White-Asian actor and because Japanese-White mixed race actors are already popular and frequently admired in Japan's contemporary popular culture (Rivas, 2015; Törngren, 2018). On the other hand, for the past century starting since at least Japan's colonization of Korea, ethnic Koreans have been systemically oppressed.

Counterhegemonic Reading of Mixed-Race Difference

Although the film reproduces problematic representations that center Whiteness, it would be an intentional misreading to ignore the progressive representations of mixed-race difference in *47 Ronin*. Unlike most films that reduce mixed-race actors into monoracial difference (Nishime, 2017a), *47 Ronin* centers Kai's mixed-race identity. Kai's mixed-race heritage is salient as the witch and Lord Asano's samurai mock him as a half-breed. Because Kai has grown up with the mystical creatures of Tengu Forest, it is at first unclear whether "half-breed" is a reference to his mixed-race heritage or his upbringing as a human in a supernatural forest, even despite a White actor (Daniel Barber) playing the young Kai. The film forecloses the latter reading in the test of wills at the Tengu Forest, however. Facing off against a disfigured, demon-like mystic, Kai's opponent taunts him by sharing that Kai's mother, a peasant girl, who was impregnated by an English sailor, left the newborn Kai in the forest to die. Thus, the movie leaves no doubt that Kai's marginalization is not because of his mystical past but his mixed-race present. This is an important counterrepresentation because by positioning Reeves, a mixed-race actor, as a mixed-race character, and centering his identity in the plot, it pushes against the pattern of attributing monoracial difference onto mixed-race Asian actors such as Nancy Kwan, Dean Cain, Chloe Bennett, and Reeves. Rabin (2012) notes, "To assert one's multiracial self-identification is contingent upon a discourse of race that already exists—one that is always already linked to the hegemony of monoraces" (p. 396). This filmic assertion, then, troubles the fixity of racial categories by demonstrating race's complexity and fluidity.

47 Ronin's clarity about Kai's mixed-race ancestry is also necessary to advance a superficially progressive message about racial tolerance. Its clear moral argument is that bigotry against mixed-race people is wrong. This is represented by Kai's eventual acceptance by the samurais, who discontinue their use of the slur "half-breed" as he earns their respect and his place among them. Because this is a meaningful subplot, there are several moments where his fellow samurai brethren demonstrate their growing acceptance. After Oishi finds Kai on the "Dutch Island," a slaveholding commune, Oishi petitions Kai to return to help him save Mika, but Kai questions why he would follow Oishi's command. Oishi confesses that he failed Lord Asano when he did not take seriously Kai's warning about seeing a witch. Reflecting contrition and honoring Kai, he offers Kai clothes while bowing his head. Prior to that point, Kai is seen wearing gray-colored clothing made of what appears to be rough material akin to burlap while the samurai wear colorful red outfits. Although the clothes Oishi provides are the humble clothes of farmers, they are similar to the clothes worn by Oishi and the other *ronin*.

Later in the film, Basho (Takato Yonemoto), one of the *ronin*, succumbs to his injuries that were sustained while saving Yasuno (Masayoshi Haneda) during the *ronins'* failed assassination attempt. On his deathbed, he confesses that he threw stones at Kai during their childhood. By seeking forgiveness from Kai and claiming in his final breath that Kai is a "good man," he demonstrates Kai's worthiness. The following morning, Yasuno, who is represented as the most cynical toward Kai, offers his apologies for not revealing that Kai had saved his life during the film's early hunting sequence against a mythical beast. Echoing an overwrought theme of honor, Yasuno says, "A samurai does not take credit for victories of others." Then he offers Kai Basho's sword, saying that a samurai carries two swords, which signals Kai's full acceptance by Lord Asano's former samurais. Further clarifying the point, Oishi invites Kai to write his name on the pact and to seal it with blood, thereby becoming the last member of the forty-seven *ronin*. At the film's conclusion, Kai commits seppuku with the rest of the restored samurai, thus dying an honorable death together.

The theme of Kai's acceptance, however, does not mean that Kai is the primary hero figure. Unlike most representations with White (presenting) actors in lead roles, Oishi is the moral center and the leader of the *ronin*. He is established early in the film as the leader of Lord Asano's samurais, acting as an advisor and assisting Lord Asano's seppuku by beheading his lord. Most important, he drives the narrative action by formulating the *ronins'* revenge plot. Oishi frees Kai, who would otherwise have continued to fight in a murderous stupor in the gladiatorial arena on the "Dutch Island," gathers Lord Asano's former samurai, creates the battle plans, and has the *ronin* sign a pact of duty and self-sacrifice. In most films with White heroes, on the other hand, sympathetic locals are almost always relegated to sidekicks or supporters (Tierney, 2006).

In addition, representations of the White Self are usually constructed as more moral than the Oriental Other (Benshoff and Griffin, 2004; Dyer, 1997; Oh and Kutufam, 2014; Pieterse, 1992; Said, 1978; Shohat and Stam, 1994). Oishi, however, symbolizes the film's understanding of Bushido, which is described by the shogun as the "old ways" of the warrior. He and his men depart on a journey to avenge their master to restore Lord Asano's honor despite knowing that their act will result in their own demise. The film secures this reading of honor, as even the shogun (Cary-Hiroyuki Tagawa) recognizes Oishi's value to the nation. On the day of the men's mass seppuku, the shogun has a sudden change of heart and allows Oishi's son, Chikara (Jin Akanashi), to live and maintain Oishi's bloodline, suggesting that Oishi's honor and moral goodness are too valuable for the Japanese nation to lose.

In contrast, Kai is represented as an ambivalent antihero, who strives against the misanthropy and magical arts of assassination he learned in the Tengu Forest. Indeed, he joins Oishi's men, not because of duty or honor, but because he wants to rescue Mika, Lord Asano's daughter, whom he has loved since childhood. Thus, it is the Japanese hero rather than the mixed-race White-Japanese man, who establishes unwavering, albeit fetishized, moral duty that is ascribed to samurais in the Western popular imagination. In further contrast, other White men are represented as philanderers and barbaric heathens. Although the film does not establish whether Kai's father knew Kai's mother was pregnant, the implied meaning, given his profession as a sailor and the theme of abandonment, is that he left Kai and his mother just as his mother left Kai in the Tengu Forest. Further, there is little room for semiotic interpretation for the Dutch, who are represented unidimensionally as barbaric and immoral. It is revealed that Kai is sold into slavery, so the implication is that the Dutch are slave traders, who operate a dishonorable gladiatorial arena on one of their ships for their own gambling amusement. There, they pit the most marginal members of society against one another, including the "half-breed" Kai against a gigantic, monstrous man, who is badly scarred and deformed. The Dutch also lead the unknowing Oishi into the gladiatorial arena, forcing him to fight against Kai, whose bloodlust leaves him unaware of the man before him. Thus, the inclusion of a mixed-race Japanese-White character creates room for counterrepresentational meanings that were encoded into *47 Ronin*.

White Grievance, the Antihero, and White Heroism in a Mixed-Race Body

Despite its counterhegemonic possibilities, *47 Ronin* reifies White racial hegemony. Its insertion of Kai into the legend shifts from the specifically Japanese people and meaning of the story to one that incorporates Whiteness. The logics of White racial hegemony and the for-profit interests of Universal Pictures in a high-budget film disciplines the text to fit dominant ideologies. *47 Ronin* does this by establishing Whiteness as a site of racial grievance while also advancing a neoliberal, postracist story of acceptance through individual effort.

Before elaborating on this argument, it is first important to grapple with the mixed-race difference of Keanu Reeves and the character he plays, namely, how can a mixed-race character be argued to stand in for White grievance and heroism? This is both through the elisions in the casting and story as well as the way mixed-race bodies have historically acted as racial signifiers. Beltrán and Fojas (2008) write, "Hollywood traditions of whiteness also continue to serve as potent frames of understanding, even in films and other media texts that foreground mixed race actors and/or a multicultural aesthetic" (p. 11). Mixed-race actors hint at exotic difference that is increasingly marketable in Hollywood, leading to an upswing in racially ambiguous mixed race actors playing leading roles in Hollywood, including, most prominently, Vin Diesel and Keanu Reeves (Beltrán, 2008; Beltrán and Fojas, 2008). Mixed-race actors' early career choices often shape how they will be read, and because Reeves has played racially unmarked characters for most of his career, starting in his breakout role as Ted in *Bill & Ted's Excellent Adventure* (1989), he is commonly understood to be White. For many fans, then, even though he plays a mixed-race character, their extratextual knowledge of his body of work will likely have them read Reeves as White, fitting with the representational trope of White heroes in faraway Asian lands.

In *47 Ronin*, there is another mixed-race actor in the cast; the villain of the story, Lord Kira, played by Tadanobu Asano. His biography as a mixed-race child raised in Japan reads more closely to Kai than does Reeves's. It is only Reeves's mixed-race difference that is acknowledged on screen, however. This is to say that Japanese-presenting mixed race difference is ignored while White-presenting mixed race difference is recognized. This is a consequential choice as it reveals the intentions of the producers to mark whose mixed-race identity matters. For viewers with intertextual knowledge of Tadanobu Asano, this message would be clear. Because of the phenotypical expression of Lord Kira's mixed-race body, it would reveal that tropes of "hybrid degeneracy," the belief that being mixed race produces emotional instability and biological inferiority (Beltrán and Fojas, 2008, p. 10), matter only for the Japanese-presenting mixed race man. Indeed, as Nishime (2014) clarifies, representations of mixed-race people include "images of both the degenerative *and* the heroic multiracial" (emphasis not mine) (p. 16). This becomes racially marked such that hybridity is redemptive when Whiteness physically manifests but is degenerative when it is latent. Unlike Kai, who has rejected his upbringing in dark magic and who lives in humility and service to Lord Asano and his court, Lord Kira embraces ruthlessness and greed. For instance, he strikes, and perhaps kills, a prone sparring partner; uses the witch's magic to deceive the shogun into ordering Lord Asano's death; and forcibly takes Mika, Lord Asano's daughter, to be his reluctant bride.

White Grievance and the Neoliberal Postracist Antihero

Despite its location in a fictionalized, ancient Japan, *47 Ronin* can be read as a film about White grievance. It is not the revenge fantasy of *Falling Down* (1993) in which D-Fens (Michael Douglas) embarks on a campaign of retribution against a racially diversifying, increasingly gender-equal society (Kennedy, 1996; Mukherjee, 2006), nor a heroic last stand, such as *300* (2006), against an incoming, overwhelming threat of a multiracial enemy (Oh and Kutufam, 2014). Rather, it is a representation of "wounded white masculinity" that functions to ironically secure White heterosexual men's position atop social hierarchy by arguing for its victimization (Kelly, 2018, p. 162). Its repeated, manifest theme of mixed-race mockery and social ostracization in Japan against a White-presenting mixed race character reflects White attitudes about so-called reverse racism. As critical race theorists have argued, White Americans believe that they are victims of systemic racism, while simultaneously believing that people of color are no longer marginalized by the harmful consequences of White racial hegemony (Bonilla-Silva, 2006; DiAngelo, 2011). White people tend to view themselves as victims and claim that people of color have advantages denied to White Americans and are thus at fault for their own racial marginalization (Johnson, Rich, and Cargile, 2008). These beliefs in anti-White racism find form in the characters' mistreatment of Kai for his visibly White difference.

Before making the connection between the White grievance film and the increased visibility of the White antihero, it is important to first clarify what is meant by an antihero, though perhaps it can be taken for granted since the character has become so easily recognizable (Vaage, 2015). The antihero is almost always a White man with ambivalent, conflicted morality (Mittell, 2015). Although he engages in despicable acts, he is usually reconciled by his moral code and effectiveness where orderly behavior and coherence to civilized norms cannot (Vaage, 2015). Indeed, he is redeemable for his noble qualities, despite his moral flaws and errors in judgment (Triana, 2018). The antihero is sympathetic because he is necessary to stop a more obviously villainous figure (Vaage, 2015). Relative to the villain, the antihero is represented as good, a necessary "evil," in opposition (Mittell, 2015).

In *47 Ronin*, the two villains are cartoonish in their lack of complexity and their evil desires. Lord Kira is represented as coveting the village of Ako, and he engages in trickery and magic to achieve his goals. His reasons are unclear, but it is implied that he covets Ako because of its bountiful resources as a sunny village set in an idyllic background of forests, rivers, and lakes. In contrast, Lord Kira's village consists primarily of a stone castle set atop a rocky, snowy mountain. As CGI-produced effects swoop upward and zoom into his lair, it shows a dreary, dark location that is marked by stone and shadows with light peering through barely lit corridors. The coldness, darkness, and treacherous location are in marked contrast to the warmth, light, space, and bounty in Ako. Lord Kira's desire to possess Ako, already feminized with its connection to fertility and nature, is further embodied in his sexual desire to possess Mika and to have her produce his heirs. While waiting for the shogun's imposed one-year mourning period to end so that he can wed Mika, he snarls at her continued lack of affection, saying, "You may look down on me, my lady, but our children, and their children will be one blood." His threat of sexual possession and control of her body resonates with fears of Asian men as rape threats, a fear that is associated with the "yellow peril" stereotype (Hamamoto, 1994; Marchetti, 1993; Ono and Pham, 2009).

Unlike Lord Asano, who is magnanimous in his treatment of Kai, Lord Kira is represented as petty and cruel against those with less power, and against those with more, he leans on trickery and magic. In the Western imagination, hedonic power signifies feminine power, and it has been demonized in relation to agonic power, which is represented by masculine strength and direct action (Kogan, Hoyt, Rickard, and Kellaway, 2004; Oh and Kutufam, 2014). Because Asian masculinity is commonly gendered feminine in U.S. media (Espiritu, 2004; Oh, 2012; Ono and Pham, 2009; Sun, 2003), "yellow peril" threats are, consequentially, dangerous because of their hedonic minds rather than their agonic brawn. Usually, this is represented in Asian villains' corruption of science and technology with mystical practices of an inscrutable Orient (Hamamoto, 1994; Oehling, 1980). Although Lord Kira does not directly use magic, he combines his trickery with the witch's enchantments. The most important of these is the deception and manipulation of the shogun's laws of nobles that sets the narrative in motion and that allows Lord Kira to take Ako.

Perhaps the more dangerous threat is the witch as it is her enchantments and tricks that give Lord Kira the ability to stage his takeover of Ako Village. The witch, however, is deprived of agency as she is not represented with her own motivations. The witch is far more powerful than Lord Kira, having the ability to shape-shift into a fox, a dragon, an octopus-like hybrid creature, and a floating piece of cloth; to enchant; and to cast fire. Yet she freely submits to his goals, urging him to action but not acting for her own benefit. There is no narrative justification for her support, such as affection because of shared history, romantic desire, misplaced faith, psychological need for his acknowledgment, or limitations because of a patriarchal, magic-averse society. Instead, she is a flat character, whose only purpose is to help Lord Kira possess Ako. In the only scene where she expresses her desire to kill Mika, the witch reveals that she has promised to not harm Mika while seductively slithering atop her prone captive. Instead, the witch suggests that Mika harm herself, leaving her a dagger.

In this way, the witch fits the stereotype of the dragon lady, a sexually manipulative Asian/American woman who works on behalf of her Asian/American male partner to ensnare and/or compromise the hero (Espiritu, 2004; Ono and Pham, 2009). Both villains, then, are constructed as a feminized, hedonic threat, a scare that resonates less with ancient Japan than with the contemporary U.S. cultural terrain, with male anxieties about femininity infiltrating masculine spaces and with the racist fears of feminized yellow peril threats.

In contrast to his enemies, Kai has spurned his magical powers and chooses to fight honorably as a (man) samurai, despite being deprived of this status during his life prior to joining the *ronin*. His only uses of magic are against other magic users, including the lord of the Tengu forest during the test of wills and the witch in his final battle. Despite Kai's rejection of magic, his ability to use it more effectively than his opponents is reminiscent of Tierney's (2006) argument about the White hero's supraethnic viability. That is, the White hero is able to master the martial and mystical techniques of racialized Asian ethnics more quickly and more effectively than his teachers and opponents.

The White Antihero and the Postracist Savior

The recent popularity of the antihero coincides with White professional men's fears of losing status in a diversifying society and becoming feminized in white-collar labor (Larabee, 2013; Vaage, 2015). In this way, it is connected to the construction of hegemonic masculinity, which is a reaction to the societal transformations wrought by social justice movements, starting in the 1960s (Ducat, 2004; Kimmel, 2006). In this movement, men defined themselves in opposition to femininity rather than holding fast to traditional Christian notions of masculinity in the United States that valued self-restraint and stoicism (J. K. Kim, 2015; Kimmel, 2006). While freed of stoicism, the opposition to femininity constrains acceptable emotional expression to anger and violence, hallmarks of a newly forming hegemonic masculinity (Kimmel, 2006). "Masculine victimhood encourages white men to speak about common human vulnerability as if it were systemic structural oppression" (Kelly, 2020, p. 8).

Kai, as an articulation of the antihero, is morally flawed but redeemed as his heroism intersects with the Western imagination's construction of Japan as a space to explore Western subjectivity (Blouin, 2011; Oh, 2017; Oh and Wong Lowe, 2016). Although this is not true of the character of Kai, it is for the Western audience for whom *47 Ronin* is intended. As Blouin (2011) writes, Japan is a "dream-world positioned beyond the limitations of the physical" (p. 318). It is no surprise, then, that the Japan of *47 Ronin* is a fantastical, mystical world based in but separate from the historical legend. In this imagining, Japan is not only a space to appropriate but also to save. This satisfies White America's desire to paradoxically erase its historical role as an Asian Pacific colonizer by imagining itself as heroic in ancient Japan's salvation from itself.

To this end, it is necessary to understand *47 Ronin* as also fitting the White savior trope.

The White savior trope features a White man or woman, who saves a victimized community of color either from their own communities or from White villains in the antiracist film. Murphy and Harris (2018) write, "the White savior is a primary trope that serves to fuel the toxic ideology of the perceived 'legitimacy' and validity of White innocence" (p. 61). That is to say that the White savior narratively erases the history and structures of White racial hegemony. In non-White worlds, it inserts White heroism to point to its own supremacy (Shome, 1996). In White spaces, the White hero is confronted with the moral ugliness and violence of White racists, prevailing against them to symbolically present White people as heroes rather than people of color, who have had long struggles to overcome racial injustice (Madison, 1999; Schultz, 2014). Rather, empowerment for people of color only comes through the aid of White saviors (Griffin, 2015). Thus, the function of the White savior is to both demonstrate the White character's superior moral goodness and their superior physical strength and intellect (Benshoff and Griffin, 2004; Fitzgerald, 2013; Murphy and Harris, 2018; Schultz, 2014). Specific to Asian/American communities, the White savior is represented as a figure that is more (sexually) desirable because of his superior masculinity (Nakayama, 1994). He has "supra-ethnic viability," which allows him to appropriate and master the skills and techniques of Asian peoples more effectively than his rivals despite a limited period of time to train (Tierney, 2006, p. 609).

Although Kai does not gain the skills of the samurai, he is represented as their most capable fighter. In the early hunt to kill the beast that was rampaging through Ako, Kai defeats the beast single-handedly after it runs roughshod through the samurais, and he saves an ungrateful Yasuno in the process. Further, in the final fight scene, he overcomes the witch, who has transformed into a serpent-like dragon. In addition, in the Dutch gladiatorial arena, Kai overcomes Oishi, who is only able to escape death by invoking Mika's name, which breaks Kai's bloodlust. Most important, however, Kai is the linchpin for the successful completion of the mission to save Mika and the village of Ako from the tyranny of Lord Kira.

Under Oishi's leadership, the *ronin* face two major setbacks—to arm his men and to assassinate Lord Kira. In the former, Oishi takes his men to a village renowned for its sword makers, but they find the village burnt and empty of its inhabitants, save for three of Lord Kira's samurai. When the men's disguise as farmers is uncovered, they stand stunned and weaponless until Kai springs into action, defeating the armored, enemy samurais. Kai convinces Oishi that all of the villages with weapon makers would be similarly destroyed, urging Oishi to go to the Tengu Forest to gain enchanted weapons by overcoming a test of wills. Without Kai's knowledge and skill, Oishi's plan to assassinate Lord Kira would have failed.

Further, Oishi's plan to assassinate Lord Kira during the lord's trip to his family home also ends in a tactical defeat as Lord Kira has lured Oishi into a trap. As they walk into a field filled with straw formations in the dark of night, the witch appears and casts fire, which spreads rapidly across the straw. Lord Kira's samurai then shoot arrows at the fleeing *ronin*, leading to Oishi's military failure. After their defeat on the battlefield, Oishi's spirit is broken until Kai tells him that they now have the element of surprise and that Oishi should not lose hope. His encouragement allows the eventual, successful infiltration and assassination of the witch and Lord Kira. Although Kai arguably plays a secondary role as a tactician and supporter, it is only through his encouragement and later heroism that the plan succeeds. Kai, as a White savior, is not the superior moral figure, an impossibility because of his antihero character, but he is a physically superior warrior and a necessary member for the *ronin*'s success. This retelling, even as a fantasy, diminishes the heroism of the *Japanese* samurai by incorporating a White antihero savior whose contributions are necessary for the legend of the forty-seven *ronin* to be established. As a point of comparison, this would be akin to the filmic retelling of the historical legend of the three hundred Spartans by introducing a Japanese character as the superior warrior without whom the Spartans would not have had the physical or tactical ability to win. This undermines the specific ethnic meanings articulated in the legend, introducing Whiteness as necessary even in Japan's most iconic story of heroism and honor.

Despite the obvious racial implications, the White antihero's racialization is narratively hidden. This is, of course, similar to the function of whitewashing—to be invisible in spite of its hypervisibility. In the only article that examines this paradoxical racing and nonracing, Wayne (2014) argues that the Whiteness of the antihero is made invisible through his multiracial friendships.

> Regarding race, images of diversity including Black-White friendship and multicultural cooperation validate the "end" of race by providing visible evidence of integration and the success of race-neutral, neoliberal political and economic arrangements while the absence of White animosity perpetuates the myth that Americans have left racism in the past (p. 198).

This is similar to the ways multiracial buddy films and television shows use friendships as a way to advance postracism, the belief that racism no longer has deleterious impacts on the lives of people of color (Ames, 1992; Artz, 1998; Gates, 2004; Thornton, 2011) or as cover to hide racist meanings (Oh, 2012; Pham, 2004; Wald, 2009). As such, postracism is intertwined with color blindness, the liberal belief that White people do not see race or that not seeing race is the ideal condition on which interracial friendships are built (Bonilla-Silva, 2006; Jayakumar and Adamian, 2017; Mueller, 2017). In addition, it claims that everyone is universally guilty of, and victim to, racism (Alcoff, 1998; Oh and Banjo, 2012). Postracism, and its concomitant counterpart, color blindness, are liberally expressed, but its impacts and purposes are to roll back antiracist gains (Ono, 2010) or, at a minimum, to not acknowledge the specific functioning of White racial hegemony (Alcoff, 1998; Giroux, 2003). The White antihero also is constructed as a postracist figure by distancing himself from White groups that are used as foils to prove the antihero's nonracism (Wayne, 2014). Likewise, White savior films emphasize clashes with "bad" White people to demonstrate benevolent Whiteness that is free of racism (Fitzgerald, 2013; Hughey, 2010). For instance, rural White Americans in Appalachia are consistently represented as ignorant and racist to demonstrate their difference from "good" White people.

Similarly, *47 Ronin* establishes the "bad" White people as the Dutch slave traders. Not only are they narratively evil through their purchase of slaves, pleasure in human death matches, and gambling, the film visually marks them as evil. Like Kira's mountaintop fortress, the Dutch dock and ships are enveloped in the darkness of night, and the interior of the ship is dimly lit. The harbor shots use a blue filter to signify darkness, and the hallway to the gladiatorial arena is also darkly lit with several candles flickering on the sides of the wooden hallway. Its darkness works in concert with the narrative action on screen to establish the immorality of the Dutch. Further overdetermining the point, a shirtless Dutch foreman is shown with his face tattooed with dark circles around his eyes, a triangular dark tattoo around his nose, and the outline of teeth and a jaw to resemble a human skull. His body is also marked heavily with his torso covered in dark ink except for a few patches of visible skin on his ribs and the outline of a backbone. The tattoos form the image of a living skeleton, further signifying the depravity and moral death of the Dutch.

By placing the Dutch slave traders in opposition, Kai is not only a more acceptable antihero; his difference distinguishes him as a "good" White person. This is similar to the operation of antiracist films that insert White heroes who protect people of color from White villains. For instance, this is the message of the historically reimagined film *Mississippi Burning* (1988), which crafted FBI agents into heroic figures fighting against White supremacy, despite the FBI's historical complicity (Hoerl, 2009). Dutch racism, however, plays a small role in *47 Ronin*. The source of most racist resentment, as described earlier, comes from Japanese villagers, samurais, and the witch. The film thus represents the grievances of Whites, who see messages supportive of anti-White racism; it also provides a conservative, postracist message of victim blaming and recovery. Like conservatives who argue that there would be less racism if people of color would stop discussing racism and stop "playing the race card" (Gandy, 1998; Lipsitz, 1998), the film adheres to the color-blind faith that acceptance comes to people of color who work hard and do not complain (Giroux, 2003).

It is perhaps not coincidental then that Kai's other "half" of his mixed-race identity is Japanese. This is because the myth of racial meritocracy is given substance through the model minority myth, which was historically constructed to discipline Black Americans by claiming that Japanese Americans succeeded through self-reliance (Hamamoto, 1994; Nakayama, 1988; Wu, 2002). Prashad (2001) writes, "Asians are used, in this instance [anti-racist programs], then, as a weapon against the most modest form of redistribution devised by the state" (p. 42). As a model minority figure, Kai's primary goal is to be accepted, which is realized when he is granted seppuku with his fellow samurais. Despite being an antihero, he gains acceptance, not through resistance, but rather through working hard and quietly accepting his marginalized status.

This is exemplified in his romance with Mika, particularly as U.S. films tend to deal with forbidden love, like the Shakespearean play *Romeo and Juliet*, by having their characters rebel against their families and other structures that keep them apart even if it ends in tragedy for the lovers. *47 Ronin* disrupts this familiar narrative trope by having the two lovers accept their different social station. When Kai returns from the hunt early in the film, he is met in his lowly hut by Mika, who tends to his wounds. The dialogue that ensues is instructive.

KAI: This is no place for you, my lady.
MIKA: Are you sending me away? Look at me and tell me you don't love me.
KAI: I will always love you, but you have your place, and I have mine.

This works both as Hollywood's exoticized understanding of obedience and strict hierarchy in East Asia and as a message about not fighting against marginalization. Indeed, only by assimilating to the expectations of Japanese society and by not complaining does Kai achieve the inclusion he desires. The message, then, is that if racially marginalized people assimilate, do not complain, and work hard, they will be fully accepted into dominant culture because it is not structural racism but individual attitudes that matter. This message links to postracist, neoliberal prescriptions for marginalized people of color to achieve inclusion through individual effort rather than systemic change (Enck-Wanzer, 2011; Hasinoff, 2008; Jones and Mukherjee, 2010; Oh and Banjo, 2012; Prashad, 2001).

Using Kai as a mixed-race antihero that both signifies Whiteness and mixed-race difference, *47 Ronin* is a mishmash of filmic tropes that include White grievance, White anti-racism, and the White savior. Kai's mixed-race difference matters, as it allows even more fluid racial discourses than is possible in the monoracial body. Signifying Whiteness, the film argues that he is a victim of racial discrimination and marginalization, replicating the White grievance film. Unlike the typical White grievance film, however, he does not lash out or fight against the forces that oppress him. Instead, signifying Asianness, he is narratively constructed as a model minority–like figure, who overcomes racism through assimilation and a willingness to accept his own devalued status. He is accepted as a samurai only when he proves his worthiness on the battlefield and his fealty to the Bushido code. As such, he is also a romanticized, exoticized figure of the Western imagination. Thus, it romanticizes his suffering as an "appropriate" minority response. That it is shown to succeed, like all model minority and color-blind antiracist films, minimizes systemic racism and argues for postracist, individual effort instead. In this case, however, it boils these problematic discourses down to the single site of the mixed-race body.

Imagining Kai as Zainichi

Mixed-race Japanese celebrities are a visible part of Japanese media culture (Horiguchi and Imoto, 2016; Oshima, 2014; Törngren, 2018). Indeed, their visibility has given rise to a neologism *haafu* or *hafu*, which is simply a transliteration of "half." In particular, *haafu* children with a Japanese and White parent are considered especially attractive and the most desirable mixed-race child (Rivas, 2015, p. 714; Törngren, 2018). As Iwabuchi, Kim, and Hsia (2016) claim, "The Japanese popular culture has valued mixed-race *hafu* celebrities with images of good looks, exoticism, and cosmopolitanism" (emphasis is theirs). It is for this reason that I reimagine Kai as not mixed-race White and Japanese but mixed-ethnicity Korean and Japanese. This move is intended to partially intervene in the lack of interest in the postcolonial condition of Japan's colonized subjects (Chapman, 2007; J. K. Kim, 2015). This is an unfortunate gap in the literature because it hides (post)colonialism's articulations outside the sphere of the West.

My interest in Korean residents in Japan is because they are the largest group of foreign nationals in the archipelago (B. Kim, 2006, 2008; Tai, 2004). Korean residents are commonly referred to as "Zainichi," though the word's literal meaning simply refers to someone residing in Japan (Dew, 2016; Htun, 2012). When used as a noun, it is commonly understood as Korean because of Zainichis' more than century-long presence that dates to Japan's colonial period, starting in 1910 (Chapman, 2007; Htun, 2012). I retain the use of the word despite its ambivalent connotations because "it is a term that came to prominence in the 1970s to recognize and confront the denizenship of Koreans in Japan, whose identity was defined in part by the cultural memories and traumas of the colonial period and its immediate aftermath" (Dew, 2016, p. 2). It is an in-between identity that expresses a lack—of not being Japanese or Korean (Chapman, 2007)—rather than, for example, the both/and discourse commonly expressed among mixed-race Americans (Matsunaga and Torigoe, 2008).

Although it is beyond the scope of this chapter to include a full historical review of discrimination against Zainichis in Japan, a quick review contextualizes current discrimination. Most Zainichis are third- and fourth-generation descendants of Koreans, who were forcibly brought to Japan and forced to work in labor camps during Japan's buildup to war (Chapman, 2006; Htun, 2012; Tai, 2004). Although Zainichis were considered Japanese, they were treated as second-class citizens. After the Great Kanto earthquake, for example, thousands of Koreans were killed on baseless suspicions that they poisoned Tokyo's water supply (Itagaki, 2015). As colonial subjects, they did not fit within cultural logics of citizenship, which viewed native Japanese as having the strongest claim, *naichijin*, the internally colonized Ainu and Okinawan, as having secondary claims, and overseas colonized citizens from Korea and Taiwan as having tertiary claims (Tai, 2004). After the Allied Occupation ended in 1952, per the San Francisco Peace Treaty, even their limited rights were lost (Chapman, 2006; Htun, 2012; Itagaki, 2015; B. Kim, 2006; S. Park, 2017; Tai, 2004). With Japan in sovereign control, it passed legislation that made Zainichis stateless within its borders (Dew, 2016; Ryang, 2014).

> By 1952, the estimated 600,000 Korean residents in Japan had lost the right to political participation, the right to permanent residence, access to social security, health insurance, income benefits, and national veterans/bereavement pensions, the right to overseas travel, and access to certain educational and occupational opportunities. (Dew, 2016, p. 5)

They were required to carry alien registration documents at all times and were required to be fingerprinted, an indignity that only criminals experienced (Tai, 2004).

Their rights improved in the 1970s as Zainichis led a civil rights movement to claim equivalent rights to native-born Japanese without giving up their Korean identities and names (Chapman, 2006; Tai, 2004), and because of their efforts and because of international pressure, Japan eventually granted legal rights, although everyday discrimination still exists (B. Kim, 2008). Zainichis are still considered foreigners despite living in Japan up to four generations (Htun, 2012), and they face systemic and daily discrimination (Visočnik, 2014). The ideological root of the discrimination is because of a persistent view of a homogenous national identity that emphasizes Japanese monoethnic uniqueness and exceptionalism (Chapman, 2006). Because of the monoethnic ideologies driving national identity, citizenship is still understood as assimilation into

Japaneseness, despite multicultural movements and discourses about coexistence (Chapman, 2006).

Challenges to this construction of nation has been met with rising antiimmigrant sentiment rooted in a belief in monoethnic exceptionalism (Tai, 2004). Anti-Korean backlash targeted at Zainichis has been manifest in yet peripheral but highly visible hate speech on- and offline. Iwabuchi (2017) argues that it is a reaction to Korea and China's growing economic and cultural influence, which some Japanese experience as a relative loss as it is no longer the only industrialized non-Western global power. Itagaki (2015), however, understands it as a form of "victimhood racism" that is due to exaggerated fears of being victimized by its minority population. Fueling the backlash are reactions to transnational Korean television shows and popular music, which are viewed as a cultural threat (Itagaki, 2015; Iwabuchi, 2017; Yamaguchi, 2013) and contempt for Korean and Chinese historical disputes (Iwabuchi, 2017; Yamaguchi, 2013).

There are now more than two hundred "hate books," including a 2005 best seller titled *Hate Korean Wave Manga*, and more than one thousand antiimmigrant hate speech protests as reported in a governmental survey (Iwabuchi, 2017). Hate speech protests against Zainichis are not infrequent (S. Park, 2017; Yamaguchi, 2013) and receive support by the Liberal Democratic Party, the ruling conservative party (S. Park, 2017). According to Itagaki (2015), anti-Korean "hate" is not a fringe element of Japanese society as commonly argued but systemic and historically based in Japan's relationship to its colonies. Common hate speech includes referring to Zainichis as "cockroaches" to suggest infestation into the metaphorical Japanese home and as malcontents, which is a historical referent to Korean colonial subjects who were seen as not appreciative of Japan's "benevolence" (Itagaki, 2015).

Understanding Kai as Zainichi-Japanese spotlights the discrimination faced by Zainichis. The mocking "half-breed" comments would not be linked to his visible difference as there are no obvious distinguishing differences between Japanese and Koreans. Rather, they would reveal the ethnic bigotry that Zainichis face (Iwabuchi, 2017). Kai's lowly status and his hut on the literal periphery of Ako would symbolize the discrimination Zainichis experience as peripheral members of society. Because Japanese view overseas colonized people as the least Japanese in a center-periphery model of citizenship (Tai, 2004), Kai's liminal existence between the society in Tengu Forest and his partial adoption by Lord Asano into the village but not his household could be read as similar to the dozen-year stateless existence of Zainichis from the end of Allied Occupation to the normalization between South Korea and Japan in 1965.

However, Kai's desire to leave the Tengu Forest and join the village of Ako might also provide problematic messages that support governmental efforts toward assimilation into Japaneseness that erase Korean ethnic identities

(Chapman, 2006). Though not its dominant meaning, it would only require reading slightly against the grain to interpret the Tengu Forest as symbolic of Korea, Ako as symbolic of a benevolent Japan, and Lord Kira's base as symbolic of anti-immigrant protesters such as the Zaitokukai. In this formulation, Korea would be read as a less desirable place than a benevolent Japan not only because of Kai's desire to escape but also because of its mysticism and misanthropy. Indeed, it might affirm right-wing fears that Zainichis are a domestic national security threat (Shipper, 2010). Furthermore, by contrasting Ako and Lord Kira's stronghold, it vilifies hate groups, an ideologically easy message, while suggesting that the correct path is joining and finding acceptance in Ako.

Because Japan does not grant birthright citizenship, Zainichis do not automatically receive citizenship, so Kai's journey could be read as symbolic of Zainichis' legal and psychic choice to naturalize. It would suggest that despite the indignities that are experienced and the marginalization received, the most affirmative choice is to accept one's place in Ako. This provides a superficial liberal message of acceptance but on the illiberal precondition of silently accepting their second-class citizenship. Indeed, this is visible in the love story with Mika. Kai's acceptance of his inability to actualize his love for Mika and his eventual seppuku leaves no room for a counterreading of the symbolic union of Zainichi and Japanese through marriage. This would perhaps also function to produce a distortion of contemporary ethnic relations as the inability to marry could be read as located in the historical past because Zainichis and Japanese are now legally able to wed.

Yet even with its clear assimilationist message, Kai as a mixed-ethnicity Zainichi would challenge representations of desirable mixed ethnicity/race as only children of White and Japanese parents (Törngren, 2018). Although there are real-life mixed ethnicity celebrities with Zainichi and Japanese parents, there is no such mixed-ethnicity Zainichi and Japanese character representations of which I am aware. The closest prominent example is perhaps *Go* (2001), a story about a Zainichi adolescent who struggles with whether to integrate fully into Japan, despite its anti-Zainichi discrimination. Unlike that story, Kai is *haafu*, and he is a savior figure. Most *haafu* children of Zainichi and Japanese parents subsume their Korean heritage into a Japanese one as their parents usually register them as Japanese to receive the benefits of citizenship and as they usually do not identify as Korean (Tai, 2004). Kai's heroism could legitimate *haafu* identities that reclaim Korean heritage and Zainichi communities.

As a savior figure, a *haafu* character that does not represent visible Whiteness challenges the White savior trope by providing a counterrepresentation in which Japan is saved through the intervention of a non-White hero; it also provides a counterrepresentation of Zainichis that runs against the common tropes of criminality, threat, victimhood, and societal burden. It might, however, construct Korean masculinity as more physically powerful and with connections to the Tengu Forest as more primordial. This could align with colonial views of the colonized as less civilized (Pieterse, 1992). That said, it could also fit into existing desirability for a Korean "soft masculinity" that is marked by a muscular, hard body but a soft, emotionally feminine demeanor (Jung, 2006, n.p.).

Different casting that includes a *haafu* Zainichi would produce ambivalent meanings that progressively challenge the tropes of Zainichi in Japan but that ironically would argue for assimilation, which viewed otherwise is an erasure of Zainichi communities. For U.S. Americans, unfamiliar with the ongoing social dynamics between Japanese and Zainichis, the film would argue for the salience of this specific ethnic discrimination. This could lead to a more complicated understanding of ethnic difference in East Asia that challenges racialized understandings that treat Koreans and Japanese as largely undifferentiated. The easy assimilationist messages, however, would still amplify the same messages of passive, submissive belonging that would affirm the model minority stereotype. Although it would remove White grievance from the film's narrative meanings, a reading of the film as relevant to the United States could produce universalist messages that further affirm that color or ethnic blindness is the ideal, liberal outcome.

Conclusion

47 Ronin is spectacular in its attempt to draw together multiple threads of the White racial imagination—illiberal views of White grievance and assimilation and liberal views of postracism. The whitewashed representation through the mixed-race body allows the film's producers to take on multiple subject positions—the marginalized racial other and the White self—that conveniently advance White views of race. Kai's mockery as a "half breed" for his visible White difference connects to beliefs about systemic, racist disadvantages against Whites, particularly working-class Whites; his identity as Japanese, however, allows the film to leverage model minority discourses about the proper role of minority assimilation into dominant culture. The postracist assumption is that all it takes to change society is the effort of the person of color. Most obviously, his visible Whiteness connects to beliefs in White superiority, heroism, and salvation. The whitewashing of Kai, then, is necessary for the film to do this multiple ideological work. Without it, *47 Ronin* might still have problematic messages that are analogs to White racial thinking about postracist assimilation, but its links would be more abstract, and its links to the White savior trope and to White grievance would be erased.

4

Satire and the Villainy of Kim Jong-un

● ● ● ● ● ● ● ● ● ● ● ● ● ● ● ● ● ● ● ●

The Interview

The Interview (2014) is infamous for its central role in the Sony Pictures hack and subsequent document release that embarrassed the studio, created dialogue about gender pay disparities, and stirred geopolitical tensions. It so offended North Koreans that the movie was considered an "act of war" (Frizell, 2014, n.p.). Indeed, North Korea vowed countermeasures and the North Korean ambassador to the United Nations, Ja Song-nam,[1] sent a letter of protest to U.N. secretary general Ban Ki-Moon to block the release of *The Interview* ("North Korea continues protest," 2014). Retribution was realized in November 2014 when hackers, Guardians of Peace, released internal company documents, caused the delay of the premier ("Sony backtracks," 2014), and scared four major cinema chains, Cinemark, Regal, AMC, and Carmike, from screening the film for fear of violent reprisal (Barnes and Cieply, 2014). The movie's release was ultimately delayed, only played on a few hundred screens, and was primarily distributed online.

As Hornaday (2014) put it, there was a huge "kerfuffle" caused by a pedestrian, adolescent comedy (p. C01). The movie was rewritten by the prolific comedy screenwriting duo, Seth Rogen and Evan Goldberg, whose previous work include the adolescent coming of age comedy *Superbad* (2007), the stoner comedy *The Pineapple Express* (2008), the apocalyptic comedy *This Is the End* (2013), the raunchy cartoon *Sausage Party* (2016), and several others. Perhaps because of its more serious subject matter, *The Interview* was pilloried by film critics as unremarkable, juvenile political satire (Brownstein, 2015). In addition, the film was criticized for its hyperviolent pleasure in the filmic killing of North Koreans. Discussing the film's conclusion after the titular interview that exposes Kim[2] as an ordinary person, film critic Ann Hornaday (2014) noted: "so inspiring is a sequence that seeks to unseat totalitarianism by way of the press rather than guns that the hyper-violent sequences following it seem lazy and gratuitous. This goes double for the now-notorious stunt in which Kim's head graphically explodes" (p. C01). Indeed, his fictional death is unprecedented in cinematic history, as it is the first time a sitting world leader has been killed on screen (Barnes and Cieply, 2014).

Perhaps because North Korea has come to occupy the space of a near cartoon villain in the Western imagination that deserves to be mocked and vilified, film critics did not comment on the representations of North Koreans that fit long patterns of racial stereotyping of Asian/Americans. This argument, however, was not missing entirely as self-identified Korean American authors on nonmainstream websites pointed to characters with accented English, a "dragon lady," and jokes that relied on racist mockery (Builder, 2014). These are obvious criticisms, but perhaps because of the sensitivity in discussing Whiteness within the logics of postracism (DiAngelo, 2011), I found no criticism of the whitewashed White savior narrative. In leveling their criticisms, the authors engaged convenient analysis that largely ignored the function of satire, which was a dominant metacriticism in the comments sections. I argue, however, that the humor and satire in *The Interview* rhetorically justifies the caricatured, infantilized fears of masculinized North Korea as a yellow peril threat and the heroism of White masculinity.

The Interview is a satirical comedy about two White American men who are recruited by the Central Intelligence Agency (CIA) to assassinate the leader of North Korea, Kim Jong-un (Randall Park). The bungling duo include Dave Skylark (James Franco), the host of a popular entertainment talk show and Aaron (Seth Rogen), his friend and show producer. When the CIA learns that Dave and Aaron are traveling to North Korea for an interview, they are tasked with assassinating the young dictator. The narrative conflict arises when Dave wants to abandon the mission because of his belief that Kim is misunderstood. This reading is overturned, however, when the film reveals that the North Korean head of state is, indeed, a cruel dictator. Though bumbling fools, à la Maxwell Smart in the television series *Get Smart* (1965–1970), they succeed in proving on live television that Kim Jong-un is an ordinary person and not a god. Then, they assassinate him and spark democratic revolution. In the following chapter, I begin with a summary of North Korean representations in the U.S. cinematic imagination, then describe the use of satire to provide ideological cover for anti-Asian racism and White masculine superiority, and conclude with a reimagination of the films' meanings with Korean American men in the lead roles.

Representing North Koreans in the U.S. Imagination

Research on U.S. representations of North Korea is limited to a handful of studies on recent films such as *Die Another Day* (2002), a James Bond film; *Team America: World Police* (2004), a puppet-based political satire by the creators of *South Park*; and two movies about North Korean attacks on the United States, *Red Dawn* (2012) and *Olympus Has Fallen* (2014). This is despite the fact that North Korea has figured disproportionately in the U.S. imagination since its inclusion in George W. Bush's terrorist Axis of Evil (J. Kim, 2015). It has occupied a unique place as it connects both old threats of a Communist "Red" danger with the new threats of global terrorism (J. Kim, 2015). In shifting geopolitics, it allows the "yellow peril" to persist as a perceived threat through Western characterizations of North Korea as a rogue state (Seo, 2009).

The threat is not represented simply as a frightening presence, however, but as an infantilized danger. The representation of North Korea tends to be of a petty, juvenile threat that is nonetheless ruthless and cold-blooded. In J. Kim's (2015) study of *Team America: World Police* and *Die Another Day*, two films that present North Korea as an existential danger, she argues that they both work as satire of post-9/11 discourse. While clearly true for *Team America: World Police*, this is a peculiar reading of *Die Another Day*, as the Bond films work allegorically but not necessarily ironically. She claims that the movies present the trope of North Korean danger ambivalently while providing space to critique the United States.

In *Team America: World Police*, the infantilization of the North Korean threat is personified in its representation of Kim Jong-il, who is not only the North Korean head of state but the leader of a global terrorist network. Despite his position, Team America does not take his threat seriously, which J. Kim (2015) argues satirizes U.S. stereotypes of Asian masculinity. In *Die Another Day*, J. Kim (2015) reads the film as a critique of White supremacy as the villains Zao and Colonel Moon are presented as rational critics of U.S. neocolonialism and Western military hypocrisy. I would argue, however, that these critiques are given space but ultimately overturned in the film through Zao and Moon's transracial surgeries that convert them into White men, becoming what they say they despise. In addition, the narrative construction of the men as unambiguous villains subverts the films' critiques of the United States. Although satirization of White privilege through racial transformation is an available negotiated reading (J. Kim, 2015), I would argue that it is not the dominant meaning of the text. Rather, the transformation is encoded as a transgressive, invalid long-ing for White privilege that necessitates its disciplining. It is a straightforward argument for racial essentialism rather than a critique of it.

Despite her relatively generous reading of the movie, J. Kim (2015) recog-nizes some problematic representations, such as the inclusion of a woman dominatrix figure, who tortures Bond (J. Kim, 2015). In films about a North Korean threat, Pollard (2017) also notices similar characters in *Red Dawn* (2012) and *Battleship* (2012), linking it to the stereotype of the dragon lady. Although different from historical characterizations of the dragon lady as an Asian vil-lainess who violates standards of proper feminine morality by sexually seduc-ing and betraying the White hero (Ono and Pham, 2009; Shimizu, 2007), the dragon lady is often understood today more simply as a racialized femme fatale (Balmain, 2009). In addition, Pollard (2017) notes that the films include a men-acing yellow peril that delights in torturing White men but is not fully com-petent in its ambitions. The point, then, is to demonstrate White men's greater will power, determination, tenacity, and ability (Pollard, 2017). These represen-tations, of course, are not new to North Korea but rather draw on the racial-ized treatment of Asian/Americans in Hollywood and broader popular culture (R. G. Lee, 1999; Ono and Pham, 2009).

Satire and Racial Mockery of the North Korean Other

Whiteness can only be given form through its opposition to racial Others (Dyer, 1997; Nakayama, 1994; Oh, 2012). It is defined not by what it is but by what it is not. As such, for satire to uphold White racial hegemony, *The Interview* must clarify racial stereotypes of Asians generally, as well as ethnonational peculiar-ities of North Koreans specifically, to define itself in contrast. Indeed, the film uses satire as a way of engaging racial mockery (and White goodness) under the cover of satirical humor. This is a banal strategy of racial humor in Holly-wood (Oh and Banjo, 2012). Even when producers intend for the humor to have counterhegemonic meaning, it often fails because it relies on knowledge of a racial stereotype for the joke to work (Schulman, 1992). The direction of that failure, then, falls disproportionately on people of color, and in the U.S. cul-tural terrain, racial humor has historically been used to advance White racial hegemony (Boskin and Dorinson, 1985).

Racial satire can also be problematic because it is ideologically fraught to link racist humor with pleasure (Sienkiewicz and Marx, 2009). When the racial humor amplifies stereotypes, the "joke can demand a suspension of empathy, with the target being an object of ridicule not sympathy" (Billig, 2001, p. 268). Finding the joke funny requires accepting stereotyped beliefs (Billig, 2001). Despite these concerns, satires such as *Family Guy* (1999—), a televised cartoon, has largely escaped criticism because the rhetorical deployment of satire excuses manifest meanings present in the text. Because *Family Guy* does not justify its racist mockery with narrative context and closure, the representations stand as decontextualized vignettes that draw humor through the exaggeration of common stereotypes and the centering of White masculinity (Sienkiewicz and Marx, 2009). *The Interview* similarly centers White masculinity through its use of racial mockery. It is not racial satire, nor is it even political satire. North Korea is represented simply as it is understood in the Western imagination. Instead, the satire is the lampooning of the spy genre with the inclusion of two inept, unlikely White heroes.

It should be made clear that satire does not necessarily function to challenge the objects of its exaggeration; it can also reinforce existing hegemonies (Lacroix, 2011). Satire scrutinizes an object for study and ridicule to either subvert hegemonic commonsense by revealing the inanity of the belief or to uphold hegemonic common sense through exaggerated mockery (Thompson, 2009). Differentiating between what Gring-Pemble and Watson (2003) refer to as comedic satire and burlesque satire, they claim that comedy draws audiences into identification, whereas burlesque pushes audiences away through essentialized notions of the ridiculed Other. Because satire appears superficially similar in form in either case, it is relatively easy for satire to slip between meanings and for audiences to adopt heuristics that assume the intention that fits their worldviews (Perks, 2010).

In contemporary discourse in which color-blind racism, the belief that only privatized racism exists rather than systemic racial discrimination (Prashad, 2001, p. 38), there is discursive space for so-called equal opportunity racial humor. Within this space, racist jokes are able to break the taboo against overt racism (Billig, 2001) that is still vigorously disciplined in Hollywood despite the newfound openness manifest in the Trump administration. Color-blind racism, while arguing that racism no longer matters, uses openly racist jokes that are excused by claiming that all races are equally targeted for ridicule (Oh and Banjo, 2012). This so-called ironic racism allows shows that are self-conscious of their own racist representations to claim they are not meant to be read straightforwardly while representing racism straightforwardly (Dubrofsky, 2013). As such, casual racism is argued to be ironic and not meant literally (Sienkiewicz and Marx, 2009).

The Interview ridicules North Korea, using impressions of satire to reinforce Western understandings of the North Korean Other. For instance, the taglines on movie posters read:

이 무식한 미국놈들을 믿지마세요! (Do not trust these ignorant Americans!)

From the Western capitalist pigs that brought you "Bad Neighbors" and "This is the End."

Despite using a North Korean standpoint, the purpose is clearly not to identify with North Korean perspectives but rather to read it ironically. This was an explicit concern of Rogen and Goldberg, who discussed in the DVD commentary their worries that Kim Jong-un's turn as a villain would not be compelling enough after Randall Park's affable, sympathetic portrayal in the early scenes (Goldberg and Rogen, 2014b).

In *The Interview*, there are three notable North Korean characters, Kim Jong-un, Park Sook-yin (Diana Bang), and Guard Koh (James Yi). Through positioning the characters differently, the goal is to have the audience disidentify with the "bad" North Koreans and to identify with the "good" U.S. Americans and their North Korean helpers. Reflecting the gendered and racialized construction of Asians (Espiritu, 2004), Sook-yin, the only North Korean woman featured in the film, is a "good" character. She works alongside Dave and Aaron to overturn the regime, and she has a sexual relationship with Aaron. On the other hand, all but one North Korean man, an unnamed guard who helps Dave and Aaron escape, support the authoritarian regime. Thus, *The Interview* reifies a binary construction of good Asian women as supporters of White men and bad Asian men as yellow peril threats.

Like earlier representations of North Koreans (Pollard, 2017), however, the guards cannot defeat even the most inept White American men. When Dave and Aaron first encounter Guards Koh and Yu (Paul Bae), their handlers, Dave's attempt to hide his ricin strip among a pack of gum is nearly foiled when Guard Koh questions the contraband. Being told sheepishly that the poison is gum, Guard Koh chews it, which leads to his eventual violent, retching death. In an extended sequence that delights in the visual humiliation of a North Korean man, Guard Koh suffers dramatically after ingesting poison. He discharges projectile vomit before heaving on the floor in agony. Once on the ground, sound effects and his lifted buttocks imply that he has also violently defecated. Before dying, he removes his gun, ostensibly to commit suicide but shoots his partner, Guard Yu, in the face instead. The pleasure in the humiliation and mutilation of people of color recalls the violent history of White supremacy, which turned the public killing of people of color into a spectacle for White rage and pleasure.

This is also represented in the filmic killing of a North Korean television producer, who tries to stop broadcasting Dave's interview with Kim, leading to a prolonged sequence of bodily mutilation that was criticized by reviewers. In the DVD commentary, Rogen explains that the scene was added to build tension and increase pace with the relatively slow interview between Dave and Kim. Rogen and Goldberg also admit on the director's track that the scene was "one of the most highly debated moments of the movie" (Goldberg & Rogen, 2014b). In the scene, the producer bites off two of Aaron's fingers, and Aaron bites off one of the television producer's fingers in return, a subtle reference to

The Lord of the Rings: The Return of the King (2003). With blood spray reminiscent of a Takashi Miike movie, the two men struggle before the "anal impalement joke" in which Aaron lifts the producer onto a camera control stick. With the producer's anal penetration, the producer is raped and emasculated. Thus, the producer's death is resonant with the emasculation of Asian/American masculinity in Hollywood (Espiritu, 2004; Sun, 2003), and it is also consistent with the filmic treatment of Asian/American men's lives as worthless (Sun, 2003).

Asian/American men's filmic disposability was made clear in the escape of Dave, Aaron, and Sook-yin. During the escape, Sook-yin uses a large-caliber machine gun to mow down an entire hall of North Korean guards who rush the control room to forcibly stop the broadcast. More graphically, during their escape in Kim's tank, they run over a caravan of jeeps, carrying North Korean guards. Treating North Korean lives, and more notably deaths, as objects for audience pleasure, the camera moves to a medium shot of a North Korean guard lying on the ground in horror before the tank's tread squashes his head, causing it to explode in a spray of blood. Controversially, in the final showdown between Dave and Kim, a slow-motion sequence set to Katy Perry's "Firework" shows a cannon shell hitting the tail of Kim's helicopter, leading to a slow-motion explosion that is shown creating blast pressure against Kim's face before it is enveloped in flames and inexplicably explodes, causing him to literally lose his top. Showing the filmic assassination of a sitting leader of a sovereign nation, in particular, demonstrates *The Interview*'s pornographic pleasure in the gratuitous killing of North Korean men and the elimination of a "yellow peril" threat.

Before that moment and up until the film's second act, however, the representation of Kim Jong-un holds counterideological potential with an interracial bromance in which the Asian man is the really "cool" guy in the pair and in which the all-White bromance is displaced. This is short-lived, as Kim's portrayal as a sympathetic figure is subverted through the revelation that he is petty and despotic and that he has "honeydicked"[3] Dave. Kim's explanations of North Korea as a misunderstood regime are overturned as he, along with a North Korean grocery store, is revealed to be fake. This is a nod to Western hopes that simply exposing North Koreans to government propaganda will lead to revolution. The manipulation of Dave is also clearly connected to yellow peril stereotypes in which the emasculated Asian villain does not rule with brute strength and masculine excess but through manipulation and trickery, hedonic power that is gendered female in the Western imagination (Kogan, Hoyt, Rickard, & Kellaway, 2004). Indeed, the evil Asian dictator, who manipulates toward nefarious ends, is a common trope of the inscrutable "yellow peril" (Hamamoto, 1994; Marchetti, 1993). Although the target of the manipulation is often a White woman, *The Interview* turns the racialized + gendered configuration around with its playful treatment of homoerotic attraction in the bromance.

Kim's threat, however, is neutralized through his emasculation. While he bonds with Dave in the film's second act over their shared resentment of their respective fathers' disapproval, Kim's "daddy issues" are rooted in sexualized disappointment as being "gay" for liking Katy Perry and margaritas. At first, the film redeems this interest, suggesting a more progressive, expansive understanding of normative masculinity; this is challenged in Kim's death, however. In the controversial scene, the scene is rife with overdetermined sexual metaphors with the long muzzle of the tank's cannon and the shell itself signifying phallic meaning while the tail of the helicopter as the impact point signifying a sexual "bottom," a term used in gay male communities for the penetrated male. This is a role White gay men frequently presume Asian/American men should embody (Eguchi, 2015). The explosion of the ship and Katy Perry's chorus "Firework" complete the sexual metaphor with its links to ejaculation, or perhaps more appropriately in this case, a cum*shot*. Although Perry's song is about individual empowerment and self-worth, the emphasis on the word "firework" in the context of this sexual metaphor provides other signs to link to the emasculating sexual metaphor, as Dave's (cum)shot destroys Kim. Like *Team America: World Police*, the threat of North Korea is not taken seriously through its emasculation of Asian masculinity (J. Kim, 2015).

While North Korean men are represented as disposable or infantilized threats, Sook-yin's character occupies a more ambivalent position. In her introduction to the film, she disembarks a helicopter behind armed guards who grab Aaron on a deserted Chinese mountaintop. She strikes the classic image of a dominatrix with her knee-high leather boots, form-fitting military uniform, and hair pulled back in a tight bun, and she barks ultimatums at Aaron. Later in the film, she uses sex to draw Aaron into a scheme to delegitimate Kim with the ultimate goal of leading a revolution to overthrow the Kim family's dictatorship. Although it is left open for the audience to conclude whether she manipulated ("honeypotted") Aaron, Rogen and Goldberg (2014b) claim in the DVD commentary that they hope audiences read her sexual interest in Aaron as an intentional manipulation, albeit for a good cause. This is the gendered difference between Sook-yin and Agent Lacy's (Lizzy Caplan) manipulations of Aaron and Dave, respectively, and Kim's manipulation of Dave. In the latter, the Asian men's manipulation has nefarious intentions, whereas the Asian and White women's manipulations serve a noble purpose—the end of dictatorship.

While Sook-yin's manipulation does not function to betray White men as the dragon lady representation often does, she can be read as partially doing so—similar in form and function but dissimilar in purpose. While her representation as a dragon lady is ambivalent, her interest in White masculinity is straightforward. It is common in films about White adventurism in Asia that the White man is presented as more virile and desirable than Asian men as a mere function of White racial identity and through the emasculation of Asian men (Espiritu, 2004; Hamamoto, 1994; Sun, 2003). When Sook-yin visits Aaron in his room, she confesses that she has been attracted to him since their first, brief encounter on the mountaintop. When she rips off his shirt, she proclaims: "You're hairy. Hairy like a bear. Your nipples are so pink. I love it." Because Aaron is presented throughout the film as frumpy and less charismatic or sexually desirable than his buddy Dave, her attraction is not explained. Indeed, her comments read as comedic because his physical traits are not those that are typically understood as attractive. As such, the film suggests that her attraction to Aaron is simply because he is a White man.

It should be stated that the film's satirical nature and Goldberg's reading that her manipulation is intentional are arguments that the film is, in fact, interrogating and questioning White male desirability. This possibility, however, is given little room in the film's denouement. In one of the last scenes, Aaron is shown talking to Sook-yin through Skype, maintaining a long-distance relationship. Therefore, even if she is argued to have manipulated Aaron, the movie positions her as having developed romantic feelings for him, and the normality of their relationship overturns the excess required in satire. Indeed, much of the conversation is a discussion about Aaron naming his dog "Jong-un." The naming is unusual, but the conversation about a pet's name approximates a banal, domestic conversation.

As Whiteness gets constructed in relation to the villainous Asian Other, it is presented as more moral and desirable. Although Dave and Aaron are represented as excessive in their pursuit of hedonistic pleasure and Dave is represented as narcissistic, their moral failings only cause harm to themselves. As such, they are imperfect heroes but heroic nonetheless when compared to the tyranny of the North Korean men. Moreover, they possess heterosexual virility. Despite the film's homoerotic overtones, Dave and Aaron's story moves away from the bromance to watch them physically apart and with the two men in heterosexual relationships. The final scene during Dave's press tour for his new book about his adventures in North Korea shows Agent Lacy smiling in the crowd as their gazes connect, suggesting that although she "honeypotted" him, she has fallen for him. In parallel fashion, although Sook-yin may have honeypotted Aaron, they maintain their relationship. With Dave and Aaron's heroic turn and their heterosexual romances, they are masculinized, in contrast to Kim Jong-un.

Where the movie functions as satire is in its commentary on the spy genre and bromances. Some of the literary elements of the bromance in the spy genre that are satirized are generally beyond the scope of this analysis and less relevant to the social meanings around Whiteness in the film, but this is not to say that satire as form does not configure at all in its social meanings. The satire matters insofar as it questions White heroic masculinity. This is clearest in the presentation of Dave and Aaron as spectacularly unintelligent. One movie critic referred to the Dave character as a "dunderhead journalist" (Hornaday, 2014, p. C01), and Rogen and Goldberg, on several occasions, joke about how unintelligent the character is meant to be (Goldberg & Rogen, 2014b). Like the bumbling spy depictions of Maxwell Smart and Inspector Gadget, Dave satirizes the White superspy. Where they succeed through a combination of luck and their high-achieving women partners, Dave succeeds through his ability to emotionally connect, thus partially embodying the gendered construction of the new man (Kimmel, 2006). As such, *The Interview* interrogates and questions the lone wolf, masculine hero of the spy genre, such as in the Bond films and the Bourne franchise. Neither Dave nor Aaron are hypercapable, much less capable. To the extent that the spy hero also signifies Whiteness, the satire questions White masculine heroism.

This progressive representational turn, however, is ambivalent as it is the representational rationalization that allows the film's racial mockery to work. Specifically, as Perez (2013) explains in his participant observation of stand-up comedy, comedians are taught to engage in "negative self-presentation" to make provocative jokes, including racist jokes (p. 490). So long as White comedians insult themselves first, they have earned discursive space to approach the "hurtline," the social boundary between acceptable and unacceptable humor (Perez, 2013, p. 487). In *The Interview*, the representation of Dave as extraordinarily shallow and unintelligent creates the semblance of equal opportunity jokes. The difference is that there are not existing racial stereotypes of White men as less intelligent that pervade popular culture, such that Dave can be generalized broadly to White men. Rather, the humor works to mock the specific character and the spy genre. As such, the satirical treatment of the superspy challenges White masculinity as superior through its use of buffoonish White men spies, but it is this very challenge that is employed as negative self-presentation to obfuscate the straightforward racial and geopolitical mockery of North Korea.

Imagining a Korean American Bromance

In D. Kim's (2014) criticism of *The Interview,* he briefly imagined a film without White leads, saying that having Asian American leads would convert the interracial dynamics of the film into a U.S.–North Korea standoff instead. Similarly, I conclude the chapter with a sustained intellectual imagining of this alternative casting choice, envisioning Dave played by Korean Americans such as John Cho or Steven Yeun and Aaron played by Ken Jeong or Bobby Lee. The practice of this representational imagination can be counterhegemonic by detaching racial signifiers and applying them to another group (Perks, 2010). As Shugart (2001) notes, "Subversive parodic performances may be a particularly effective way to denaturalize these hallmarks" (p. 108). In the case of *The Interview*, using Korean American actors in lead roles would work similarly to the inclusion of John Cho and Kal Penn in *Harold and Kumar Go to White Castle* (2004). Like that film, an imagined Korean American bromance would be counterhegemonic in its connoted meanings, but it would not be fully subversive. There are still ideological limitations that are manifest in the text.

Perhaps most substantially, having two Korean American leads would challenge the notion of the model minority, particularly because the characters' lack of intellectual acumen and discipline decouples the model minority from hard work and intelligence. As a stereotype developed to discipline Black families and to deny them civil rights benefits (Hamamoto, 1994), the decoupling of the model minority with Asian Americans would allow more space for Black–Asian coalition and would make a small representational contribution to defang one of White supremacy's more effective discursive strategies. It would also lessen the threat of the model minority as an overachieving cyborg-like being that portends fewer opportunities for White American children. As Kawai (2005) has persuasively argued, there is a dialectic between the model minority and the yellow peril. In their roles in this film, Korean Americans would instead be represented as patriots who choose nation over ethnicity, fulfilling the promise of multiculturalism. This would work against the pervasive view of the Asian American as an alien contaminant to the White body politic (Lee, 1999).

At the same time, color-blind racism, the dominant racial logic in the United States, would be color-conscious in the story line about Kim Jong-un's fan interests. Specifically, being a superfan of a Korean American, Dave Skylark, would avoid the problematic belief in Western desirability (Said, 1978). Exaggerating Kim's well-known interest in basketball, the Western self uses self-flattery in *The Interview* through its assumed conceit that he is also a hidden fan of U.S. cultural life writ large. Pointedly, this shifts Kim's real-life invitation of a Black American basketball player, Dennis Rodman, to White American men. It obviates the possibility of Asian admiration for Black America and the counterhegemonic potential that holds.

With Korean Americans as the leads, Kim's fandom might be understood as developing through extended kinship with a celebrity coethnic. Although it is not peculiar for ethnic similarity to generate transnational affective connections and fandom, it is representationally peculiar. In mediated discourses, Asian/Americans are assumed to admire and emulate White people, a discourse that echoes colonial era beliefs about mimicry and White superiority. There are running jokes about U.S. celebrities endorsing products in Japan or Asian/Americans getting eyelid surgery. By changing the object of desire to a coethnic, it would transform the logic of affective connection from White to coethnic desirability. Although it would challenge White racial hegemony, it would replace it with ethnonationalism. The ideological danger would be narratively displaced, however, when Dave chooses to support benevolent, democratic governance over coethnic authoritarianism. Thus, in the end, the movie would reify notions of U.S. goodness and moral authority. While it would challenge White racial hegemony, it would do so by asserting the virtue of the United States in geopolitical relations and as a melting pot. This would also be true in Dave and Aaron's victory over North Korea. While it would no longer be heroic White masculinity that prevails, it would be heroic Asian *American* masculinity that does. This is still problematic but ideologically preferable to the original, which does both simultaneously.

Furthermore, Dave and Kim's discussions about their fathers would be layered with additional meaning. Having two ethnic Korean men sharing similar family struggles would transform their connection over "daddy issues" into commentary about intergenerational conflict. Dave and Kim's lingering doubts could be read as the costs of striving to be model minorities. It would move intraethnic conversations out into public view. This would have the progressive effect of making second-generation Korean American experiences better understood, yet it would do so by strengthening the association between "tiger parenting" and notions of loveless Asian patriarchs.

Where love would be given expression is in the sexual and romantic relationships that Dave and Aaron form with Sook-yin and Agent Lacy, respectively. Both would be representationally valuable, as Asian American men are rarely seen in relationships with any women, including other Asian/Americans. Providing a space for Asian American sexuality would challenge White masculinity's (post)colonial stake to Asian women's bodies (Kang, 2002). Instead of Sook-yin being rescued from coethnics by a White man, she would be represented as developing a relationship with a coethnic. On the other hand, Dave's relationship with Agent Lacy would be representationally provocative and counterhegemonic as it would challenge the pattern of films in which Asian/American men's relationships with White women are set in fears of manipulation and rape (Marchetti, 1993). Instead, as Espiritu (2004) has stated, on-screen relationships with Asian/American men and White women would work against the often visualized construction of White men with docile "lotus blossoms" and "geisha girls." In either case, the characters would move away from the common representation of asexual Asian American masculinity (Ono and Pham, 2009). Recasting the film with Asian American leads would lead to more complexity in ideological meaning. While it would not be entirely racially or geopolitically progressive, it would at least trouble the whitewashed meanings present in the heroic tale of White masculinity and its violent destruction of a yellow peril threat.

Conclusion

Including *The Interview* is an arguably controversial choice for a book on white-washing. The characters do not replace Asian people, co-opt Asian stories, or appropriate Asian culture. Despite this, *The Interview* was included because it is important to consider representations of North Korea, which have taken an outsized place in the U.S. popular and geopolitical imagination. Like many films with White men in Asia, it is a common story of White saviors, who succeed despite the odds that are stacked against them. In this satire of the bromance and spy genre, it is their own incompetence that they overcome to defeat the yellow peril threat of North Koreans. Satires such as this that have featured North Korea are especially effective in providing ideological cover while engaging in straightforward anti-Asian mockery. Thus, North Korea becomes a useful foil because it allows the recycling of Asian/American stereotypes that are otherwise limited in a cultural terrain that endorses color blindness as a post-racist logic. Thus, what is whitewashed about the story is its forceful insertion of White men heroes against a despotic yet demasculinized threat. Its racial mockery constructs White masculinity as normative. Although the White men are problematized in *The Interview*, they emerge in opposition to the North Korean threat as morally superior for their support of freedom and as having desirable masculinity that is denied to their North Korean hosts. *The Interview* expands boundaries of Whiteness by creating representational room for even problematic heroes, reflecting the modern anxieties of White men. This is to say that despite the challenge of counterdiscourses of White masculinity, the film's whitewashed representation soothes these concerns through its mythical representation of White heroism in the face of a North Korean threat.

5

White Survival in
Southeast Asia

• • • • • • • • • • • • • • • • • • • •

No Escape and
The Impossible

> *No Escape* and erasure films: Holly-
> wood's version of #AllLivesMatter
> —*The Mary Sue* website

> Whitewashing *The Impossible*
> —*Sydney Morning Herald*

In a cinematic world in which White lives are more valued than others, it is not surprising that disaster movies center around White people's survival. Two such films that were criticized for their centering of Whiteness are *The Impossible* (2012) and *No Escape* (2015). The former is about a White British family whose Christmas vacation in Thailand is shattered by the 2004 tsunami that devastated countries across Southeast Asia. The latter is about a White American family who flee from unidentified Southeast Asian rebels, who have overturned the government and are indiscriminately killing people in their violent rampage. *The Impossible* was praised in some corners for its portrayal of the tsunami's destructive power, the acting quality of Naomi Watts and newcomer Tom Holland, and the touching family story of hope and serendipity, but it was also widely criticized for its double erasure—the real Spanish family on which the story is based and the Thai survivors. *No Escape*, on the other hand, found little critical support and was widely panned for its overt portrayal of a menacing yellow peril.

Despite *The Impossible*'s Spanish writing team, including the actual survivor, María Belón, and its largely Spanish production, it replaced the family with a British one, headlined by Naomi Watts and Ewan McGregor. It also cast relative newcomers, Tom Holland, Samuel Joslin, and Oaklee Pendergast, as the children. Because of its casting replacement, the film was heavily criticized for the implication that a Spanish family would not elicit the same audience sympathy and interest. In response, the director of *The Impossible*, Juan Antonio Bayona, claims that it was easier to get a large budget for an "international" movie with well-known (White) British actors (von Tunzelmann, 2013). This explanation is problematic as its euphemism of "international" implies that White, Anglophone stories are global whereas others are only locally specific. "In other words, only white people can stand in for the human race as a whole. For this reason, Thailand and its people are mere backdrops for the story of a Caucasian family who learn the hard way that even western privilege is no match for the brute force of mother nature," noted columnist Ruby Hamad (2013, n.p.). On the DVD's special features, Belón defends the casting choice by claiming that the movie is a "human" story so ethnicity and nationality do not matter (Bayona, 2012b). She takes on a "postracial ethos" that claims that race is irrelevant while simultaneously centering (British) Whiteness (Dubrofsky and Ryalls, 2014, p. 400).

It is not quite right to call the replacement of Spanish people with British people whitewashing, however, because Spanish people are often read as White. Instead, the casting decision points to the entrenchment of hierarchies in which northern and Western Europe are understood as more purely White whereas southern and Eastern European nations are understood as inferior (Brodkin, 2004). Although Whiteness has expanded to include more ethnic groups, ideological remnants of these old hierarchies remain, at least in the internalized belief that White British actors have more perceived market draw than White Spanish actors. To rationalize the choice for the Spanish director, writers, and producers, the availability of postracist discourses are used to emphasize the "color-blind" nature of a universal story. Despite the interest in this particular criticism, it is somewhat outside the focus of this project. Instead, this chapter is interested in the insertion of Whiteness in a Southeast Asian tragedy, the third type of whitewashing representation in the typology described in the book's introduction.

Although the film is based on a true story, it is one of tens of thousands of stories of families torn apart, so the production choice to highlight this particular one speaks to White privilege in global cinema. Despite the general inattention to this present absence, mine is not the first such criticism of the film.

A few socially minded film critics pointed to the missed opportunity to comment on racial, class, and global privilege in a story about White European survival and the erasure of Thai survivors (Cox, 2013; von Tunzelmann, 2013). Naomi Watts reportedly has justified the focus on the White family by arguing that half of the victims were Europeans (Cox, 2013), but according to Hamad (2013), less than 4 percent of those killed were foreign tourists, roughly 9,000 of the 227,000 people who died. Another defense of the film that the writers and director have argued is that Thai people are represented as good, saving Maria from her nearly fatal injuries (Cox, 2013). As so frequently happens, the producers of *The Impossible* mistake morally good representations for sympathetic, humanizing ones. The Thai people, as will be described later, are not given agency but are simply represented as "magical minorities," whose purpose is to rescue the White family (Cox, 2013, n.p.)

No Escape, on the other hand, is overt in its dehumanizing portrayal of unnamed Asian others and its subjectification of the sympathetic White American family. With less redemptive narrative quality and its lack of subtlety in representing the Southeast Asian danger, it was widely panned for being xenophobic (see Ehrlich, 2015). According to the director's track, the story was conceived when the Dowdle brothers, the cowriting team for the film, were set to visit Thailand (2015b). Their trip coincidentally happened during a bloodless coup d'état to overthrow the pro-U.S. government. Drawing on an Orientalist imagination, the revolution was reimagined as violent and bloodthirsty instead. In Jones's (2015) criticism on the *Mary Sue* website, she writes, "The film is also a typical Hollywood film in that it places white characters at the center of a film that features the suffering of non-white characters as set dressing" (n.p.).

Although *No Escape* might not be understood as a typical disaster movie, there are similarities in narrative style, emotional intention, and setting that connect the films in this analysis. First, both of the films are located in Southeast Asia. *The Impossible* is set in the resort town of Khao Lak, Thailand, and *No Escape* was shot in Thailand and imagined as a fictional world that hints at being Cambodia with the signage in upside down Khmer script (Ehrlich, 2015). Indeed, Cambodian officials refused to allow the film to be exhibited in the country (Ehrlich, 2015). Second, both of the films feature survival and escape as key themes. Southeast Asia is represented as a threat, whether it is because of natural or human dangers. While *No Escape* is not a disaster film per se, "[m]odern terrorism and disaster film share a common emotional strategy: the dramatic impact on audiences through formulas of panic, phobos in classical tragedy" (Sánchez-Escalonilla, 2010, p. 10). Finally, both films feature the survival of the particular White family.

Disaster films can be perniciously conservative in their ideological rendering of human survival in the face of disasters (Kakoudaki, 2011). They especially reinforce the traditional family with its renewal acting as a major theme (Sánchez-Escalonilla, 2010), establishing the father as the protector in times of crisis (Kakoudaki, 2011). The films suggest that the restoration of the family unit is the solution to the problems that the filmic survivors face. Generally, the survival narrative points to nightmarish threats or utopian fantasies, including the end of racial difference. Who survives is rife with ideological critique in dystopian stories of survival. Stories that feature the Global South have the opportunity to critique the predominantly White Global North and its privileged ability to save itself during disasters (Kakoudaki, 2011), but this is rarely, if ever, the case. In practice, they portray the survival of White people in the Global South as disaster narratives. In these disaster and terrorist stories set in Southeast Asia, I argue that the films subjectify White terror and the survival of the White family, while reducing Asian people to helpers or villains. To support this argument, I begin with an explanation of how White mothers are constructed as postfeminist heroines, which provides a progressive veneer to hide the films' support for White patriarchy. I then argue that the films construct White victims as worthy of sympathy, while erasing the survival, loss, and heroism of Southeast Asians. Next, I point to the binary construction of good Asians as those who help White people and bad Asians as those who oppose White people. Finally, I conclude by reimagining the heroic families as played by Southeast Asian/American actors.

White Survival and Renewal

The restoration of the White family is a common theme in both *The Impossible* and *No Escape*. In *The Impossible*, it is the family's physical reunification that drives Henry's story line. After being separated from his wife, Maria, and his son, Lucas, and after separating himself from his sons, Thomas and Simon, Henry is represented as tirelessly looking for his other family members until the moment when fortune and persistence intersect in an emotional family reunion at the hospital where Maria struggles with near-fatal injuries. In *No Escape*, the restoration is psychological. Through their survival together, the couple renews their love for one another, pointing to the theme expressed on the director's track that a family that sticks together can persevere through any calamity (Dowdle, 2015b).

Yet in this story of survival, not all of the family members are equally important in the struggle to renew their families. The selective survivors' stories articulate conservative ideological meanings that are justified by the characters' circumstances and somewhat disguised by postfeminist aesthetics and emotionally overwrought stories of family survival. The films suggest that when families are stripped away from the complications of modern life and convenience that it is White men who are emergent as protectors of the family (Kelly, 2020;

Kimmel, 2006), particularly in *No Escape* but visible in both films. The difference from openly White supremacist discourses is in degree rather than type.

The problematic nature of the representations is somewhat obscured by the superficially progressive representations of women in the films' postfeminist aesthetic. Postfeminism works by arguing that feminism's systemic critique of patriarchy is no longer necessary and that what matters now is a woman's individual empowerment (McRobbie, 2006). One way postfeminism works in film is to represent women characters as equal to men, albeit usually at a cost to their personal happiness or social well-being. The postfeminist representations are necessarily different in these films because of the disaster narratives and the women's roles as mothers. They do not enact individual liberation through consumption, sex, or corporate power but rather are more similar to the postfeminist heroines in recent dystopian stories such as the *Hunger Games* and *Divergent* series. In multiple analyses of the *Hunger Games*, scholars argue that despite Katniss's discomfort with romance as well as her disavowal of traditional notions of femininity and of being a mother, she demonstrates an innate maternal nature, protecting Rue and taking care of Peeta (Brown, 2019; Dubrofsky and Ryalls, 2014). Her superficially feminist authenticity disguises the traditional construction and makes acceptable Katniss's limited agency in which she subjugates her own interests in favor of secondary men characters. This substantiates rather than subverts patriarchy (Brown, 2019).

The maternal-figure-as-postfeminist-hero becomes more fully realized in *No Escape* and *The Impossible*, as the character is no longer the figurative mother but the literal one. In this idealized construction, the White woman is praised for her devotion to her children (Guillem and Barnes, 2018). Indeed, her goodness extends to the protection of other children. As Shome (2014) observes, "what is unremarked is that in world history, it is only white women who have risen to the level of mythology, and it is only white women around whom narratives of universal love and desire tend to be scripted" (p. 4). To present the White mother as especially virtuous requires the negation of non-White femininity, a symbolic erasure of mothers of color (Shome, 2014). The postfeminist heroine, too, is raced as White (Ruthven, 2017), and representations of White women can be (post)feminist while also advancing White racial hegemony (Ghabra, 2018; LeBlanc, 2018).

Unlike modern postfeminist heroine texts that provide enough ambivalence in the representations to make counterreadings possible (see Lusksza, 2015; Ruthven, 2017), the agency of Maria, the mother in *The Impossible*, and Annie (Lake Bell), the mother in *No Escape*, is limited, and it is specific to the ways they satisfy their roles as good mothers and supportive wives. Maria's grave injuries limit her agency to the disaster and its immediate aftermath. After being swept away by the raging tidal waters, Maria holds onto a palm tree while yelling in primal anguish and fear. Her pain turns to hope, however, when she sees

Lucas struggle past her. She lets go of the tree and swims toward him while being injured by floating debris. Their attempts to find one another are further threatened when a second wave strikes the mother and son. Lucas sees his battered and bloodied mother floating in the water, and after yelling for her, they finally reunite, embracing each other tightly. As the water subsides, the extent of Maria's injuries is revealed, showing a large tear in the back of her thigh, a large tear in one of her breasts, and multiple abrasions.

Lucas is asked to take the lead, thus shifting, by narrative necessity, the agency of the two characters. He helps his mother toward a tree when they hear the shouts of a young boy. Although Lucas refuses to help, arguing that they have to take care of themselves first, Maria imparts a lesson about caring for others even in times of personal peril. Looking deeply at him, she says, "Even if it's the last thing I do." Thus, her primary act of agency is to act as a good mother by protecting children and imparting moral courage onto her own son. From this point forward, Lucas becomes the caretaker and the agent who reunites his family as Maria succumbs to the life-threatening nature of her injuries. Thus, *The Impossible* provides Maria with limited agency that is conveniently ended when her maternal obligations are completed. This is, of course, largely rationalized by the film's choice to follow the real-life traumas on which the story is based and the gender composition of Maria's family, but it is important to note that no other woman character in the film is shown with agency and that the film was comfortable changing the ethnicity of the characters but not the children's genders.

In *No Escape*, Annie is superficially empowered because she is not solely a passive partner. At times, she enacts agency to be the good wife and mother. To the extent that she is a capable mother, she enacts heroic action to save her children, and as a good wife, she rescues her husband in times of crisis. As the writing duo state on the audio commentary on the DVD, she is in "mama bear mode." It is important to note that during her disagreements with Jack (Owen Wilson), the film makes it clear that if he had listened to her, the family would not have survived. Thus, Annie's agency is activated only in ways that support her husband's plans. This form of agency does not subvert patriarchal power but rather is complicit with it (Kornfield, 2012). Women's agency is partnered with White masculinity so long as it is subordinate and helpful to it. Annie performs the aesthetic of the empowered postfeminist heroine, but she does not even have the postfeminist heroine's ambivalence.

In a scene that marks the end of the second act, Jack and his family are hiding in a local man's garden when the rebel leader and a band of gunmen search for the Dwyer family with red flares to light the darkness. Knowing that it is only a matter of time until his family is found, Jack moves to take a rifle that has been placed against a tree. On his approach, Jack steps on a branch, alerting the suspicions of a nearby rebel. To distract the guards, Annie crawls out from the bushes with her hands up and is immediately apprehended and struck by the rebel leader. As such, she makes herself into the damsel-in-distress to save her husband. During the final showdown with the rebel leader, Annie's agency as good wife and mother is most fully realized. When her daughter, Lucy (Sterling Jerins), rushes to her father, this imperils them both. The rebel leader forces Lucy to point a gun at her kneeling father, commanding her to shoot him. As her daughter stands traumatized and crying, Annie emerges behind the rebel leader and strikes him in the head with a shovel, killing him and creating a commotion that allows the family to survive another threat. Thus, she is the postfeminist good wife and mother, acting to suppress (Oriental) threats to the White family.

Taken in analytical isolation, there could be an argument for her agency as the family's protector. Her agency is constrained, however, because it is meant to support rather than lead the family, a role that is reserved for Jack. A reading of Annie as a feminist rather than postfeminist heroine is foreclosed in multiple scenes in which Jack defies Annie's wishes to save his family. After escaping to the roof with other hotel guests and workers, their respite ends when a helicopter rises above the rooftop. As the helicopter rotates to its side, Jack spots a rebel gunman and moves his family to safety while others are slaughtered around them. On the rooftop, other rebels push past a barricade, and Jack convinces Annie that they have to jump across an alley onto the rooftop of a neighboring building. Although Annie wants to hide and is afraid of the perilous leap, Jack utters what becomes a repeated mantra in the film, "All I know is, we got to keep putting ten steps between us and them."

When Annie runs in a slow-motion sequence that emphasizes the dramatic nature of the escape, she halts at the building's edge as she is wracked with fear. Emphasizing the urgency of the situation, the film crosscuts to three gunmen in the background walking casually in front of the opened rooftop door while dead bodies are strewn about in the background and as flames burn in the foreground. After her leap and hard tumble onto the nearby rooftop, Jack tricks his youngest daughter, Beeze (Claire Geare), and tosses her to her mother. Lucy, however, runs away, and he has to chase her down, but when he tries to throw her, she grabs his neck, which puts herself in danger, holding onto her father while dangling from the building's edge. In this early scene, it can be read as a metaphorical argument that White women put themselves in danger when they exercise their own agency by disobeying the benevolent, capable patriarch. Once across, they see that an Asian man, who was helping Jack, is shot mid-jump, attempting a similar escape. The film conveniently sacrifices the Asian man, a possible patriarchal competitor, to secure Jack's role as protector.

In the other major scene in which Annie defies Jack, the family is riding together on a scooter, disguising themselves as locals. Turning a corner, they see a mob full of rebels that are between their path to the U.S. embassy. Upon seeing the mob, Annie pleads with Jack to turn around, but he insists that they ride slowly through the crowd. Their ride includes a sequence of fast cuts and multiple close-ups that emphasize their physical contact with the rebels and the proximity of the danger around them. It also includes their detection by a rebel, who allows the family to slip through. Despite the improbability that they would escape detection, Jack's decisive choice allows the family to continue to put distance behind them and the rebels. As such, the audience reads Annie's attempts to enact decision-making influence as a gendered lack of courage that would lead to the family's demise. This dynamic is complicated only once in the film when Annie thinks the embassy is too quiet. Jack scouts ahead only to see rebels emerging from the embassy while an explosion blasts through the second floor of the building. The rebels chase after him, leading to the aforementioned confrontation in the groundskeeper's garden.

The narrative reason for Jack's wrong decision is to insert Hammond (Pierce Brosnan), a scruffy, jaded British agent. Unlike Brosnan's most well-known role as James Bond, Hammond has a somewhat unkempt greying beard and greasy hair while wearing casual outfits of short-sleeved shirts that are loosely buttoned to reveal his white undershirt and leather necklace with a tiger's tooth. Unlike Jack, Hammond is an antihero, who represents qualities of hegemonic masculinity. In his first conversation with Jack about why he likes Thailand, he expresses patriarchal, colonialist attitudes, saying: "The women. They're so eager to please. You know what I mean." In addition to his demonstrably heterosexual, racist sexism, he is a hegemonically masculine figure through his uncanny rescues of Jack and the Dwyer family.

Hammond's most dramatic, second rescue happens in the garden after Annie's distraction. Although her courage allows Jack to decisively grab a rifle and become the knight-in-shining-armor, he belatedly learns that it has no ammunition. Instead of killing Jack immediately, the rebel leader silently gestures to his men to rape Annie while other rebels pin Jack to the ground and force him to watch. Moments later, Hammond inexplicably appears, pretending to be captured by his Asian confederate, "Kenny Rogers" (Sahajak Boonthanakit). Together, they shoot several rebels and rescue the Hammond family, thereby demonstrating his superior capability. While Hammond is drawn as a hegemonically masculine antihero, his continued rescue of the Dwyer family has little on-screen motivation, and it is not narratively explained how Hammond happened to find the Dwyer family to rescue them. The only motivation described later in the film is Hammond's sense of responsibility to protect Jack's family since he believes his work as a Western agent has led to the rebels' anger.

Hammond's role, then, is primarily as a narrative sleight of hand that allows the Dwyer family to escape from certain danger. In addition, he is an ideologically useful figure who establishes Jack as an everyman. The heroic, everyman father is a representation that is nearly exclusively limited to White men. Men of color, even if they are represented as White in their film roles, tend to play exceptional characters, such as Dwayne Johnson in the disaster movie *Sky-scraper* (2018) and Jason Momoa in the adventure film *Braven* (2018). The White everyman's heroism is not because of exceptional ability, character, or physical strength; it is because of his ordinariness imbued by racial superiority. As an ordinary White man, he embodies what Kelly (2018) refers to as "Hollywood's *wounded man*" (p. 163). He is a White character who is marked by a sense of grievance at masculinity that has been lost, a melancholic version of the "new man." The wounded man is similar except that his feminization is not his own choice but rather is caused by a shifting world that has devalued his racialized masculinity (Kimmel, 2006). Whether in the grievance expressed in the wounded man or the mockery expressed against the new man (Hatfield, 2010), a restoration of heteronormative White manhood is represented as desirable. Hammond's later sacrifice to protect the Dwyer family can be read as a symbolic transferal of masculinity. In this sense, Jack's Whiteness is not coincidental to the film but is consistent with the trope of victimized White men, who must restore their masculine vigor.

In *The Impossible*, the transferal of masculinity happens in Lucas's coming-of-age story in which he transforms from a somewhat self-absorbed teenage boy to a precocious son, who learns his mother's lesson to help others who are less fortunate than himself. In the hospital, he does not actively search for his own family, believing them to be dead, so instead he helps in the reunion of other parents and their children. After Maria instructs him to help people, Lucas walks cautiously into the hall, his steps uncertain and his shoulders slouched. Moving into the hall, an agitated man (Douglas Johansson) grabs Lucas by the shoulder to face him and yells at him in Swedish. Showing a family photograph, Lucas understands that the man is looking for his loved ones, shouting their family name, Bernström, and the names of his wife and children. Lucas tells him to calm down and says he will help. In a montage, Lucas is shown walking around different rooms in the hospital, speaking the names of the Bernström family. Along the way, he is stopped by multiple White European adults and one Thai elder woman, who asks Lucas to find members of their family. At the end of the montage, as Lucas repeats the names, Mårten Bernström (Emilio Riccardi) hears his name, and after a short exchange in different languages, Lucas fulfills his humanitarian mission by reuniting Mårten with his father in a touching reunion. Because the father is not injured, there is no narrative reason the father could not have searched for his son on his own, so the story of unification is primarily to demonstrate the lesson Lucas has inherited from his mother. It serves a conservative ideological function that suggests that a woman's proper function is to be a good mother who raises good boys, who in turn have the agency to create better, more humane societies.

In contrast, Henry does not impart such lessons on Thomas (Samuel Joslin) and Simon (Oaklee Pendergast), the youngest of the Bennett brothers.

Indeed, Henry temporarily abandons them at a mountain refuge while searching for Maria and Lucas. As such, his role is to act as an active agent, searching for and reuniting the family. These are clearly gendered messages about the role of White men and women and their functions within the family. In a controversial scene, a shirtless Henry leaves Thomas and Simon on a truck that is headed to a mountain refuge on high ground, asking a White woman to look after his boys. Despite Thomas's pleas that they stay together, Henry says that he must continue to search, despite the darkness of night that has fallen on the area and the debris and rotting structures that endanger his search. His nighttime search proves futile as he falls through a building into standing water that extinguishes his flashlight. Forced to abandon his search, he encounters a rescue truck that takes him to a shelter, where he meets other White survivors. Although his search has failed, a German man (Sönke Möhring) gives him his cell phone to call home. Henry breaks down in tears but promises to continue the search.

The following morning, in a montage of Henry with the German man, they are shown looking at body bags, looking through debris, locating a map to find area hospitals, and looking at bulletin boards with lists of the injured and deceased. There, he finds the woman to whom he had entrusted Thomas and Simon, and she informs him that the children were taken from her. Even with this news, he does not look for them, but he continues his search for Maria and Lucas, arriving at a nearby hospital. At the hospital, Lucas sees his father from afar and chases after him. At the same time, Simon disobeys his brother, Thomas, and runs off a truck to urinate, and Henry has resigned himself to another failed search. At the front of the hospital, Lucas yells loudly in a fit of desperation, calling for his father. Thomas and Simon hear their older brother and they run to him while Thai children in the truck look on. They hug tightly, sobbing uncontrollably. At the same time, Henry sees a red ball, which his children received for Christmas a day earlier, so he gets off the truck to explore further. There, Henry sees Lucas and his other sons, leading to the reunification of the Bennetts. Although the film points to coincidence or perhaps fate as a reason for their reunion, it is facilitated because of Henry's persistence and Lucas's growth as the agents of family restoration. The films gesture toward gender-equal agency, but they construct White women as having only partial agency related to their roles as good wives and mothers, and they construct White men as restoring the nuclear family, reproducing patriarchal ideologies of men as protectors of the White family (Kakoudaki, 2011).

Worthy and Unworthy Victims

While all survivors in the films, including the extras, are victims of natural and human disasters, I focus narrowly on instances in which characters are deprived of agency, suffer physical or emotional trauma, and whose suffering is important to the stories. In these two films, it is only White characters who fit these criteria, including Jack, Annie, Lucy, and Maria. Indeed, in *The Impossible*, all of the survivors in the shelter are White, all of the survivors in the mountain refuge are White, and the vast majority of the patients in the hospital are White. There is an overdetermination of Whiteness as victims. This is true in cinema generally, and it is also true of local news (Dixon and Linz, 2000; Entman and Rojecki, 2000). This points to a White supremacist belief that White people's lives are more valuable. The ideological commitments to White humanity are reflected in studies that show that White people have greater sympathy for the victimization of White people (Ben-Porath and Shaker, 2012). The only times in which people of color are primarily represented as victims are those cases in which White humanitarianism is shown as necessary to save pitiable racial Others (Balaji, 2011). The centering of the White Self in the mediated imagination of the United States means that sympathetic stories of people of color surviving and having agency is outside the ideological framework of what is conceivable in film. This is not necessarily to say that this lack of empathy usually comes from an intentional desire to exclude the stories of people of color but rather that for White filmmakers, including Spanish ones, White characters of Anglo and Nordic origin are at the center of the White racial imagination.

The only one of the victims that is not a White woman is Jack. However, his victimization occurs in conjunction with the victimization of his wife, Annie, and his oldest daughter, Lucy. In the garden scene, she is slapped violently across the face before the rebel leader orders her gang rape. Notably, the scene is framed as a wide shot, which positions the audience from Jack's vantage point, subjectifying him and his reaction to his wife's mistreatment even in her act of agency. The attempted rape is particularly pernicious because it literalizes yellow peril fears of Asian men as rape threats who endanger White women (Hamamoto, 1994; Marchetti, 1993; Ono and Pham, 2009). Later in the film, Lucy is emotionally victimized as the rebel leader forces her to kill her father lest he shoot her in the head. Held on his knees by other rebels and because of his paternal love for Lucy, Jack gives her permission to shoot him to lessen her guilt and to prevent her death. Lucy's victimization constructs her as a docile object through which Jack can demonstrate that he is a loving, courageous patriarch and through which Annie exercises violent aggression to protect her husband and daughter.

Of course, it is not surprising that the films primarily construct White women and girls as victims. This fits with a long-held discursive configuration of White women as victims, which lionizes White men's protection (Frankenberg, 1993). It converts the White men's possession of White women from racialized, patriarchal control into a romantic, flattering story of the damsel-in-distress (Bogarosh, 2013; Fulop, 2012). In *The Impossible*, Maria loosely fits the stock character as she moves from an empowered agent in the unification of her family to a victim of the tsunami and the multiple injuries it has inflicted. Of her family members, she is the only one shown in pain during the tsunami and in its aftermath as the film shifts from "disaster porn" to medical "torture porn." Although she is not saved by a man's heterosexual romance and heroism, she finds medical help because of her son and Thai villagers, and she reunites with her family because of her son and her husband. In this way, they rescue Maria from death.

As a victim, she is immobilized, only lying down throughout roughly the last three-quarters of the film. Her face is badly bruised, she has multiple abrasions on her face and body, dried blood has coagulated across much of her shoulders and arm, and she violently retches blood and stringy debris. Maria's condition continues to worsen as she becomes ghastly in appearance. In two scenes, she asks Lucas to look under the blanket at her leg. In the first, he says her leg is red, which she says is good as long as it does not turn black. In a later scene, he checks again and turns away in revulsion, suggesting that her leg has, indeed, blackened, but he lies to comfort his mother, telling her that her leg is the same as before. Lost for a time as hospital staff accidentally misidentify her, she and Lucas are reunited when Lucas says that the belongings he is shown are not his mother's, alerting the staff to their mistake. This implies that Maria was too infirmed to realize that the wrong woman's name had been written on her arm. As such, she is dependent on the medical staff to heal her and on her male family members to reunite the family. Her victimization, then, serves two purposes. It compels audiences to sympathize with her as a victimized White woman, and it subjectifies her eldest son and husband into heroic action.

As critics have also noted, the emphasis on White survivors and victims implies that Thai survivors and victims matter less. They are symbolically rendered unworthy of audience sympathy. In U.S. media, people of color are routinely dehumanized, represented in stereotyped ways or treated as a monolith without individual difference and value. Where dehumanization differs is in the form of the stereotype. For Asian/Americans, our lives are often represented as having less inherent value with cinematic depictions of dehumanizing barbarism and cruelty (Locke, 2009), as inauthentically human as the cyborg (R. G. Lee, 1999), and as less interested in the lives of our own people. Arguably, this takes form in the tiger mom stereotype, too, which constructs the callous mother as depriving her own children of love and care. In all of these cases, Asian Americans are constructed as having a deficit of humanity. The whitewashing of the stories through the insertion and foregrounding of White families deprives Southeast Asian families of the same humanity and empathy. As Hamamoto (1994) argues, this can have disastrous consequences when U.S. foreign policy and military adventurism takes less seriously the value of people's lives in Asia.

Even if I am to concede to the imagined economic logics that center White survivors, it does not have to come at the expense of humanizing portrayals of Southeast Asians as survivors. In *No Escape*, innocent Thai victims are shown merely as dead bodies, set dressing to emphasize the perils faced by the Dwyer family. Just a bit more imagination might have shown a local family fleeing from rebels in a mosaic-like story, which leads to the two families' intertwined destinies. This, however, would imagine a different story, perhaps with the local family rescuing the Dwyers instead of Hammond. In *The Impossible*, on the other hand, several sympathetic survivors are shown in addition to the Bennett family. This includes the White boy, Daniel (Johan Sundberg), whom Maria and Lucas first rescue, and Mårten Bernström, who Lucas reunites with his father. Their reunions with their fathers (never their mothers) are both included as poignant moments of hope amid calamity. Daniel's reunion also validates Maria and Lucas's moral choice to help others even in times of personal tragedy.

In the montage sequence with Lucas, there are six adults who are featured on camera and who ask for help finding a family member. Of the six, the first five are White, with one Thai elder. Her inclusion reads as token inclusion to argue for the film's diversity while being primarily focused on White Europeans and Americans. Indeed, the names the audience hears on screen are Mårten Bernström (Swedish), Peter Berry (U.S. American), Anna Marie DeBrauwn (French), Renata Castorini (Italian), and Tatiana Cherneshova (Russian). In the shelter, six White survivors are featured on camera, sharing their stories, and the only other survivor besides Henry to share his is a German man. In both places, the background extras who act as survivors are predominantly White. Indeed, in the shelter, there is no person of color visible on screen, including aid workers. The only instance in which White people are not predominantly featured as survivors is on the truck with Thomas and Simon. It seems there is some room to represent Thai children as victims when their cuteness, innocence, and lack of agency evokes sympathy. In *The Impossible*, then, not only does the film not tell the stories of a Thai family, it intentionally erases stories of Thai victims even in the multiple stories of other survivors that receive brief glimpses in the film.

On the audio commentary featured on the DVD, Bayona, the director, does not critique but instead values the centering of Whiteness in the film. "Yeah, this is why I think it's so important to tell the story from the Western point of view because the movie tried to explain not just the tragedy but tried to make it something universal, make it something to talk about our own lives, about the end of our world of innocence, our illusionary world, of materialistic things and self-security, false sense of security, and I thought that was interesting" (Bayona, 2012b). This statement, of course, contradicts Belón's frequent color-blind arguments about a universal humanity by particularizing universalism;

understanding a "Western point of view" as universal only makes sense if he believes that Thai stories are not universal and that White stories, by their nature, are. This is consistent with filmic views of Whiteness that sees itself as normative and universal (Projansky and Ono, 1999). Both films imagine Southeast Asia as a setting for White people to find family and to learn to value their lives together. It is a place of adventure *for* White people.

Good and Bad Asians

The two movies' simple narrative structure constructs simplistic notions of good and bad people. In *No Escape*, like many movies set in Southeast Asia, it is a picture of economically and technologically backward societies that have corrupt and unstable governments and whose people are irrationally violent and anti-American (Pollard, 2017). When action movies or thrillers are set abroad, the threat of violence is consistently oriented against U.S. Americans rather than what is more geopolitically likely, a threat from U.S. Americans (Wilkins and Downing, 2002). To construct the threat, there are two readily available versions of the "yellow peril" stereotype on which to draw. One is a feminized mastermind, the archetype of which is Fu Manchu (Hamamoto, 1994; R. G. Lee, 1999). Unable to physically fight, he uses his twisted mind instead to rule or destroy humankind. Because this version of the yellow peril stereotype is strongly associated with East Asians, such as Chinese and Japanese, this is not the form the stereotype takes when representing Southeast Asia. As a developing region, the threat is instead constructed as barbaric hordes (Hamamoto, 1994).

In *No Escape*, the rebels are constructed in this way. In the first street confrontation, the rebels clash with police, who are wearing riot gear. Unable to quell the mob violence, the police are overwhelmed, suggesting the instability and lack of capability of the government. The rebels then turn their violence indiscriminately to innocent bystanders and overrun the hotel where the Dwyers are staying. When Jack returns, he witnesses a U.S. American businessman being dragged out, forced to kneel, and shot in cold blood. In the hotel, the rebels slaughter guests with machetes. Although the killings are not shown, women's bloodcurdling screams of desperation are heard, men with machetes are shown prowling, and the bloodied corpses of White women lie on the floor.

Because only the rebel leader is shown in at least a medium shot and because none of the rebels, including the leader, ever speaks, the film produces a sense of a monolithic Asian terror. One critic described the film as similar to the zombie film, *World War Z* (2013), except with Southeast Asians as the faceless, undifferentiated, and dehumanized threat (Winn, n.d.). In a chase scene, the movie crosscuts between the fleeing Dwyer family, made more chaotic by slightly shaky camera work and multiple, quick cuts, to a menacing shot of calm rebels, walking with deliberate and unrushed steps. The sequence is reminiscent of slasher movies, such as *Friday the 13th* (1980) or *Halloween* (1978). The primary menace is the rebel leader (Hiran Bunyaain). Even though he is featured on screen, he functions primarily as an unnuanced symbol of evil. As such, when Hammond explains later in the movie that the rebels are angry at Western corporations' control of the local water supply, the explanation has little rhetorical potency as it is undermined by the indiscriminate brutality, the visualization of terror, and the rebels' dogged pursuit of the Dwyer family. Instead of adding nuance, Hammond's explanation reads like a shield to justify the overtly stereotypical yellow peril imagery.

Just as bad Asians are represented as opposing White people, good Asians are represented as helping White people (Tierney, 2006). In both of the films, there are a few Southeast Asians shown as "good Asians," whose morality is manifest in the ways they help the White survivors. As Dubrofsky and Ryalls (2014) note, people of color are included only to the extent that they center White characters; people of color are not allowed to be the heroes of their own stories but to authenticate the heroism of White people. In *No Escape*, the Dwyers are aided by Kenny Rogers and two elder Thai men, a groundskeeper (Somwang Ritdech) and a boatman (Danai Thiengtham). The elder groundskeeper recognizes the danger the Dwyers are in and hides them in his garden, and the canoe owner hides Jack under the boat after he barters his shoes. On the DVD's audio track, the Dowdle brothers, the writing duo, mention that they included the characters to clarify that not all of the local people are bad (2015b).

The other "good Asian" is Kenny Rogers. When the family first arrives at the airport, Hammond calls a Kenny Rogers–themed van to take them to their hotel. Wearing a blue denim vest, a cowboy hat, and a turquoise bolo tie, he has gained the nickname because of his intense fan interests. The Dowdles mention that the character is because of a Steve McQueen–themed bus they saw in Egypt (2015b). As such, the reason for this characterization is for mocking humor and to give him an easily digestible Western nickname. Furthermore, the only implied motivation Rogers has is his loyalty to his partner, Hammond. The sidekick works to center Whiteness while keeping people of color at the periphery (Gates, 2004). Having a person of color as a partner provides a superficial gesture toward multicultural inclusion while limiting his subjectivity and masculinizing more dominant or more sympathetic White heroes (Artz, 1998; T. K. Nakayama, 1994). Characters of color are not allowed to be the heroes in the stories but to simply authenticate the heroism of the White protagonist (Dubrofsky and Ryalls, 2014).

On *The Impossible*'s audio track, Belón remarks that she is grateful for the generosity of the Thai people, who took time to help her when they were looking for their own families. She says she wanted to demonstrate her gratitude by showing them as caring people rather than as victims (Bayona, 2012b). She misses the point, however. What is dehumanizing about victim representation is not the pitiable circumstances in which characters find themselves; rather, it is when people are represented as having no agency in these circumstances. As a consequence, the film erases Thai victims and limits Thai people to being care-takers of White people. Their humanity is limited to their usefulness to White families. This includes a frail, elder Thai man, who drags Maria through the mud to his village, where elder women silently dress her wounds and where men remove a door to use as a stretcher so that she can be transported to a nearby hospital. At the hospital, an English-speaking nurse manages Lucas and other survivors' children and comforts Maria before her surgery. In every case, they serve the needs of traumatized White people. They are deprived of their own agency and sympathetic stories of searching for and reuniting with their own families. It is a twisted liberal vision in which Asians are accepted and liked not because of their own humanity and their own stories but because of the ways they benefit White people.

Reimagining Asian Survivors

Reimagining the Bennett family of *The Impossible* and the Dwyer family of *No Escape* as Southeast Asian families from the United States and England would act as only a partially counterhegemonic corrective if there is not a full reimag-ining of the story. It still would center English and U.S. American families, replicating the same Western centrism that ignores the stories of local South-east Asians. It also would continue to understand Southeast Asia as an unsta-ble, threatening place that cultivates terroristic dangers, and it would still continue to relegate Thai people in roles as helpers of European and U.S. Amer-ican families.

In the White imagination, the "Third World" regions are exotic places of adventure that threaten White people's safety. By having a Southeast Asian American family in the roles of the Dwyer family, this decenters racialized meanings and converts them into national anxieties instead, that is, the belief that U.S. Americans are endangered for their national belonging and citizen-ship rather than their Whiteness. Although its geopolitical meanings would be largely unchanged, it would counter the conflation of U.S. Americanness with Whiteness, and it would work against xenophobic representations of Asian Americans as "perpetual foreigners." While different casting choices alone would not remove the exoticizing nature of the representations, having South-east Asian American actors set in places with people who look like them would weaken the racialized, exoticizing tendencies in the film. Southeast Asia as a place and its people would not escape the exoticizing lens, but exotic difference would be limited to cultural difference rather than biological difference if the actors shared the same ethnoracial identities.

Casting actors of Southeast Asian descent would also decenter Whiteness in stories of disasters. Different casting choices would work symbolically to insinuate that the lives worthiest of audiences' sympathies are not only White people. The counterhegemonic potential of showing Thai families from the West would challenge ideas of who deserves sympathy. In the West, it has typically been White women who are constructed as victims most deserving of audiences' sympathy (Frankenberg, 1993). This is because White women are constructed as moral guardians of the nation-state (R. G. Lee, 1999) and the colonial project (Coloma, 2012). By casting an actress of Southeast Asian descent in the role of Maria, this would challenge these naturalized associations. It would still retain its gendered meanings, and if too prevalent, it could become a trope of its own that borrows from the hyperfeminization of Asian/American women, but in limited representation, it would invite audiences to care about and sympathize with the struggles of women of Southeast Asian descent, who are affectively drawn into the imaginary body of the nation-state. While the damsel-in-distress is a sexist gender trope that denies women's agency, it has also been a White supremacist trope that imagines White women as the most morally pure and most beautiful. Casting women of color in those roles can disrupt at least the White supremacist part of the construction.

If Maria was a Thai English character, it would also change the subtextual meanings in her relationships with the locals who help her. Instead of caring for her because of her Whiteness, it might suggest that there is a diasporic bond because of their shared ethnic identities. Although this would not be expressed directly, her treatment by the villagers would lose its racialized meanings. It would be even more visible in the hospital where Maria would be surrounded by White Europeans. The nurse's attention to her would subvert the idea that people of color should subvert their interests for White people. This would decenter the subservient filmic relationship of people of color to Whiteness, but it would, on the other hand, connote an ethnocentric message.

Because of Annie's maternal and spousal protection, a Southeast Asian American woman would read as counterhegemonic. Usually, Asian/American women are represented as passive and obedient "lotus blossoms" to their White male lovers, or when represented as aggressive, they are represented as "dragon ladies" that sexually manipulate White men (Espiritu, 2004). Neither would be true for Annie. Most obviously, if the family is cast as Southeast Asian American, then her actions would not be for or against a White man. In addition, her character's acts of aggression would be represented as morally justifiable. This is a limited corrective because her character would complicate stereotyped constructions of Asian American women, but it would still be in line with the postfeminist heroine that has come to dominate White women's representations recently.

Having actors of Southeast Asian descent play the men in the stories also holds counterhegemonic potential. In Western cinema, Asian men are rarely depicted on screen as heroic figures unless it is in occasional roles as a martial arts expert (Hamamoto, 1994). It is instead White men who are configured as the heroes who are agents of the action on screen (Dyer, 1997). By having patriarchs of Southeast Asian descent, they become constructed as protectors of the family. Because family acts as the primary metaphor through which the nation-state is understood (R. G. Lee, 1999), this would work as counterrepresentation that imagines a multiracial nation-state, and it would help deconstruct the idea of White men as protectors of the West. Furthermore, it would challenge the current racialized politics of desire that represent Asian men as undesirable romantic and sexual partners. The films' inclusion of loving relationships between spouses produces idealized constructions of who is a desirable life partner. What would not be challenged, however, is the sexist and heteronormative nature of the representations. It would still imagine the family, and by metaphorical extension, the nation-state, as defended by men. To produce intersectional, progressive meanings would require not only different casting but a reimagination of the stories.

Thus far, I have used a generic expression "actors of Southeast Asian descent" because to the best of my knowledge, there are few prominent actors of Southeast Asian descent. To the extent that there are Southeast Asian actors in the United States, they are Filipinx or Vietnamese Americans. There are no prominent Thai, Cambodian, Malaysian, or Indonesian American actors of whom I am aware. To the extent Filipinx American actors such as Rob Schneider, Vanessa Lachey, Lou Diamond Phillips, Phoebe Cates, and Dave Bautista are on screen, they are often not read as Asian. The most prominent contemporary Vietnamese American actor is arguably Lana Condor. However, her most prominent roles have been Jubilee, a Chinese American, and Lara Jean Covey, a Korean American teenager. Because of the dearth of Southeast Asian American actors in the United States, the construction of Asianness in U.S. media culture is dominated by images of East Asians. As such, a decision to include actors of Southeast Asian descent would complicate the racial imaginary in the West about who constitutes Asianness.

Conclusion

Disaster films are an understudied genre because their narratives are seen as simplistic and lacking artistic merit (Maeseele and van der Steen, 2016). Perhaps reflective of it being understudied, there are no studies of disaster films that focus on racial meanings in them, although a few make observations about race or national difference. For this reason, this chapter is additionally important. It not only examines whitewashing but also expands the literature by including a race-centered analysis of disaster movies. The chapter also links the affective intention in disaster movies with stories of terroristic violence.

In the disaster movie, there is a consistent theme of survival (Keane, 2006). In this narrative crucible, it burns away other complexities and produces straightforward ideological meanings about who or what is the threat and who deserves to survive. Even in films that are not set in foreign lands, the choice of whom the movie centers as sympathetic figures produces, even if unintentionally, ideas of whose lives are most valuable. It is, for example, a common trope that in slasher movies, Black Americans are the first to die, the implication of which is that multiracial representation and friendship are acceptable, but ultimately there is a hierarchy of human worth. This is the same for disaster movies, and it is why it is important to understand them and to call into question their ideological assumptions. During the Black Lives Matter protests, there were occasionally mocking criticisms claiming that White people's lives were implied to be less valuable. Especially in disaster movies, the opposite is true. White-dominated media culture has asserted that not only do White lives matter but that White lives are all that matter.

6

Whitewashing
Anime Remakes

• •

Ghost in the Shell and
Dragonball Evolution

Hollywood has a decades-long history of whitewashing anime, the hand-drawn animated style of cartoon from Japan (Berman, 2017). Its whitewashing is usually rationalized because of anime's "culturally odorless" quality in which it is drawn to intentionally obscure its Japaneseness (Iwabuchi, 2004, p. 55). "The propensity of Japanese animators to make their products appear non-Japanese is evidence that a Western-dominated cultural hierarchy continues to govern transnational cultural flows" (Iwabuchi, 2004, p. 59). It becomes easy, then, for Hollywood producers to imagine anime's racial ambiguity as racially White, particularly as anime figures' exaggerated wide eyes are read as a signifier of Whiteness in the Western racial imagination.

Fans, however, have rejected live-action adaptations that have imagined the leading characters as White, despite the *mukokuseki*, or racelessness and nationlessness, of anime's visual style (Iwabuchi, 2004). This was even true for M. Night Shyamalan's adaptation of *The Last Airbender* (2010), which was adapted from a U.S. cartoon rather than a Japanese one. Because of its mishmash of Asian aesthetics in a fictionalized pan-Asian world and its clear homage to an anime visual style, fan-activists organized and resisted after the lead roles were cast as White (Lopez, 2011). For adaptations of much-loved manga/anime, films have been routinely criticized for their casting choices, although the language of whitewashing did not emerge as popular culture lexicon until recently. This includes recent films such as *Speed Racer* (2008), *Dragonball Evolution* (2009), *Death Note* (2017), and, especially, *Ghost in the Shell* (2017).

For the latter, there was palpable anger over the casting choice of Scarlett Johansson in the role of Major Kusanagi long before the film was released (Rose, 2017), and fans' dissatisfaction was renewed with promotional photos of a close-up of Johansson's face in a side profile. With the bomber jacket and her hair dyed black in a bob cut, she was framed in the same way as a signature image from the anime (Berman, 2017). Fans' dissatisfaction worsened when news articles revealed that visual effects were attempted to make Johansson appear more Asian (Berman, 2017). This sparked anger over digital yellowface (Sampson, 2016). Asian American actors Constance Wu and Ming-Na Wen lent their voices to the chorus of critics, who decried the choice of a White actor in a role that could be more easily imagined for an Asian American actor (Loughrey, 2017).

Dragonball Evolution, similarly, was reviled by fans (Dennis, 2017). Though it did not receive as much attention, perhaps because of its smaller scale, lack of an A-list star, and/or sociohistorical moment before whitewashing was as salient in the popular imagination, it is, at the time of this book, the seventeenth lowest ranked movie on the Internet Movie Database (IMDB) with a rating of 2.7 out of 10 stars. The backlash for the film was so strong that the screen-writer, Ben Ramsey, later penned an apology for seeking a payday rather than being respectful of the source material (Dennis, 2017). Both *Ghost in the Shell* and *Dragonball Evolution* are so notorious that they made it onto *IndieWire*'s top twenty-five list of the worst whitewashed movies. I focus on these two films because of their visibility in the politics of whitewashing anime. They are exemplary because of the scale of the outrage due to *Ghost in the Shell*'s casting choices and the scale of the mockery directed toward *Dragonball Evolution*. They also share a loosely similar plot point as they both feature White saviors' existential questions about their own (racial) identities.

Given whitewashed anime adaptations' inability to succeed at the box office (Frank, 2017; Kilday, 2017), it is remarkable that they continue to be made in a media industry that is averse to risk (Hesmondhalgh, 2007). Despite a long string of financial failures, there is an established history of whitewashed roles (Berman, 2017). For *Ghost in the Shell*, Paramount Domestic Distribution Chief Kyle Davies is on record saying that the whitewashing controversy hurt the film's box office performance (Loughrey, 2017), though it is not possible to quantify directly (Kilday, 2017). The failures, however, have not slowed interest in anime adaptations with plans for other highly popular properties such as *Akira* (1988), *Astro Boy* (1952–1968), *Cowboy Bebop* (1997–1998), and *Naruto* (2002–2007). All but *Cowboy Bebop* and *Akira* are said to be filming with or pursuing an Asian or Asian American cast. Even then, *Akira* was once connected to a White actor, Garrett Hedlund, before those plans were shelved, likely because of recent whitewashing controversies (Couch, 2019).

So if the film industry, which is marked by a high degree of risk, seeks to minimize it by choosing safe, successful formulas (Croteau and Hoynes, 2014; Hesmondhalgh, 2007), then whitewashing speaks to producers' faith that it is not whitewashed casting that has doomed the films. Indeed, the faith betrays rational economic logic. This is not to claim that the choices are motivated by an explicit desire to promote Whiteness even at the cost of profit. Rather, it is the affective commitment to White racial hegemony that makes it possible to believe that White casting is a reasonable investment in spite of the over-whelming evidence to the contrary (Frank, 2017; Jasper, 2017). It is the benefit of the doubt given to Whiteness that people of color do not receive. Media workers of color behind and in front of the camera carry additional stresses because they know that White executives will blame a box office failure or ratings "bomb" on Asian American casts or leads rather than on the quality of the project or the whims of audiences. Yet even a string of live-action anime failures is not attributed to the casting of White leads in the remake of Japanese cultural products. As Yuen (2017) observes, Hollywood corporate suites are among the least diverse in comparison to all other major industries. As such, there is a collective faith in and promotion of Whiteness.

Despite Hollywood's penchant for adapting and whitewashing anime, researchers have not turned their attention to them. It should be pointed out that in adaptations of comic book movies, such as the Marvel Cinematic Universe or D.C. films, fidelity to the source material is often used as a justification for reifying White-centric casting. For instance, even in problematic cases such as the Orientalist *Iron Fist* (2017-2018), which was produced as a series on Netflix, it cast Finn Jones, a White actor. In other cases, claims to progressive racial politics have led to the replacement of Asian characters with White-presenting ones, such as the Mandarin (Ben Kingsley) in *Iron Man 3* (2013) and the Ancient One (Tilda Swinton) in *Doctor Strange* (2013). Both films could have reimagined Asian characters in ways that are not Orientalist or could have replaced the Asian characters with non-Asian actors of color rather than White actors. Thus, source fidelity is used as a shield to protect White representation but discarded when it inconveniences White racial hegemony. With East Asian adaptations, the stated concern for source material fidelity is usually cast aside. U.S. remakes of East Asian horror cinema, for example, retain only the narrative form while stripping stories of their cultural specificity, thus containing the transgressive potential of the remake (Wong, 2012). In another example, the televised remake of a South Korean travel reality show that featured celebrity elders, *Better Late Than Never* (2016–2018), retained the structure of the original while adapting the remake to favor Whiteness and to Orientalize East Asia (Oh, 2018a). Studying remakes and adaptations of East Asian texts and specifically anime is important because of the ways it reveals the logic of Whiteness as casting and narrative choices cannot be hidden under the umbrella of source fidelity. Rather, the transnational, transracial borrowing reveals White racial hegemony's appetite to consume, transform, and profit from difference.

The Postracist White Hero and the Yellow Peril

Postracism has multiple paradoxes. First, it expresses hope in the end of race while maintaining racial chauvinisms (Watts, 2010), and second, it expresses racelessness (as color blindness) while requiring explicit images of visual, racial difference (Thornton, 2011). In postracist media, race is in the background of the narrative and is not addressed directly, suggesting that race and racism do not matter in the characters' lives (Drew, 2011); this is the form taken in these anime adaptations. It should be noted that this is different from postracist antiracist movies, racial comedies, and interracial buddy films that explicitly center race to argue for its contemporary irrelevance. Instead, these films' postracism is maintained through the narrative unimportance of race. It is simply, like the metaphor of *Ghost in the Shell*, our exterior but not our actual selves. In a color-blind fantasy, characters are oblivious to each other's race, even when not noticing lacks verisimilitude.

Cinematic postracism works cynically as White people are centered in non-White worlds (Shome, 1996). In this centering, White heroes are frequently represented as moral and good (Benshoff and Griffin, 2004; Murphy and Harris, 2018), civilized and complex (Madison, 1999), and rational, authoritative voices against racially coded disorder (Giroux, 1997). The White hero is represented as racially, culturally, and morally superior whereas racial others are marked by corruption, excess, and depravity (Oh and Kutufam, 2014). Indeed, s/he is represented as a "metonym for benevolent White supremacy" (Fitzgerald, 2013, p. 98). It is as Schultz (2014) says, a filmic update on the "White Man's Burden" (p. 207). In Asia-centric stories, the White hero is frequently represented as having what Tierney (2006) refers to as supraethnic viability, the ability to quickly become the most capable warrior after appropriating the martial arts of Asian people and combining it with his biologically superior body. In martial arts films, "good" Asian characters support the White hero's intrusion into their lives, acting as sidekicks or teachers (Tierney, 2006). In *Showdown in Little Tokyo* (1991), Nakayama (1994) argues that the White hero is represented as the protector of Asian Americans, creating envy and desire to be the White man by his Asian American partner and sexual desire from Asian American women (Nakayama, 1994). In *The Wolverine* (2013), the White hero protects a Japanese woman from the patriarchal abuses of her family, killing nameless hordes and a techno-Orientalist cyborg threat (Oh, 2016). Thus, the threat is located in Asian patriarchy, a common colonial trope used to justify the possession of Asian women and territory (Espiritu, 2004).

To disguise these desires and to avoid criticism within a postracist framework, Whiteness is hidden with the prevailing logic of color blindness. Color blindness, in turn, silences race talk, preventing antiracist action and presenting a utopian multiculturalism devoid of systemic inequality (Esposito, 2009; Ono, 2010). As Cobb (2011) writes, "Strangely, even in its earliest iterations, postracial practice invoked ideals of racial visibility to evidence a new form of colorblindness" (p. 407). Within a multiracial framework, it provides ideological cover to resituate Whiteness as progressive while simultaneously recycling stereotypes of people of color (Ono, 2010). These representations flatten such characters so that they are developed only insofar as they are useful for the character development of the White heroes (Griffin, 2015). In the interracial buddy cop genre, their utopian friendship fantasizes relationships that are unburdened by structural racism and differences in lived experience (Artz, 1998; Thornton, 2011). Because multiculturalism is a salient, highly visible signifier of progressive racial politics, its inclusion can hide and smooth over problematic representations of Asian/Americans and White superiority (Oh, 2012; Pham, 2004).

Ghost in the Shell's "international" representations, Japanese team members, and the narrative conceit of the raceless shell hide its problematic centering of White heroism, appropriation of Japaneseness, and yellow peril representations of Japanese masculinity. For *Dragonball Evolution*, the Chinese American teachers, grandparents, love interest, and sidekick legitimate the White hero. Thus, I argue that the movies use postracism to hide the salience of race while advancing problematic representations and tropes of Asian people and culture. To build the argument, the chapter explores the characters' journey to not only fight an existential threat but to choose their (White) humanity, the long-standing trope of the White savior fighting against existential yellow peril threats, and the binary construction of "good" and "bad" Asians. To conclude, I reimagine the films with Asian/American lead characters.

Heroic Journey toward White Selves in Asian Families

Ghost in the Shell and *Dragonball Evolution* are essentially about the lead characters' search for their true identities and choosing their humanity. *Ghost in the Shell* is set in a dystopic neo-Tokyo reminiscent of *Blade Runner* (1982). Major Mira Killian (Scarlett Johansson) is the most extreme version of cybernetic merging as her brain is implanted into a "shell," a robotic body with a human appearance, and she is presented with a choice—to defeat Kuze (Michael Pitt), the villain who has abandoned his humanity to live as a cybernetic presence within computer networks or to join him after learning that they were both victims to the same corporate experiments to merge a human brain into cybernetic shells. *Dragonball Evolution* is a straightforward hero's journey. The hero, Goku (Justin Chatwin), a high school–aged boy, is tasked by his grandfather Gohan (Randall Duk Kim) to recover magical dragonballs so that an evil alien presence, Piccolo (James Marsters), cannot fulfill his ambition to use the dragonballs to destroy the Earth. In the final battle, Goku learns he is the human embodiment of Oozaru, Piccolo's powerful beastly helper, thus setting up a nature versus nurture conflict, choosing between his true self, a destroyer of worlds, or his human self, who was raised by his loving grandfather. In both films, the leads choose their humanity.

Although the analytical focus of the book, thus far, has been on character analysis, the narrative parallels between the two films are too striking to ignore despite their manifest differences—U.S. versus Japanese setting, mystical versus technological power, and lighthearted versus heavy tone. The similarities reveal White fantasized relationships to Asia and to Asian people that is made possible through the representational project of whitewashing. The value of Asia and Asian people is to allow White people to fully realize their self-identities and to legitimate White heroism. In both of the films, the heroes begin their journeys in isolation. When Gohan is killed by Piccolo and his assassin, Mai (Eriko Tamura), Goku is left orphaned. Although his grandfather's uplifting words to "Always have faith in who you are" do not have particular meaning in the moment, it proves pivotal to Goku's discovery of his true self. In *Ghost in the Shell*, Major begins her journey, believing that she is not only orphaned but that her body was destroyed in a terrorist attack. The story reveals this deceit in what is essentially an identity film—what makes a person who they are? Although the original anime explored the existential question of what humanity is in a future age of advanced robotics and high technology, the filmic retelling is layered with questions of race because of Johansson's visible presentation as a White woman. Learning about her past means not only grappling with her former human self but also learning about her living Japanese mother and her former Japanese identity. Although the movie formally questions who she is—her ghost or her shell—the racial subtext is unavoidable. Should she embrace her former Japanese self or be her cybernetically embodied (White) shell? As critics have written, it is especially problematic that the movie reveals that a Japanese woman has been implanted in a White body (Egan, 2017) with the unstated assumption being that Hanka Robotics would consider a White person a more desirable shell in neo-Tokyo (Goldberg, 2017).

Dragonball Evolution fits the trope of the hero's journey in which tragedy spurs the protagonist, who is unsure of his own ability, into action and discovery of his true purpose. In addition, it also fits a trope of self-discovery that is only made possible when White people are alienated by the inscrutable, exotic difference of the Asian other (Blouin, 2011; Marston, 2016; Oh, 2016; Oh and

Wong Lowe, 2016). Although *Dragonball Evolution* is set in the western United States, it is populated with a Chinese American grandfather, Chinese teacher, an Asian American sidekick, a dragon lady villain, martial arts, and monks that evoke imagery of Shaolin Temple, a fixture in kung fu films, and in addition, many viewers are likely to have intertextual knowledge that the movie is based on a popular Japanese anime (Tsukawaki, 2017). The complexity of this choice could be because James Wong helmed the film, providing a limited challenge to the trope of White self-discovery in Japan/Asia, but nonetheless it still is likely to be read as at least partially an Asian world because of Goku's relationships and the Chinese iconography.

For viewers of *Ghost in the Shell*, their identification with Major as a White woman renders the dystopian, near-hallucinogenic digital landscape an alienating environment; this builds on the character's narrative isolation. On the ground level, the buildings are worn and in decay, while the streets are damp despite the lack of rain. The dampness does not make the streets glisten or wash away the grime but rather works together with the representations of slum-like dwellings and the monochromatic gray buildings and streets. Its visual suggestion is that the real, multicultural world of neo-Tokyo is, despite its technological advances, decaying and eroded. Far above the streets, frequent aerial shots establish the city as a postmodern, illusory world. Its beauty and life are digitized and commercialized in building-sized holograms that appear as phantasms loosely attached to the buildings that anchor them. The bright holograms dominate the cityscape with Japanese signifiers such as koi fish, an oversized Asian man's face with visor-like sunglasses, and frequent Orientalist images of geishas.

Whether as homage or as the director's own techno-Orientalist imagination, the scenes hearken to *Blade Runner*'s visualized fears of reverse colonialism and a multicultural world dominated by Japan (Yu, 2008). "This image of Japan as a forward outpost of the future has long permeated popular culture" (Paulk, 2011, p. 478). Japan becomes a world of robots and cyborgs, a place in which people are not quite human (Paulk, 2011). Unlike *Blade Runner*, however, it locates the mechanized, nightmarish future world over there in East Asia rather than here in the United States. It furthers techno-Orientalist myths in which Japan's technological advances have come at the loss of its humanity (Morley and Robins, 1995). In this world, then, audiences are invited to disidentify with the multicultural, postmodern dystopia and to recognize Major's dilemma of seeking to restore her humanity as she embodies Whiteness in this place—made to live lifelessly but with a shell of Whiteness that provides hope for restoration.

It is, for this reason, that her identity crisis is resolved through her embrace of her White shell. On its face, this does not make narrative sense because she chooses to abandon her human self as a Japanese woman. However, it makes ideological sense because postmodern Japaneseness has so strongly been associated with soullessness (Morley and Robins, 1995; Oh, 2016). Thus, choosing to be White fits an ideological common sense to become human. Ideologically, being Japanese is to be the cyborg even if, in the narrative, being Japanese is human while being White is to be the cyborg. Her Japaneseness exists merely as a ghost, memories of a past life. Although the character does not appropriate Asian skills, the film appropriates Asian lineages to produce a more interesting life story for the character. This is not unlike White Americans' frequent claims of Native ancestry. It is a way of claiming the Other to create a more interesting Self, and it is occasionally a means to claim resources meant for historically marginalized U.S. Americans. It is an optional, often fictional, identity that enriches White Americans' beliefs about their own heritages but that does not bear the racial marking and oppression of visible difference.

Dragonball Evolution, on the other hand, is set in the present, but as Goku journeys from his California suburbs into the desert, he not only moves geographically away from "modern life" but temporally, too. His training on the parched soil, his travels to the monk's temple, and his battle against Piccolo in the wilderness move increasingly away from technology and toward mystical fighting arts and centuries-old legends. As such, Goku's heroic journey is also an adventure into Asia's premodern past. The overvaluing of the past fixes Asia into a culturally temporal space in which mysticism and tradition are overdetermined (Darling-Wolf and Mendelson, 2008; Oh, 2018a; Oh and Wong Lowe, 2016). Interest in the past is to claim Asian authenticity, uncorrupted by modernity, as a way of also reclaiming the adventurer's humanity. Yet it is not simply about appreciation of Asian historic pasts but consuming it and claiming expertise. These are the two poles of Western fascination with East Asia—as postmodern technofuture and premodern ancient past. The encounter with Asia is almost never with the present.

As Goku moves backward into the past, his identity crisis occurs when he learns that he is Oozaru, the disciple of Piccolo who will wreak havoc on the Earth.

GOKU: "I will defeat Oozaru, and I'm here to destroy you."
PICCOLO: [Chuckles] "Destroy Oozaru? When the blood moon eclipses the sun, you will become Oozaru."
GOKU: "What? No."
PICCOLO: "There is no denial. Goku's time is over. Goku is a shell. This is who you are."

In both films, they use the metaphor of the "shell" to suggest that the characters' physical (White) bodies are not their real selves. Unlike *Ghost in the Shell*, however, Goku's shell is what links him to Asianness. His grandfather, Gohan, had adopted and raised Goku in an unambiguously Chinese American household and has trained him in a mystical form of kung fu that harnesses qi to manipulate air. Because Goku reads as White, his family home, his grandfather, his kung fu, his Chinese teacher Roshi (Chow Yun-Fat), and his Asian American sidekick Yamcha (Joon Park) are necessary to overdetermine Asianness. Goku's alter ego, Oozaru, on the other hand, is neither White nor Asian. Instead, he is an apelike beast. Indeed, Oozaru roughly translates to "great ape." His beastly transformation includes a furless face, large nostrils, a protruding jaw, dark brown fur, and oversized arms.

Goku's identity story does not begin in earnest until after he transforms into Oozaru. While pinning Roshi by his neck and strangling him, Roshi tells Goku/Oozaru: "Only with faith can you win. Don't let Oozaru destroy the Goku in you." Roshi's words then trigger a vision of his grandfather, who is standing in front of their family home and the bucolic setting of his youth. With the shot colored in an ethereal blue and with mist covering the ground, the frame evokes both his faded memories and a peaceful netherworld. Against this dream-like image, his grandfather's familiar words resonate and finally have clear meaning: "Always have faith in who you are. You are special, Goku." With multiple paternal reminders, Goku returns to his (White) "shell" while incorporating Oozaru's power with his own. Like Major, he chooses (White) humanity without giving up extraordinary ability and power. It is in his White body that he can possess different selves—culturally Chinese American and physically alien. Indeed, as he incorporates Oozaru's power, he does not become a hybrid but rather returns to his original appearance as Goku. As such, he returns to his White shell, which like Major, is the only worthy vessel.

These representations are reminiscent of cultural appropriation in which White people "eat the other" as a way of enriching their lives (hooks, 1992). That is, of course, the point of appropriation—to perform superficial signifiers of the other to advance White subjectivities (Oh, 2017; Yoshihara, 2002). This is visible in the direction of the cultural borrowing. Appreciation draws attention to, edifies, and praises another's culture and people, while appropriation draws attention to, edifies, and praises one's self for the plundering and performance of otherness. It is not cultural borrowing itself that is morally unjustifiable but rather for whom and for what reason borrowing happens that determines its moral rectitude. Film directors, writers, and producers often argue that their interests are out of appreciation for Asian culture, including anime in this case, but as Hamamoto (2000a) notes, "Asiaphilia is a deceptively benign ideological construct that naturalizes and justifies the systematic appropriation of cultural property and expressive forms created by Yellow people" (p. 15). The Whiteness of Asiaphilia in the remakes of Japanese anime produces the dislocation of Asianness as heroic figures in favor of White heroes that conquer dangerous Asian foes.

The White Savior and Yellow Peril

Both *Ghost in the Shell* and *Dragonball Evolution* represent the White leads as savior figures, and as savior figures, they resonate with the frontier hero in Westerns. For Major, her fight is in a new, dystopian cyberpunk frontier, where the world is chaotic and ordered only by a stoic, cyborg hero. For Goku, the story's location in the U.S. American West, including a desert showdown, visually locates *Dragonball Evolution* in this filmic space. In the Western, heroic cowboys such as the Lone Ranger emerge as savior figures to save frontier towns ravaged by unchecked, lawless men (Fitzgerald, 2013; Miller, 1996). In this uniquely U.S. American morality tale, the hero demonstrates the benevolent supremacy of the White hero (Fitzgerald, 2013; Kollin, 2010). As Murphy and Harris (2018) also point out, the Western frontier myth and the White savior have many overlaps. Unlike the cowboy who saves a single town, Major and Goku save all of humanity. Major fights against a technological threat while Goku fights against a millennia-old alien power. I am not arguing that the films can be read straightforwardly as Westerns, but there are resonances with these anime adaptations.

Despite the obvious White savior tropes in both films, the yellow peril villains are less well defined. The primary villain in *Ghost in the Shell* is Kuze, whose shell is physically White, and the menacing figure in *Dragonball Evolution* is a green-skinned, nonhuman space alien named Piccolo. Despite their superficial, obvious differences, they can be understood as Asian. Indeed, as Paulk (2011) notes, a common representation of the Japanese, and arguably Asians, more generally, is as aliens and androids. The connection is more explicit with the visibly Asian subordinates who work for or are controlled by the villain. In *Dragonball Evolution*, Piccolo is aided by a dragon lady figure. The dragon lady is most prototypically represented as a dangerous threat to White men, who seduces and tricks them to advance the plans of a villainous Asian man, that is, the yellow peril (Hamamoto, 1994; Shimizu, 2007). In other representations, she is a hypersexual, racialized "femme fatale" (Balmain, 2009), who performs kinky sexuality and dominates White men (Espiritu, 2004; Sun, 2003).

Though Mai does not use her sexuality, she is visually sexualized. Mai's typical outfit is a burgundy-colored, lacy bodysuit that has a cutout of an upside down, rounded triangle, revealing her cleavage. Thus, her chest and face are the only parts of her body that reveal her skin. She is further eroticized with matching burgundy gloves and leather knee-high boots. The outfit is completed with a wide belt and a gun holstered to her upper thigh. Her hair is cut in a simple bob with straight bangs covering her eyebrows. Although her sexuality is not dangerous per se, her work as an assassin representationally couples her hypersexualized outfit with her work. Indeed, in her first appearance, she is shown in a rural Japanese village, encountering a maternal figure, who wears a simple, earth-colored, flowing one-piece dress, who sacrifices herself in order for her daughter to remain undetected. In opposition to the self-sacrificing, idealized mother, Mai is defined as a callous femme fatale.

Further embodying the stereotypical dragon lady, Mai infiltrates a temple where Goku is training to steal the final dragonball. To slip past the team, she transforms into Goku's love interest, Chi Chi (Jamie Chung). When Mai, who has transformed into Chi Chi, fights against the real Chi Chi, she is knocked to the ground and manipulates Goku by calling plaintively for his help. Falling for her deception, Goku knocks out the real Chi Chi, and Mai escapes with the dragonball. It should be noted that like typical representations of the dragon lady, she has no clear motivations of her own but works in service of an Asian villain. Piccolo is, thus, transformed into an Asian villain figure because his association with Mai. This is furthered because of his alien desire to destroy the world through the practice of magical, mystical arts. As Lee (R. G. 1999) points out, Asian Americans have long been imagined as a contaminating, alien presence. Although Lee does not mean space aliens, the idea of Asians as a foreign threat that will destroy Western society has been a popular fear (Locke, 2003; Ono and Pham, 2009). The archetypal figure is Fu Manchu, a feminized threat who is dangerous because of his ability to manipulate others and because of his dangerous intellect that mixes Western science with Eastern mysticism, posing an existential threat to the world that the White savior has to police (Hamamoto, 1994).

In *Ghost in the Shell*, the clear yellow peril threats are established early in the film during Major's fight sequence against a group of sadistic, perverted men at a gangster club and the mindless yakuza assassins and robot geishas, who are controlled by Kuze. During Major and her partner Batou's (Pilou Asbaek) investigation, they find an underground yakuza bar, evoking old Chinatown stereotypes of hidden dens of opium, gambling, prostitution, and other vices (Chang, 2003). It is a space of decadence and decay, fitting for its underground location. In the club, Major is met by two Asian men in black suits, one of whom has a large, cybernetic jaw. They take her to a private room with a dancing pole, and they cuff her hands around it. There she encounters an elder Asian man in a suit and a man with a shaved head, who is wearing a blazer but without a shirt. The elder man is dressed like a late-period Elvis Presley with a pompadour hairstyle, large sunglasses, patent leather purple shoes, and a face glistening with an oily, unnatural substance. He questions Major while moving closely behind her and whispering in her ear. When she does not respond to his questions, he sits voyeuristically, chanting for her to dance while his henchman electrocutes her with a shock baton. His uncomfortable touching, whispering, and voyeuristic chants for her to dance are evocative of the yellow peril as a rape threat that endangers White women (Hamamoto, 1994; Marchetti, 1993).

In an earlier sequence, the yakuza assassins that Major kills are reminiscent of another version of the yellow peril stereotype—an invading horde (Hamamoto, 1994). Defeating the inhuman horde demonstrates the White protagonist's heroism by fighting against the odds to defeat the great numbers arrayed against her/him, such as in *Lucy* (2014), *Kill Bill, Vol. I* (2003), and *Rambo: First Blood Part II*. In addition to their numbers, the hordes are dehumanized and frightening because of their cruelty. In an earlier scene, yakuza assassins are literally mindless because of Kuze's ability to hack into people who have received cybernetic upgrades. In the scene, the men are nearly indistinguishable, wearing the same black suits, black shoes, and cybernetic enhancements over their eyes. Using identical submachine guns, they murder an African delegation and Hanka executives. The film then cuts to Kuze kneeling in the dark with a single shaft of light from above. This reveals the many wires attached to his skull, confirming that Kuze is the mastermind behind the operation. Cutting back to the yakuza men, their role in the film quickly ends when Major dives into the banquet room. Although Kuze does also control two White waste disposal workers later in the movie, they have some character development, dialogue, more time on screen, and are much more difficult to defeat. The Asian men, on the other hand, have no dialogue or backstory and are on screen only for mere seconds, further emphasizing their disposability and devalued humanity.

Asian disposability and techno-cybernetic threat is most fully realized in the robot geishas. Although the geishas are represented as clearly robotic, they also signify the hypersexualization of passive Japanese women, who are submissively available to the sexual desires of White men (Espiritu, 2004; Marchetti, 1993; Shimizu, 2007). The diminutive robot geishas kneel behind the men, pouring drinks and wearing kimonos that are worn loosely on their shoulders, suggesting their sexual availability. The featured geisha robot, played by a major Japanese actress, Rila Fukushima, has a face that is porcelain white with a large red dot. Her face is literally stamped with the Japanese national flag, overdetermining the robot's ethnoracial identity. Subverting the usual stereotype, the geisha is corrupted by Kuze's influence, becoming a murderous presence. Under Kuze's control, she hacks into the White Hanka executive's spine, extracting information and his life force. Her danger is physically embodied as her joints dislocate, and she transforms into a frightening spider-woman hybrid. She becomes the cybernetic yellow peril threat, the logical extension of techno-Orientalism in the White imagination (Oh, 2016). The yellow peril is threatening because of its distance from humanity.

This is most fully realized in Kuze, who has abandoned humanity to live in the network. Like Major, his brain was transplanted into a shell, but unlike the hero, he does not embrace his physical body and his role in human society. He is both like the Fu Manchu archetype (Fong, 2008), who threatens to destroy the world through his sinister cruelty and his intelligence, and he is like the cybernetic techno-Orientalist threat (Oh, 2016). It is important to note that like Major, Kuze has a White shell he can occupy but a backstory as a real Japanese man. The choice to reject his physical White body, then, can be understood as the reason he is represented as evil. In other words, Major rejected her former Japanese self to become more human while Kuze rejected his White shell to become more cyborg-like. As such, Whiteness is connected to humanity, and Asianness, specifically Japaneseness, is denied humanity and associated with a robotic threat. Kuze's treachery, then, is represented as not only a rejection of humanity but specifically a rejection of Whiteness.

The other major villain in *Ghost in the Shell* is Mr. Cutter (Peter Ferdinando), an executive at Hanka Robotics. Although he is not an obvious yellow peril threat, ignoring his role would be ignoring the ideological complications he presents. Mr. Cutter's racial identity is straightforward. He cannot be reasonably read as Asian except to the extent that he works for a Japanese company that has collaborated with the government to create antiterrorist cyborgs. Although the film is ambiguous about whether Mr. Cutter's superiors know about his actions, the film clarifies that the Japanese government was unaware of the extent of his company's experiments. This was fully realized when Mr. Cutter orders a strike on Section 9, the joint antiterrorist force that is supported by Hanka Robotics but run by Aramaki (Takeshi "Beat" Kitano) at the direction of the prime minister. When Mr. Cutter turns to shoot Aramaki during his arrest, Aramaki outdraws him with his six-shooter, thereby taking on the figure of the "Wild East" cowboy against the capitalist villain.

Mr. Cutter represents the threat of masculine technology and the moral abandonment of his humanity. This is where perhaps he might be interpreted as at least Asian-adjacent. His work for the company means an abandonment of his own humanity because of his greed and militarized technological fetish. This is clearest on two occasions: when he kills Dr. Ouelet (Juliette Binoche), a mother figure for Major and when he tries to assassinate Major by remotely controlling the spider tank, a giant, heavily armored robot. As Schaub (2001) notes, the gigantic robot is linked to masculine excess and danger while the feminine becomes a vessel that contains the power of the robotic while maintaining humanity. The feminine, in anime, is often used to defeat masculinized greed (Giresunhu, 2009). Although he is not an Asian man, it is possible to read his adjacency to Asianness as the reason he abandoned his humanity, thus, like Kuze, rejecting Whiteness and embracing "Asianness" instead.

Good Asians and Multicultural Cover

Both of the films, but especially *Dragonball Evolution*, incorporate Asian helpers, that is, mentors and sidekicks. In martial arts films, Asians become marked as "good" and "bad" by their support and opposition, respectively, of the White hero's entitled right to appropriate Asian people's cultural practices (Tierney, 2006). Asian mentors pass on knowledge and ordinary Asian people demonstrate their worthiness through their fawning appreciation of the White hero's superiority (Espiritu, 2004). Asian/American men sidekicks admire and envy the White man's virility and power (Espiritu, 2004; Nakayama, 1994), and Asian/American women sexually desire him (Espiritu, 2004). In plainer language, the Asian/American man wants to be the White man, and the Asian/American woman wants to be with him. In either case, they support and acknowledge his superiority, providing ideological cover for stories that are, in essence, plainly White supremacist ones (Fitzgerald, 2013; Tierney, 2006).

Because James Wong, a Chinese American director, and Ben Ramsey, a Black American screenwriter, were the primary creative forces for the *Dragonball Evolution*, the men who support Goku are slightly more ambivalent than the usual representations of the White savior's sidekicks. Gohan fits two stereotypes—the mentor who teaches mystical martial arts and a sexless eunuch figure, à la Charlie Chan. Gohan's other family, if they exist, are not shown on screen or included in flashbacks or exposition. This suggests that he has lived a bachelor life, particularly as no family members visit for Goku's birthday party, nor are any discussed. Although the revelation that Gohan discovered and adopted Goku appears to be an allusion to the *Superman* story, Gohan is not represented alongside a partner when he discovers the alien baby.

What complicates the character is the unconditional paternal love Gohan has for Goku. This counters stories of Asian/Americans in U.S. popular culture. Although the film does not make the point explicitly, it suggests that Gohan knew that Goku was Oozaru from the beginning. Instead of fearing the eventual destroyer of the Earth, he nurtured him, telling him to "always have faith in who you are." This picture of an accepting, loving Asian/American man deviates from common depictions of intergenerational conflict between uncaring Asian/American fathers and their culturally U.S. American children. Although loving Asian American patriarchs have become somewhat more visible on screen lately, the notion of an unconditionally loving Asian/American man has been largely incomprehensible. Perhaps it is the reason that *To All the Boys I've Loved Before* (2018) symbolically erases the Asian American father and replaces him with a loving, adoptive White, single father, why *The Joy Luck Club* (1993) mostly erases the fathers from the stories of the Chinese American daughters' lives, and why *Gilmore Girls* (2000-2007) did not show Lane Kim's father during the televisual run, only solving the "mystery" later in the Netflix miniseries.

When Gohan dies and entrusts Goku with the mission of collecting the dragonballs and saving the world, he is replaced by Roshi. As Gohan's former master, his character is understood to be Gohan's elder, but he is visibly younger, delayed in aging because of his control of his qi. Like Gohan, he is also a mentor figure who trains Goku.[1] Unlike Goku's kindly grandfather, Roshi is portrayed as a bawdy drunkard, who finds redemption through the sincerity and promise of Goku. Unlike Gohan, he is a less complex character. His sexual perversion is first revealed when Bulma finds *Bikini Quarterly* in his room and when he is shown wearing a graphic T-shirt that has a scantily dressed Asian woman in black undergarments, latex boots, and evening gloves, and it is further reinforced when Bulma, a White woman, threatens him after he places his hands on her buttocks when they sit together on her trike motorcycle. Although the film attempts to convert his sexual perversion into humor, its lack of comedic impact works toward a straightforward reading of Asian men's sexual perversion, a stereotyped representation of Asian/American men (Marchetti, 1993). His social awkwardness and inappropriate sexual harassment is represented as an outgrowth of both his sexual immorality and inexperience, despite his advanced age.

The other Asian/American man who supports Goku is Yamcha. Yamcha is portrayed as an unethical bandit who traps people in the desert and only frees them upon promise of payment. Indeed, it is the promise of a huge payday that prompts Yamcha to join the team. Unlike the two mentors, however, his primary relationship is not with Goku but with Bulma. They develop a partnership and inchoate romance. Thus, his fit with the usual sidekick is partial. Although he eventually supports the team's lofty mission and Goku's central role as a White savior, his contributions are mostly represented as separate from Goku. Indeed, his budding interracial romance with Bulma challenges notions of Asian/American asexuality, providing a counterhegemonic challenge to the politics of desire (Espiritu, 2004). The challenge is, however, a limited one as their hints of romance are not actualized with a kiss or other on-screen signs of sexuality or romance.

Chi Chi's role in the film is little more than a way of demonstrating Goku's sexual and romantic desirability. The audience's first extended scene of her is during Goku's daydream in his science class where he imagines Chi Chi sitting at her desk biting seductively into a red apple in a field full of yellow flowers while the wind gently blows her hair. The natural setting and the fruit are apparent allusions to Eve's temptation. The allusion does not advance the narrative, however, but simply presents her as an object of the White male gaze. In addition to being objectified into a decorative role, she is objectified to advance Goku's character arc. Her primary purpose in the film, then, is to demonstrate Goku's heterosexuality and his desirability. Like Asian/American women in White savior narratives, her function in the film is merely to confirm his heterosexual, masculine virility.

In contrast, Major has no Asian male love interest to confirm her heterosexual, feminine virility. Indeed, her only scene that involves hints of sex besides the aforementioned yakuza club scene is when she finds a sex worker. They do not have sex, but, instead, Major caresses the woman's face and lips at a moment in which she questions her own humanity. Thus, the filmic representation of White men's colonizing, possessing desire is denied to White women, and Asian/American male asexuality is further established as a filmic trope.

The only significant Japanese or Asian characters are her mother and her supervisor, Aramaki. Major's boss is atypical in his ideological complexity. His inclusion in the cast was announced after the controversy erupted around Johansson's casting choice in the iconic role. It is possible that his eventual inclusion was a way of quelling the whitewashing controversy that led to his ideologically ambivalent character, or perhaps it is because Beat Kitano is a highly respected actor and director such that the role had to be interesting enough for him to accept it. The final possible explanation is that because of Kitano's iconic status for fans of transnational cinema, portraying his character in ways that might be read as disrespectful to his stature would cause even more fan outrage. Fans, of course, are an opportunity and a threat for media production (Jenkins, 1992).

That said, Aramaki is a strange fit in the movie. All of the characters in neo-Tokyo speak English as the lingua franca, including the yakuza gangsters and Major's teammates (in their limited dialogue). His lines, however, are subtitled, and everyone he interacts with understands his Japanese without difficulty. His Japanese speech breaks the conceit in the film in which audiences might understand English as the decipherable language for audiences or as the new language of Neo-Tokyo, and it highlights how Japaneseness has been otherwise erased. Thus, he rubs against the grain of the text, revealing the hegemonic co-optation of the Japanese story. Aramaki is also unusual in a White savior narrative because of his detached coolness and heroic purpose. Although the character is flatly drawn, he is neither a weak, dependent Japanese man who requires the help of a White hero nor a martial artist with skills to pass down to Major. He is morally uncompromised, supporting Major at the risk of losing Mr. Cutter's technological support for his antiterrorist unit, Section 9.

When Major escapes Hanka's facility and learns the truth of experiments to implant human brains into cyborgs, Mr. Cutter orders an assassination of all Section 9 members. The setup of four attacks is revealed, but only the assassination attempts on Aramaki and Major are shown. For Aramaki, his survival conjures a Western showdown as he is outnumbered and outgunned, armed with only his six-shooter. As three enemies in full body armor and machine guns riddle Aramaki's classic Lotus Excel with bullets, the elder Aramaki emerges stoically with just his bulletproof briefcase as a shield and his pistol to kill the gunmen. As he stands over one of the gunmen, he is subtitled as saying, "Don't send a rabbit to kill a fox," before unloading his final shot. The otherwise sedentary bureaucrat, Aramaki, emerges as a full-fledged gunslinger.

The character unmistakably hearkens to the stoic cowboy in Westerns, making Aramaki arguably the coolest character in the film. In a way, then, it Americanizes the character. Thus, while his character development is flat, his counterrepresentation presents ideological complexity that allows Asian men to be imagined as the prototypical U.S. American cowboy, embodying masculine virility, heroism, and stoic coolness.

Major's mother (Kaori Momoi), on the other hand, is objectified as her only purpose is to demonstrate Major's Japanese heritage. The reveal itself does not further the narrative; her mother could have been any race for the sake of the story. It services the ideological goals of Whiteness, however, literally demonstrating that Whiteness can absorb and be any race. Indeed, the film provides no agency for any Japanese women. They are either robotic or human geishas, sexualized holograms, or mother figures who have no character development of their own. Other than Aramaki, Japanese people are largely denied agency, and other than decorative background to establish location, Japanese people and their subjectivities are erased. The film's producer, Steven Paul, justified the whitewashing and, implicitly, the erasure of Japanese people in Tokyo by arguing that the film presents an "international world" rather than a specifically Japanese one (Loughrey, 2017, n.p.), thus using globalized multiculturalism as a justification to replace Japanese people while holding onto Japaneseness as a visual aesthetic for the city.

Thus, the movie uses superficial multiculturalism as ideological cover for its whitewashing. This is a common strategy of representation—to use a multicultural veneer to hide texts' advancement of White racial hegemony (Bineham, 2015; Griffin, 2015; Oh, 2012; Pham, 2004). *Ghost in the Shell*'s presentation of a multicultural Tokyo is as critics have claimed, Tokyo without Japanese people. This is slightly overstated as Japanese characters and people of color are limited primarily to background and minor roles, but with the exception of Aramaki, the characters who drive the narrative are all visibly White—Major, Batou, Dr. Ouelet, Kuze, and Mr. Cutter. Tokyo has been filmically colonized and the story has become culturally appropriated even while based in Japan. This is different from a text like *Death Note* (2017), which reimagines its adaptation in Seattle, narratively justifying its primarily White cast, or *The Ring* (2002), which sets its remake in the United States.

Another way that postracism is advanced is through the representation of good White people fighting bad White people. Having Mr. Cutter play the role of a cutthroat capitalist taps into modern anxieties about corporate power and technology, and in this Japanese-specific world, it demonstrates the media producer's liberal awareness that the Japanese are not solely the cause of these dangers, as techno-Orientalist narratives do, and that there is White involvement in these dangers, perhaps a nod to large U.S. technology companies such as Google, Facebook, and Apple. This represents a more nuanced understanding of a racialized technological threat, but it is still a postracist veneer that generally blames Japan as Hanka Robotics is marked as the perpetrator of the threat. Furthermore, despite Mr. Cutter's evil, he is challenged by three White characters. Clashes with evil White people in media are opportunities to demonstrate the benevolence of Whiteness (Fitzgerald, 2013). Major opposes him directly, Batou opposes him indirectly through his support of Major, and Dr. Ouelet's redemption arc occurs when she violates Mr. Cutter's orders. So that Mr. Cutter does not present a generalized White threat, he is opposed by three "good" White characters.

Postracist media texts also avoid conversations about race, presenting racial utopias that hide the work of systemic racism (Cramer, 2016). In the dystopic world of *Ghost in the Shell*, whatever problems may exist because of corporate greed and technology, human differences of race, culture, and language do not act as obstacles. Indeed, even as an identity film, Major only grapples with the question of how her former self matters in her robotic body; she does not grapple with questions of ethnic and racial change and dislocation. "With exotic Whiteness, the power differential between the self and other supposedly dissolves to portray the coming-together of a common humanity that no longer is encumbered by colonialism or the problems of the color line" (Taylor, 2015, p. 21). Like color blindness, the film ignores the existence of racism while replicating racist logics (Bonilla-Silva, 2006). For instance, while the film represents race as unimportant to its characters, the film represents a new, multiracial world order that is implicitly controlled by White people and in which White shells are implied to have some inherent advantage. Despite being in Tokyo, where an Asian-looking shell might blend in more easily, both Kuze and Major are outfitted with White-appearing shells while robot geishas are Japanese. Furthermore, the characters do not question Mr. Cutter and Dr. Ouelet's abduction and experimentation on specifically Japanese people, suggesting that what might easily read as racist is not racially motivated, hiding the racism of even egregiously racist acts.

Unconventional casting choices and the presentation of a multiracial utopia also hide the racist whitewashing in *Dragonball Evolution*. Most obviously, the head of the temple is Sifu Norris, played by Black American actor Ernie Hudson of *Ghostbusters* (1984) fame. This creates a filmic world in which martial arts is not essentialized as Chinese/Asian. Although the signifiers of the temple are culturally Chinese, its adherents are not, challenging essentialist notions of cultural authenticity. Because it happens outside of the usual structures of White appropriation in film and culture, it can be read as counterhegemonic in meaning. Indeed, it resonates with resistive Black–Asian cooperation in U.S. racial politics (Anderson, 2007; Prashad, 2001). In one of the film's earliest scenes, which establishes Goku as an underdog character, he is bullied by a multiracial group of jock-like characters. The bullies are led by Carey

Fuller (Texas Battle), a Black American classmate, who runs over Goku's bicycle with his yellow Camaro. When Goku responds with indignation, Carey and his multiracial group of friends taunt Goku. The altercation ends when Chi Chi and her Black American friend arrive, creating a picture of an inclusive group of popular, mean kids. Although the inclusive casting runs against typical structures of racial representation, they also firmly establish a color-blind world in which racial differences do not matter. Coupled with Goku's surprise that he is adopted despite his grandfather's racial difference, the multiracial coalitions construct a color-blind fantasy that provides the room for Whiteness to appropriate and become all races and cultures.

Role Reversal: Asians in Anime Adaptations

Imagining casting reversals in anime adaptations in which Asian characters are played by Asian/American actors produces counterhegemonic possibilities. For the role of Major, I imagine her role cast with an actress such as Rila Fukushima, a Japanese actress who performed in U.S. films such as *The Wolverine* (2013) and who was dehumanized in the role of the robot geisha. Because she was cast after the whitewashing controversy (McHenry, 2016), it is a bit of imaginative representational justice to consider her in the role of Major, particularly as her own role is voiceless and hardly recognizable. It is a marginalizing role for someone of her acting stature, particularly as she played a major role in *The Wolverine*.

With Fukushima as Major, the story would center around Japanese heroes fighting against White antagonists. Kuze's reading as a White man with a Western accent and Mr. Cutter's unmistakable representation as a U.S. American corporate villain would mean that the villains would be read as White and perhaps White American. Although White villains are commonly represented in U.S. cinema, they are nearly always ideologically balanced by good White heroes or antiheroes. In White racial hegemony, it is particularly rare for White villains to be countered by people of color. Therefore, having a team led by Aramaki and a Japanese Major would be an oppositional challenge to the assumption of White moral superiority frequently seen in U.S. and Western media culture (Artz and Murphy, 2000; Shohat and Stam, 1994).

Because of the transformation of Japanese space into a multiracial world in which Whites occupy many of the positions of power seen on screen, the film can be read as a colonized Tokyo in which White people have largely taken over and transformed the society to be only superficially Japanese. Black people's roles in the film further suggest a world in which globalization and population flows favor Whiteness. The only speaking role for a Black character is that of a sex worker. Thus, her labor can be seen as patterns of migration in which the racially marginalized are oppressed by globalization. The only other sex workers in this space are the Japanese robot geishas and, arguably, the geishas who walk around in the background on gritty city streets. This world, then, positions Tokyo as harmed because of its colonization and transformation into a Western-ordered world. In this context, Major and Aramaki's opposition to Mr. Cutter could be read as not only against the excesses of an unchecked corporate madman but against the evils of White neocolonial takeover. This is particularly because the only people who are shown as victims of Hanka's experiments are native Japanese. Major and Aramaki's opposition to Kuze, on the other hand, would not be a challenge to the White social order because Kuze, too, is a terrorist bent on destroying Hanka Robotics, but rather their opposition to him would demonstrate their greater morality, saving humanity and maintaining public safety even in spite of their possibly aligned interests.

Another consequence of having Fukushima play the role of Major is that her identity search and resolution would lose the message about abandoning her racial and cultural self to live as the shell. With a Japanese shell, the scene with her mother would make more sense. In the current iteration's color-blind fantasy, Major is not surprised that she was formerly a different race and ethnicity. Her lack of surprise would have more verisimilitude if her ghost and her shell were both Japanese. Although the explicit message of Major's visits to Motoko Kunagi's grave is a metaphorical burial of her former self, with Fukushima in the role, it is possible for a negotiated reading in which audiences interpret Major as incorporating the ghost and the shell as a unified identity. Finally, a Japanese Major would present a challenge to usual racial + gender configurations in her relationship to Batou. A female Major is already subversive as a man is her helper and partner, challenging usual gender roles in film, but a Japanese woman as Major would present an even greater challenge. As Japanese women have been overdetermined in film as hyperfeminine, passive, and obedient to White men (Espiritu, 2004; Ono and Pham, 2009), having a Japanese woman lead a White man would directly subvert this pairing.

For *Dragonball Evolution*, I picture Ki Hong Lee in the role. He has visibility in U.S. media culture through his supporting role in the *Maze Runner* film series. An Asian American Goku would make more narrative sense because the questions of why Goku would not have questioned his family ancestry would be clearer. Although it is arguable that the film's representation of a transracial adoption in which a Chinese American elder adopts a White baby boy is counterhegemonic, this is not productively confronted in the text. Instead, it would represent a loving relationship between a Chinese American patriarch and his adopted grandson, and it would represent a mentoring relationship between a Chinese American mentor and father figure to a Chinese American boy. These common real-life relationships are rarely pictured on screen, symbolically denying humanity and love within the Chinese American household. Having a

Chinese American Goku would be a partial correction to that representational erasure.

Furthermore, his romance with Chi Chi and her inexplicable attraction toward him would be counterhegemonic as well, because Asian American men are most commonly depicted as void of sexuality on screen (Espiritu, 2004; Shim, 1998). Again, despite Asian men and women being commonly coupled, this romantic pairing is rarely depicted on U.S. American screens. While there have been some prominent counterexamples lately, including in *Crazy Rich Asians* (2018) and *Always Be My Maybe* (2019), shows such as *To All the Boys I've Loved Before* (2018), which feature Asian women–White men romances are much more filmically and televisually common. Having Asian American men in relationships with Asian American women challenges stereotypes of asexual Asian men, removes desire for Whiteness as a mediated norm, and displaces the colonizing impulse in White men's desire to possess Asian women's bodies (Kang, 2002).

In addition to his relationships, having a Chinese American Goku would produce new connotations in the typical underdog story. Most obviously, heroic stories are denied to Asian Americans in U.S. film culture, particularly when he is not a martial arts master. I cannot recall a U.S. film in which an Asian/American hero has stopped an existential threat to all of humankind, although the opposite is fairly common. A Chinese American hero would expand the racial imagination of who has symbolic value in U.S. society. Less obviously, Lee's role in the film would produce racially meaningful and different connotations to the underdog story. Asian Americans are the racial group who are the most frequently bullied (Wang, 2016). By having Lee play the role, the bullying he encounters would resonate with the experiences of Asian Americans as a particularly vulnerable underdog. As such, his heroic turn would be more meaningful. His heroism is not only to fight against Piccolo and to honor his grandfather's love and legacy, but he is fighting magnanimously for a world that has produced his racialized rejection.

Conclusion

Whitewashing in anime adaptations reserves superherodom nearly exclusively for White protagonists. Asian/Americans are excluded from comic book adaptations, citing fidelity to canon. This was particularly visible in the televisual adaptation of *The Iron Fist* on Netflix. Fan activists called on Marvel and Netflix to reconsider the White hero as an Asian American one, to redeem a problematically Orientalist story. When even animes are whitewashed, then, it means White people become overrepresented as heroes in the increasingly popular superhero genre. This is one reason the whitewashed anime adaptations viscerally feel so damaging because it reads as an intentional erasure that conveniently rejects canonical claims when it benefits White racial hegemony.

Because of the outcry about whitewashing in anime adaptations, it will soon be possible to not just imagine Asian/American actors in live-action films based on animes. For instance, John Cho is currently shooting the highly popular anime *Cowboy Bebop* as its central character, Spike Spiegel, in a Netflix-produced television series. These adaptations are opportunities for fans who have been denied Asian/American representation because of arguments about canon to argue for representation on similar grounds. Although it is a problematic argument that maintains racial essentialism in the adaptation (Lopez, 2011), it can be a tactically useful one, particularly because the adaptations have often used Japaneseness as decoration while erasing Japanese subjectivities. In moves toward cross-racial casting, what is more resistive is not racialized claims to roles but rather disrupting larger patterns of cross-racial casting such that the direction of the casting is equal. There may be an ideal of color-blind casting, but White racial hegemony means that the cross-racial casting choices are primarily unidirectional with only enough exceptions to produce consent.

7

Transnational Coproduction and the Ambivalence of White Masculine Heroism

• •

The Great Wall, Outcast, and
Enter the Warriors Gate

"Essentially a rehash of '80s favourite
The Last Starfighter with a martial arts
spin, director Matthias Hoene's *The
Warrior's Gate* plays like a relic from a
bygone era, when broad Asian stereotypes were commonplace and went
largely unchecked"
—James Marsh, *South China
Morning Post*

"*The Great Wall* is a prototypical 'white
savior' movie; a standard Hollywood
narrative in which a Caucasian male
swoops in to save non-white natives
from others (or themselves)."
—Juli Min, *Global Times*

"As things have turned out, it's hard to think of an equivalent-but-in-reverse cultural mélange that could match it [*The Great Wall*] for sheer, tin-eared fatuousness: perhaps a CGI-heavy remake of *Gone with the Wind* that swapped out Rhett Butler for Fu Manchu."
—Robbie Collin, *The Telegraph*

The quotes above refer to recent coproductions that attempt to capitalize on the size and market power of Chinese film audiences. At best, coproductions have yielded mixed box office results, particularly when a White hero is inserted into a Chinese story. The failures of coproductions are perhaps because U.S. media workers are unwilling to representationally sacrifice White racial hegemony for greater profits. Over the past several years, there have been several coproductions that have attempted to find a formula that achieves financial success in both China and the United States. The attempts thus far have followed a similar narrative structure—a reluctant White man finds redemption or personal growth, or both, through his heroism in China, falls in love with a Chinese noblewoman bound by duty to her nation, and leaves China as a better man. Recent movies that have used this unremarkable formula include *Outcast* (2014), *Enter the Warriors Gate* (2016), and *The Great Wall* (2017).

The most notable of these is *The Great Wall*, which was widely criticized for casting Matt Damon as a heroic figure. This was particularly the case during the film's U.S. marketing efforts, which visually centered Damon's character as the most important and relegated his Chinese costars, including Andy Lau, into "glorified cameos" (Lee, 2016, n.p.). *The Great Wall* is the first coproduction by Legendary East, which is a Chinese-owned venture of Legendary Entertainment, a Hollywood studio owned by the Wanda Group ("No whitewashing," 2016, n.p.). Although the film did poorly in the U.S. box office, with $45 million in sales, it did relatively well in China as the fourth highest grossing film of the year (Mendelson, 2017). On the other hand, neither *Outcast* nor *Enter the Warriors Gate* were successful in the United States or China. They were both direct-to-DVD films in the United States, and in the Chinese box office, *Enter the Warriors Gate* and *Outcast* had limited, troubled releases, earning less than $3.5 million each. Despite their relatively minor positions in both nation's popular culture, the films are worth investigating because of what may appear to be a contradiction—coproduced films with China and the United States that assert whitewashed White savior narratives.

In theory, coproductions are mutually beneficial arrangements as Hollywood gains access to China's film market, the second largest in the world, and as China gains access to Hollywood filmmaking resources and global networks that allow the export of Chinese soft power (Su, 2017). It is for this reason that there has been explosive growth in the number of coproductions between Hollywood and China (Su, 2017). Early research expressed optimism that Chinese–Western coproductions are culturally sensitive toward the different markets they seek to enter (Bosanquet, 2018) and that they promote positive representations of both national cultures that they represent (Peng, 2016). These projections, however, might be particular to the Sino-Australian context in which they are studied. In those cases, it is arguable that the Chinese film industry is better established and its market more attractive than its counterpart in Australia, allowing it more leverage in crafting desirable Chinese representations that counterbalance the global advantages of Whiteness and affiliation with the West.

Research on U.S. coproductions does not, however, point to this same optimism. Particularly when shows are whitewashed with White actors or when White characters are centered, coproductions, at best, produce hybrid ambivalence (Oh and Nishime, 2019). When there are clear differences in financing and production power, particularly with Hollywood studios, coproductions often resemble Hollywood's usual controlling images, symbolically erasing people of color and reproducing problematic racial stereotypes (Alvaray, 2013). As such, the relationship still is shaped by unequal flows of global power in which both the United States as nation-state and Hollywood as the major hub in global media flows, is still dominant. Su (2017) notes, "The 'whitewashing' criticism [of *The Great Wall*] actually speaks to a dilemma faced by all coproductions: If the major roles are played by Chinese actors, the movie will lack international appeal and the studio will be unwilling to take the financial risk associated with a 150 million dollars [*sic*] megaproduction. But if there are no major Chinese roles, the film will not qualify for 'official' coproduction status and the substantial profits that entails" (p. 486). While Su makes a specifically economic argument, I would posit that there is an ideological one, too—Hollywood is invested in Whiteness.

Before making this case, it is necessary to pause and clarify why *Outcast* and *Enter the Warriors Gate* (the U.S. titles) are included. The films are arguably poor fits for a book on U.S. film culture as both of the films are coproduced by studios that are not located in the United States. Both were produced in collaboration with French studios, so the films are arguably more representative of French film culture. *Enter the Warriors Gate*, especially, has more dubious connections to Hollywood as it is part of a coproduction deal with France's EuropaCorp and Shanghai-based Fundamental Films. *Outcast*, on the other hand, has a more complex coproduction arrangement with Arclight Films, which is located in the United States and Australia, the United Kingdom's Notorious Films, France's 22h22, Canada's Media Max productions, and China's Yunnan Film Group (Catsoulis, 2015). Despite the lack of U.S. financing, however, both films are English-speaking movies that cast actors familiar in the U.S. cultural terrain to penetrate the U.S. film market, including Hayden Christensen and Nicholas Cage in *Outcast* and Uriah Shelton and Dave Bautista in *Enter the Warriors Gate*.

Furthermore, according to a DVD special feature, the scriptwriter for *Enter the Warriors Gate* is a Hollywood screenwriter, Robert Mark Kamen, who is best known for *The Karate Kid* (1984). Its U.S. Americanness is made explicit as it is revealed that the script was written prior to and independently of the coproduction deal. Furthermore, in the DVD extras, the director, Matthias Hoene, and the screenwriter refer to the setting as a small, suburban town in "middle America," despite being filmed in Vancouver (Hoene, 2016b). As such, it is clear that the movies mean to signify the United States. Moreover, it is arguable that the films draw on U.S. film culture to inform their narratives as a strategic choice and due to the internalization of Hollywood tropes that also benefit White people outside the United States.

Outcast imagines White intervention in twelfth-century China by centering the story on Jacob (Hayden Christensen), who struggles with his past sins as a leader of Crusades. After leaving the Middle East, Jacob searches for his mentor, Gallian (Nicolas Cage), who is in China. Despite his opium addiction and lost sense of purpose, Jacob reluctantly joins a mission to escort a young prince, Zhao (Bill Su Jiahang), and his sister, Lian (Liu Yifei[1]), to safety, fleeing from their tyrannical older brother, Prince Shing (Andy On). *Enter the Warriors Gate* mixes the old with the new as it tells the story of Jack (Uriah Shelton), a high school student, who is drawn into a different dimension to save Sulin (Ni Ni) and her premodern Chinese empire from a barbarian horde led by Arun (Dave Bautista). On his journey, he gains courage and masculine vigor, which helps him stand up to school bullies and to save his mother (Sienna Guillory) from financial ruin. Of the three movies, *The Great Wall* is the only one that was helmed by a Chinese director, Zhang Yimou, a highly respected auteur. Perhaps because of its behind-the-scenes creative Chinese talent, the movie is more ideologically ambivalent than *Outcast* and *Enter the Warriors Gate*. In the film, William (Matt Damon) and Tovar (Pedro Pascal) are fugitive mercenaries and thieves. Although Tovar chooses his own self-interest, William finds redemption in China by heroically working alongside Chinese warriors and scholars to defend against an ancient alien threat called the Tao Tei.

Although the films are coproductions, they reflect White men's view of China and of themselves. It is important to note that the nation that is worth saving does not exist in the contemporary present but is consigned to the ancient past. There is a fetishization of premodern China that is imagined as an exotic location where flawed White men discover their heroism and goodness. They are racialized stories of White masculine heroism to save a temporally and geographically faraway, feminized China. This is unsurprising given the unequal power between the United States and China, particularly with their film industries, and given the U.S. origins of the screenplays. Regarding his secondary role in the *Great Wall*, for instance, Andy Lau is reported to have said: "You have to know the truth. It's a Western production from a Western production house so the main role is a foreign person. It's not a big deal" ("No whitewashing," 2016, n.p.). Despite the imprint of Whiteness, there is ambivalence in the films, which reflects Chinese involvement in the creative process. The chapter argues that the movies structure their stories using variations of the White savior trope but that there are counterhegemonic possibilities that are created through coproductions. The chapter begins with a brief review of the trope and how it is represented in the films, then discusses the representations of Asian people as villains, partners, and supporters, and concludes with a reimagining Asian *Americans* as heroes in China. As (Shimizu, 2017) notes, Asian American characters allow possibilities for audiences to see how our lives are connected to Asia and the United States.

The White Savior Trope

It requires a certain audacity to propose whitewashed films to Chinese investors, cast members, and crews, and to expect that Chinese audiences would find it appealing. This is only possible with investments in Whiteness that are so naturalized that the ludicrousness of expecting that Chinese audiences would enjoy such films is invisible. Indeed, in industries that are argued to be risk averse (Hesmondhalgh, 2007), it is economically unusual that the same formulas are tried despite their previous failures, pointing forcefully to ideological investments in a Western racial order. Indeed, Yang (2014) argues, "the white hero's venturing into the exotic land and chivalrous rescue of a Chinese woman becomes a recurrent pattern" (p. 248). She points out that in recent years, the Chinese-produced films *Pavilion of Women* (2001) and *The Flowers of War* (2011) have adopted this formula to achieve wide, international export, albeit in more ambivalent forms that simultaneously undercut the White savior trope.

The trope is a common narrative formulation that uses the character as a "metonym for benevolent white supremacy" (Fitzgerald, 2013, p. 98). The White savior is welcomed by people who are marginalized either by malevolent White people in the antiracist film or who are victimized by their own people. In each case, the White savior liberates marginalized people of color through the strength of their moral character, intelligence, and/or their physical superiority. In the antiracist film, which usually centers anti-Black racism, the trope historically (mis)represents White people as progressive heroes (Hoerl, 2009;

Schultz, 2014). Typically, the White protagonist experiences the suffering of a Black person, takes a moral stand, suffers for it, and ultimately prevails to self-lessly liberate Black victims (Madison, 1999). The trope is paternalistic, as it positions Black Americans as subservient, inferior, and lacking agency in their own liberation (Murphy and Harris, 2018). It also hides systemic racism because the presentation of the Black American victim and her/his gratitude for the White savior's moral courage reduces systemic racism to interpersonal racism and presents its remedy as interpersonal growth and understanding (Madison, 1999; Murphy and Harris, 2018; Schultz, 2014).

The other common formula for the White savior is to save innocent people of color from oppressors within their own communities. Heroic White teachers in *Dangerous Minds* (1995) and *Freedom Writers* (2007), for instance, enter schools populated by cynical students of color, who have been raised in patho-logical communities (Hughey, 2010). Through the guidance of a caring, tough teacher, who is armed with her moral authority and rationality, the students transform their cynicism into hope, overcome the chaos of their schools, and become outstanding students (Giroux, 1997; Hughey, 2010). The unsubtle subtext is that the only reason students of color do not achieve the American Dream is because of the pathology of their own communities. This same for-mula holds true when the White savior goes abroad except that instead of jus-tifying historical or current racial relations, it engages a colonial imagination of White adventurism, goodness, and moral superiority. Instead of the skepti-cism of students of color when they first meet the White savior, the overseas White savior is welcomed for his unique ability to liberate (Fitzgerald, 2013).

When the White savior travels to Asia in martial arts movies, he usually suf-fers defeat until he appropriates the martial arts of the local people, becoming better than Asians who have been practicing it for their entire lifetimes. Tier-ney (2006) refers to this as "supra-ethnic viability," the White hero's physical superiority that allows him to quickly surpass the most accomplished Asian people (p. 609). As he gains their skills, "good" Asians are distinguished for their support of the White man, whereas "bad" Asians resist his interven-tion and cultural appropriation (Tierney, 2006). Like the martial arts movie, romances are also located in a U.S. colonial and neocolonial imagination of Asia, where the interracial romance becomes a metonym for White paternal benevolence and justification for possession of a feminized Asia from the tyranny of Asian patriarchy (Kang, 2002; Marchetti, 1993; Sun, 2003). "In the cinematic construction between the dominant/masculine West and the submissive/feminine China, Chinese women have been employed as a means of belittling China and satisfying the Western gaze, with Chinese men being reduced to sidekicks" (Yang, 2014, p. 249).

In these tales of men's adventures in Asia, it is usually situated in the White man's search for existential meaning (Blouin, 2011; Marchetti, 1993; Oh and

Wong Lowe, 2016). The trips abroad provide redemptive narrative arcs but not a change in his cultural worldview; indeed, the White savior rescues and transforms his lover in his own cultural image (Marchetti, 1993). "This fantasy promises the pleasure of imaginatively breaking conventions while maintaining the inevitability of the dominant culture's right to rule" (Marchetti, 1993, p. 109). Even in Chinese-produced films that seek global circulation and commercial success, the White savior trope is reproduced but updated with representations of strong Chinese women (Yang, 2014). Although she falls in love with him for his exceptional difference, his sacrificial death by the end of the film's narrative imagines a nation in which the West has enriched the Chinese subject but is not materially present in it.

White Knight's Adventures and Character Growth

Marchetti (1993) argues that the "White knight" in Asia does not just carry the symbolic meaning of the color white as indicative of the hero's moral goodness but that it also carries racially specific meanings, particularly through the embodied colonial-era fantasy of a masculinized West rescuing and saving a feminized Asia. The White knights of these films tap into colonial fantasies by imagining White men as uniquely able to save whole nations as individual heroes, and it also engages in fictional historical revisionism, which views White men in premodern China as heroes and protectors rather than as colonizing oppressors (Sun, 2003). In each of the films, they combine the metamyth of the "hero's journey" and the colonial and filmic trope of a White man's journey for self-redemption and self-growth.

In both *Outcast* and *The Great Wall*, Jacob and William's adventures in China are the means by which they redeem themselves and rediscover their morality and goodness. Unlike Tierney's (2006) notion of supraethnic viability, neither Jacob nor William gain the martial skills of the Chinese. Rather, like Chris Kenner (Dolph Lundgren) in *Showdown in Little Tokyo*, who is superior to the Japanese Americans by virtue of his physical strength and bravery (Nakayama, 1994), Jacob and William arrive in China as fully realized warriors—Jacob as a knight of the Crusades and William as a skilled archer and mercenary. This is an increasingly common representation in films about Asia, where White American heroes succeed through their sheer tenacity and rugged individualism against more numerous, cruel Asian threats (Pollard, 2017). Thus, their journey is not appropriative but instead is about responding heroically to their call to moral action and is realized through their combat skill.

William's Heroic Turn on the Great Wall

When William first appears on camera, his face is smudged with dirt, and he has an unkempt, bushy beard. Along with his loose-fitting brown shirt and matching pants, he is a picture of drab dirtiness, which matches the degraded nature of his inner character. William and his Spanish companion, Tovar, are revealed to have traveled to China because of rumors of "black powder." While Tovar covets it throughout the duration of the film, Jacob is conflicted after he becomes more deeply involved in the Chinese effort. Ultimately, he abandons his self-interest and embraces *xin ren* (trust), which the movie defines as the primary moral value that guides the Chinese soldiers' sense of duty and loyalty.

William first demonstrates his heroism by saving Peng Yong (Lu Han), a hapless, young soldier who is charged with guarding William and Tovar, who were taken prisoner. When the Tao Tei swarm and overwhelm the Great Wall's defenses, Peng is antsy, shifting his gaze between his prisoners and the rampaging Tao Tei. Frozen in action, which is emphasized by the extreme close-up of his worried face, William tells him, "Go and fight!" Helpless against the beast, he is swatted into the air and retreats from it by sliding backward on his buttocks. When freed, William runs into danger, catches a spear that has been deflected by the Tao Tei and stabs it through the mouth, saving Peng from impending death. Continuing to rampage, the Tao Tei knocks soldiers out of its way as it turns back to attack William, who deconstructs a crossbow to use as a bow and kills the creature with a single shot. In contrast, Chinese foot soldiers fight in coordinated formation with spears and shields but are still outmatched by the Tao Tei. Indeed, during the first attack, it is only William, with the help of Tovar, who is shown killing the Tao Tei in direct combat.

The day after the battle, William and Tovar physically transform. Both have cleaner wardrobes and physical appearance, and William's transformation is especially dramatic with the loss of his bushy beard. Cleaned up, they are invited to a shared meal with the soldiers and commanders, where they are welcomed for their valor and skill in combat. In private conversation, Commander Lin Mae (Jing Tian) asks William how many "flags" he has served, and he reveals that he was raised on the battlefield and that he has fought for "many flags," implying his work as a soldier-for-hire. Lin says they are not the same and invites him onto the Wall, where she shows him the platform from which her soldiers, the Crane Corps., leap down to stab the Tao Tei with spears. After taunting him to jump and a brief exchange, she explains:

LIN MAE: Xin ren means trust. To have faith. Here in this army, we fight for more than food or money. We give our lives to something more. Xin ren is our flag. Trust in each other. In all ways, at all times.

WILLIAM: Well, that's all well and good, but I'm not jumping. I'm alive today because I trust no one.

LIN MAE: A man must learn to trust before he is to be trusted.

WILLIAM: Then, you're right. We are not the same.

Revealing the primary theme of the film, William engages a series of actions that draws him more deeply into his commitments and loyalty to Lin Mae and the Chinese soldiers, who are entrusted with saving China and, as later revealed, all of humanity.

It is worth noting that while the story conforms with the broad contours of the White savior trope, the film's moral and the centrality of China resist Hollywood conventions, perhaps because of the nature of the coproduction and Zhang's directorial decisions. Its moral of trust requires that the White hero not be a rugged individualist, who saves the inept Chinese, but rather he must rely on and trust his Chinese compatriots while maximizing his strengths as part of a team. Although most of the Chinese warriors are portrayed as relatively ineffectual, it means that at least Lin Mae is a coequal partner to William. This also resists the Hollywood convention of representing Asian women as passive damsels-in-distress, who are oppressed by the tyrannical patriarchy of their own cultures (Espiritu, 2004; Marchetti, 1993). In addition, the centering of China as the site of resistance to save the entire world from the threat of the Tao Tei subverts structured representations of the United States as the bulwark against threats to all humanity. Indeed, it is because of this centering of China that the film has been accused of propaganda by Western critics (Mendelson, 2017), who perhaps fail to recognize the inversion of a common Hollywood trope.

Before the final showdown with the Tao Tei, William is held under suspicion after Tovar has stolen gunpowder and escaped with another White man named Ballard (William Dafoe). Like the antiracist film, which features overtly racist White people as a way of showing the goodness of the antiracist White hero in contrast (Madison, 1999), Ballard (William Dafoe) is represented as greedy and opportunistic, taking advantage of the chaos of the invasion despite his twenty-five-year stay with the Chinese. Similarly, Tovar acts as a mirror to reflect who William would have been if he had not chosen to trust and fight alongside Lin Mae. That is, William would be a sympathetic yet still morally flawed and unredeemed White man, choosing avarice over selfless courage. There is quite a bit of semiotic space to read against the grain to interpret Tovar and Ballard as typical of Europeans (and perhaps White people more generally) and William as atypical in his heroic difference.

Jacob's Heroic Redemption after the Crusades

Jacob's story in *Outcast* is explicitly situated in the theme of redemption. In Christensen's interview in the DVD extras, he says: "It's a journey of self-redemption. . . . I need her and her brother for redemption. Do something good." The theme is also repeated during interviews with the director Nick Powell and one of the producers (2014b), connecting to a common trope of the

White man in Asia—to find redemption and self-meaning (Blouin, 2011; Marchetti, 1993; Oh and Wong Lowe, 2016). The redemption that he seeks stems from his disillusionment with his participation as a leader of knights in the Crusades. In his journey for redemption, he travels east to find his mentor, Gallain (Nicolas Cage), who has lost faith in Jacob. While in China, Jacob's redemptive journey takes form in an actual journey to escort the future king to Xing Yuan, where the generals will recognize the new king Zhao's succession to the throne.

Jacob's journey begins in a tavern, wearing a broad-brimmed hat that hides his face, implying his loss of self. At times, the camera shifts to a first-person perspective that is blurred to signify his opium-induced stupor. He is snapped out of his own melancholy and self-destruction when he witnesses the Black Guard capture and attempt to kill Prince Zhao and Princess Lian. Despite being unarmed and in a drugged haze, Jacob kills multiple Black Guards, rescuing the future king and his sister. Like *The Great Wall*'s William, Jacob does not appropriate the martial arts skills of the Chinese; rather, he defeats them with his previous training and experience as a Crusader, thereby representing White masculine superiority.

Despite his act of bravery, he refuses to escort and guard Zhao, dismissing her pleas, saying, "Good luck, princess." With a sigh, he turns his head toward the door and leaves, refusing Lian's entreaties. Later, as Jacob comes upon a river, he washes his face, triggering a flashback. Like *The Great Wall*, the physical cleansing is symbolic of moral cleansing. It is at this moment that he notices several Black Guard soldiers ride toward Zhao and Lian, prompting him to return to the pair and warning them of the danger. Also like *The Great Wall*, his emotional scars are healed through his relationship to a Chinese woman. Seeking to rehabilitate Jacob, Lian tosses his opium into a campfire, prompting their first meaningful conversation in which she asks whether he is "running or searching" and learning that Jacob feels the weight of committing many "crimes." Like Lin Mae in *The Great Wall*, Lian is the vehicle through which the White knight reflects on his morally depraved self and sees a path toward restoration and virtue.

When hiding in Jingshao, a desert city, he bribes a Middle Eastern caravan with the gold he has received from Lian, demonstrating that his help is not contingent on payment but based in self-sacrifice. Indeed, he suffers severe wounds while single-handedly fighting a Black Guard squadron that allows Zhao and Lian time to escape the city. Collapsing while following after the prince and princess, Jacob is nursed back to health by Lian, who validates his path to redemption, saying, "Maybe, you've repaid your debt." Represented as a one-dimensional, almost angelic figure, Lian's acceptance of Jacob signals the payment for his former sins. While his restoration is completed in that moment, his journey does not end until he defeats Shing, thus saving Zhao and delivering him to become the king. Like *The Great Wall*, Jacob also leaves, though with no fanfare, turning away silently, suggesting that his journey for self-restoration is finished. This also connotes that China's value for White men is that it is a space for restoration of the White self rather than a place to call home and to integrate. As such, *Outcast* uses typical tropes of White men's adventures in Asia as a space for self-growth, but it resists the colonial metaphor of a White man's possession of China through his romantic rescue of a Chinese woman.

Jack's Development as a Warrior

Unlike *Outcast* and *The Great Wall*, *Enter the Warriors Gate* does not feature redemption but rather a coming-of-age story about finding inner courage. Director Matthias Hoene explained on the director's track that in the beginning of the film, "Jack is a hero in the video game but a little bit of a loser in real life" (Hoene, 2016c). Unable to stand up to neighborhood bullies, Jack flees from them in a BMX bicycle chase sequence. His life changes, however, when a magician in ancient China mistakes Jack's video game character, the "Black Knight" for Jack, sending Princess Sulin and her guard, Zhao[2] (Mark Chao), through a magical basket, which acts as a portal between worlds. To hide the princess, Zhao grudgingly leaves Sulin with Jack while returning to China through the basket, which allows Jack and Sulin to spend time together enjoying adolescent life in the United States at a nearby shopping mall.

As Hoene explains, Jack's courage develops incrementally through his various combat sequences (Hoene, 2016c). At first, he ducks from invading barbarians, escaping their attacks, while Sulin valiantly fights them until she is overwhelmed by their numerical advantage. Grabbing a frying pan, Jack chases after Sulin through the magical basket where he is reacquainted with Zhao and where he meets the wizard (Francis Ng). During their travels, Zhao confronts Jack's usual tactic to run from trouble by asking, "Does that solve your problems?" This is an inflection point for Jack to realize that courage, not cowardice, is required. Unlike *The Great Wall* or *Outcast*, it is not his love interest Sulin but rather Zhao, as a buddy-mentor, who provides the space for growth. The gendered difference is also related to the nature of the men's self-journey. For William and Jacob, it is moral redemption after becoming hardened and cynical, thus relying on a gendered construction of women, particularly Chinese women, as feminine nurturers, whereas, for Jack, his adult mentor is strengthening Jack into a masculinized identity. It is important to note that Zhao is visibly older and stronger than the adolescent Jack. If they were the same age, it would question the construction of White men as a masculine ideal, particularly in relationship to the ways Asian, and particularly Chinese, men have routinely been portrayed in U.S. cinema (Espiritu, 2004; Hamamoto, 1994; Ono and Pham, 2009).

Later in the film, during Zhao and Jack's fight with a "mountain spirit" (Kara Wei), who resembles a witch-like figure with two antlers and hair shaped like curved horns, reminiscent of a ram. The witch imagery is furthered with her preparation of "soup" in a black cauldron. When she will not step aside for Zhao and Jack to pass, she fights with a mix of stylized martial arts and teleporting magic. During a precarious fight on a shifting wooden bridge over the mountain path, Zhao hangs onto the side of the crevice while the witch taunts him with her laughs and by stepping on his hands. Jack saves Zhao by throwing a wooden torch at the witch, who burns in its flames. Zhao responds, "Maybe not so worthless after all." Despite Jack's inability to fight, he still fulfills the savior role not only for the princess at the end of the film but also for his buddy, the more accomplished warrior and more masculine figure. Although Jack does not exceed his teacher as in most martial arts movies, saving his teacher symbolically associates White masculinity with heroism.

Challenges to White masculinity are erased with the film's one deleted scene. In it, a woman with a loose-fitting, torn white robe and twisted vines and flowers as a crown claims that her sister is trapped, asking for Jack's help. After bringing Jack, two of her sisters creep atop rocks and behind a tree, claiming that they are tree plants and that he's "dinner." Jack yells for Zhao, who defeats the women, who have transformed into tree-like monsters. It is an ideologically subversive scene. Indeed, Jack is feminized as a damsel-in-distress as he hangs above the women's campfire, waiting for his Chinese knight to save him. It subverts the superiority of White masculinity, and it challenges the notion of White benevolence by flipping the White man's heroism into his hubris. Although Hoene claimed that the three-minute scene was cut because it was similar to the scene with the mountain spirit, it was also an ideologically subversive fit in the movie that challenged White masculine heroism. That said, the scene, like the mountain spirit scene, is problematic because of its gendered logic of magic. When possessed by women, magic is represented as a threat to be eliminated, while the wizard enables Jack to fulfill his journey toward becoming a warrior and hero.

During the final confrontation with Arun, Sulin's hands are bound above her head while she dangles helplessly, waiting for Jack to rescue her. Although Sulin, like Lin Mae, is represented as a capable warrior, she is transformed into a passive object who requires Jack to save her to save China. Thus, the princess becomes a metonym for a benevolent, feminized China, and Arun is its barbaric, masculine alternative. When Jack kills Arun, using his video game experience as a guide, it suggests that even a capable, feminized China requires White masculine intervention if it is to be saved. It is a self-aggrandizing view of the role of White masculinity in the world. It demonstrates that even with multinational financing, coproductions reflect the unequal strength between the West and China (Su, 2017). Reflecting the trope that China/Asia is a space for

White men to discover themselves (Blouin, 2011; Oh, 2018a), Jack takes his lessons as a precocious paternal savior by creating a video game, selling it, and giving his check to his mother to save their family home. In his final act of courage, he confidently, even blithely, stands up to and subdues the neighborhood bullies, completing his transformation from a "loser" to a hero.

White Knight and the Chinese That Admire and Oppose Him

In each of the three films, the White knights partner with Chinese women, who nurture the men's self-discovery, and work with Chinese boys and men, who are either sidekicks that aid the men's journey or infantilized figures that redeem the White knights as benevolent, paternal figures. What distinguishes the "good" Asian is that s/he supports the purpose of the White savior, acting as representational legitimation of the White man's noble purpose (Tierney, 2006). The most common way that this is imagined is through the use of romance as a metaphor (Marchetti, 1993). Unlike typical U.S. cinematic representations of the White knight and his Chinese lover, however, the relationships do not result in sex, a common filmic metaphor for possession and for colonization (Kang, 2002), and none of the films represent the women as oppressed by Chinese patriarchy, a common Hollywood trope (Espiritu, 2004; Marchetti, 1993). The women are all damsels-in-distress to varying degrees, but in two of the films, they are also skilled warriors, who protect the White knight. The space for this ambivalence is likely because of the nature of the coproduction, which requires at least some sensitivity to Chinese audiences and financiers. Coproductions do not produce the wholly beneficial results that Peng (2016) has argued; instead they result in ambivalent texts that are framed by conventional Hollywood tropes, which reflect the differential in the power of the media industries (Su, 2017).

China Doll or Woman Warrior?

Of the three films, it is only *Outcast* that situates Chinese femininity within the stereotype of the "China doll" or "lotus blossom," the view of Asian/American women as passive and hyperfeminized (Espiritu, 2004; Ono and Pham, 2009; Shim, 1998; Shimizu, 2007). It is the most common representation of Asian/American women, which may explain, in part, the fetishized desirability of Asian/American women in the politics of desire in the United States and other parts of the West. Lian is represented in the film as nearly without agency as she subjugates her own desires to fulfill her father's succession plans to crown her younger brother, Zhao, as the new king. Dressed in a long, flowing white *hanfu* with golden embroidery and a matching white cloak, Lian is presented as an angelic figure. Her character's limited growth is her change from skepticism of Jacob to her romantic embrace. The only agency she attempts is to prevent Jacob's defeat in a duel by attacking her elder brother, Shing. Even this moment, however, is meant for Jacob's final heroic action. As he sees Lian lying on the ground with her white dress stained red from Shing's stab wound, Jacob musters energy to overcome Shing, killing him with the dagger that Lian had unsuccessfully used against Shing.

Unlike their filmic peers, the coproduction means that there is at least minimal sensitivity to Chinese sensibilities. This is likely the reason that none of the women are represented as oppressed by Chinese patriarchy, a common trope that requires Asian women's rescue and justifies taking women out of Asia (Marchetti, 1993; Yang, 2014). Rather than being oppressed, all of the women in the three films are privileged. One is a princess and sister to the future king, the other is a princess who becomes empress, and the third is a commander who becomes a general. Narratively, their high positions mean they are duty-bound to stay in China, although the magical world of *The Warriors Gate* allows Sulin to "vacation" in the United States to visit Jack. Thus, the films ambivalently manage the tension between colonial, White masculine possession of Chinese women and modern, Chinese assertions of self-worth through the representations of unrequited, limited romances. As Yang (2014) argues, the heroic romance satisfies the White savior trope in China-oriented films, but the symbolic expulsion of White masculinity allows a cinematic, future space of China that exists without the active presence of White masculinity.

Further departing from the stereotype of the China doll, Sulin and Lin Mae are represented as literal women warriors, to borrow from the title of Maxine Hong Kingston's most well-known book. Director Hoene noted that he did not want a typical damsel-in-distress, making Sulin a capable fighter who actively defends against her male oppressors in *Enter the Warriors Gate* (Hoene, 2016c). Indeed, Sulin is portrayed as capable of defeating multiple barbarian kidnappers with her bare hands, she deceives and stabs Arun, the leader of the barbarians, and she fights against multiple barbarians during the escape from Arun's compound. In climactic moments, however, she is reduced to a damsel-in-distress who requires Zhao and Jack's rescue.

Perhaps because of a tradition of capable women warriors in Chinese and Hong Kong cinema and Director Zhang's history of crafting three-dimensional women characters and warriors, most notably in *House of Flying Daggers*, Commander and eventual General Lin Mae is represented as the most capable and courageous Chinese warrior. Although William saves Lin Mae, who is surrounded by multiple Tao Tei, by pulling her onto a hot air balloon and away from danger, she reciprocates later in the film, grabbing William before he slips off a roof. Furthermore, in their climactic battle against the Tao Tei queen, it requires their cooperation to prevail. Intentionally subverting the trope of the White savior, the film represents William failing twice to snipe the queen as his arrows are shielded and deflected by her guardians. It requires instead that

William trust Lin Mae to make the decisive blow, fulfilling the theme of the movie, to defeat the queen. As they ride their zip line above the queen, William throws a magnetized rock to temporarily paralyze the queen's guardians, which creates the opening for Lin Mae to use her spear technique as the former commander of the Crane Corps to kill the queen. As such, William's function as a White savior is constrained, though not subverted or eliminated. This maintains the gendered cinematic, colonial relationship between the U.S./West and China but while problematizing it. Perhaps this explains in part *The Great Wall*'s moderate success in China but its box office failure in the United States.

Infantilized Boy and White Paternalism

In the absence of passive Chinese women through which to demonstrate White paternal goodness, the films about men's redemption, *Outcast* and *The Great Wall*, require other characters through which to demonstrate White masculine benevolence. While movies frequently rely on the representational trope of protecting innocent, young (White) girls, the intersection of race and gender in these films substitute infantilized Chinese boys instead, who are mentored and nurtured by their White father figures. The infantilizing representations closely resemble stereotypes of emasculated Asian/American men (Espiritu, 2004; Hamamoto, 1994; Ono and Pham, 2009; Sun, 2003). The characters' growth from ineffectual warriors to courageous young men is meant less to give the characters depth but rather to demonstrate the unique, paternal function of White men.

This is most obvious with Jacob's relationship to Prince Zhao, whose physical journey to be crowned king is meant to represent his emotional journey to become a courageous leader. As Zhao complains to Jacob, the king, Zhao's real father, would not allow him to learn to fight but only taught him "books." This fits with the common U.S. construction of the nerd or "bookworm" as a feminized figure, who lacks street smarts and physical toughness. Early in the film, Jacob calmly tightens his bowstring and shoots an arrow into a Black Guard soldier, who is riding in the far distance on horseback with a captured adolescent girl, Xiaoli (Coco Wang). As the camera cuts to an extreme close-up, Zhao is stunned as he mouths, "How is that possible?" The next day when Zhao sees Jacob, shirtless, bathing in a river, he demonstrates his racial ignorance by claiming that he thought "white devils" did not bathe before asking Jacob to teach him to become a better archer. Seeing Jacob's goodness and patience as a teacher, Lian praises Jacob for the way he cares for his brother.

Several elements of the scene require further deconstruction. First, Zhao's racism is met with kindness from Jacob that is recognized by Lian. It is important to remember that films set in the past are meant to remark on the contemporary present (Hoerl, 2009). In this case, Zhao's anti-White prejudice serves three functions. First, like much postracist discourse, it engages in a postracist universalism in which everyone can be racist, ignoring systems of racial discrimination (Gilroy, 2012; Oh and Banjo, 2012). Second, it portrays White victimization even during the Crusades and the rise of Europe. White victimization and grievance is a common theme in the White popular imagination, the function of which is to give voice to White frustrations and to deny the legitimacy of the grievances of people of color (Kelly, 2020; Lipsitz, 1998; Oh and Kutufam, 2014). Finally, Jacob's kindness, rather than indignation, in the face of interpersonal racism projects a White fantasy about their magnanimity by not "playing the race card"; this carries the implication that people of color feign racial injury for selfish gains.

As Jacob continues to mentor and train Zhao in warrior wars that the king did not, it reinforces the ideology of Chinese masculine deviance. Either it leads to underdeveloped, feminized masculinity represented in Zhao or in a cruel, hypermasculine figure in his older brother, Shing. Thus, it is only Jacob who is able to successfully raise Zhao into becoming a worthy leader and a courageous warrior. Indeed, Xiaoli's character is all but symbolically annihilated after her rescue and Zhao's early, awkward flirtations. By portraying Zhao as the childlike figure who needs White paternal guidance, it more successfully genders and infantilizes China vis-à-vis the West (Yang, 2014). Zhao's transformation is complete when he disobeys Jacob, who orders him to hide, and instead uses his bow to protect Jacob in their battle against a swarm of Black Guard soldiers.

The other feminized boy is Peng Yong, who is played by a popular pop "idol" in *The Great Wall*. He is marked in visual contrast to the other men warriors on screen because he has a thinner build than William or the commanders, he is clean shaven, he has youthful features, and his eyes are wider and more circular in shape. In each of the early scenes, he is shown as either clumsy or cowardly and responds to his mistakes with a look of pained uncertainty as his lower jaw opens and drops back and as his brows curl upward in the center. Despite serving as the guard of the cell, he fumbles the keys, which prevents the imprisonment of William and Pedro. Falling on one knee, he bows his head dramatically, raising his eyes upward, and apologizes. In the next scene, a fight on the Wall, he is shown in close-up reaction shots, uncertain about whether to fight the Tao Tei that threaten them, and he has to be rescued by Jacob as a damsel-like figure.

Later in the film, when Peng drops a bowl of sleeping potion, Commander Chen (Kenny Lin) admonishes him, saying: "Useless idiot! Report to the kitchen where you belong." This represents the commander as overly stern and unempathetic, particularly as the camera follows Peng shuffling slowly with his head hung low. Not only is this meant to render him as nearly useless, his particular punishment further feminizes him by relegating him to domestic work.

When William sees him peeling potatoes in the kitchen later in the film, he foreshadows Peng's future self-sacrifice, saying, "You're much braver than they think." Despite being hardened as a mercenary, William demonstrates more compassion for Peng than his commander, promoting an image of White paternal benevolence. The character's only function, other than to act as a vehicle to demonstrate William's paternal goodness, is to sacrifice himself by igniting gunpowder on his wrists to slow down rampaging Tao Tei. It should be noted that self-sacrifice is often cinematically imagined as feminine valor.

Because of the coproduced nature of the films, there is more ambivalence in the representations of Chinese masculinity even as the specific representations of Peng and Zhao serve a clearly ideological function by infantilizing and feminizing Chinese men. In both films, however, there are Chinese men characters, who are not feminized in this way. Strategist Wang (Andy Lau) is portrayed as a scholarly figure, but he commands authority and has filmic presence that hints at his usual leading man status. The commanders and General Shao (Zhang Hanyu) are also visually represented as physically strong with muscular builds. In *Outcast*, the king is represented as a benevolent, wise patriarch, who cares deeply for Zhao and Lian, a representation of Asian/American paternal masculinity that is rarely represented in dominant U.S. cinema. Finally, Asian/American masculinity is most complicated in *Enter the Warriors Gate*, which employs an interracial buddy formula that masculinizes the benevolent Chinese friend and mentor, Warrior Zhao. With Asian/Americans cast as the straight man in this comedic buddy pairing, Jack is feminized because of his age difference and early cowardice, Zhao's role as a paternal mentor, and gender logics that associate masculinity with stoicism, seriousness, and duty.

"Yellow Peril"

The yellow peril stereotype of Asian/Americans as a threat is the oldest, most enduring stereotype of Asian Americans in the United States (Hamamoto, 1994; Oehling, 1980; Ono and Pham, 2009; Pollard, 2017). The stereotype presents Asian/American men as a threat against Western society either because of the genius of a feminized villain such as Fu Manchu or through an invading horde. The salience of the yellow peril threat reflects contemporary fears of Asian threats to U.S. and Western global dominance (Gries, 2014; Pollard, 2017). Anxiety about China's rise as a dangerous superpower has been common in U.S. press reports (Ban, Sastry, and Dutta, 2013; Schiller, 2008); the coverage of which frequently borrows from anachronistic, racist discourses (Ono and Jiao, 2008). However, the yellow peril is problematized in the three movies because of the nature of the coproduction with its Chinese partners.

The Great Wall displaces the yellow peril threat by portraying aliens as the threatening horde. *Enter the Warriors Gate*, on the other hand, shifts the yellow peril threat onto unnamed vaguely Asian barbarians. All of the barbarians, for example, are portrayed by Chinese actors and extras, except Arun the Cruel, who is played by Dave Bautista, whose father is Filipino and mother is Greek. His movie roles, including his most prominent as Drax in *The Guardians of the Galaxy* franchise, do not specifically racialize him. This is similar to the Hollywood marketing strategy of using mixed race actors, whose heritage is ambiguous as a way of generating audience interest (Beltrán and Fojas, 2008; Nishime, 2014). His ambiguity is particularly necessary for the audience to distinguish the barbarians as non-Chinese, especially as the U.S. racial imagination sees all Asians as similar. His racial ambiguity allows a reading of Asian but while visually demarcating his difference from the "good" Chinese. His physical size also challenges the yellow peril stereotype. Although his barbarians are reduced to a simple horde, he is not represented as an emasculated mastermind or as part of the horde. He is, rather, disarmingly light-hearted, and his power is rooted in his brawn rather than an oversized brain, which challenges the emasculation of Asian/American men in the popular imagination.

The closest to the "yellow peril" threat is Shing in *Outcast*, the twisted elder brother of the future king. It is clear that he is a villainous threat as the king has chosen to not have his eldest son succeed him on the throne. The close-up of Shing's square-jawed, scowling visage encased in a dark black helmet strikes an ominous figure of cruelty and danger. In his early conversation with his father, Shing is briefly humanized as it is revealed that Shing has become a warlord to fulfill his father's expansionist desires. Shing expresses resentment for being cast aside after becoming a tyrannical instrument for the kingdom. However, the brief moment of sympathy is foreclosed when Shing threatens a guard who attempts to intervene. "Resist me," he declares, "and I will see that your children are nailed to the walls of your home one piece at a time. That your wife spends the rest of her life pleasuring my guards. Die for a king whose time has passed or choose to serve a new one." After the guard is ordered to leave the king's chamber, Shing commits patricide, using a dagger that his deceased mother had given him. Thus, he is established as a cruel, bloodthirsty warlord that the king was right to fear. At his command are the Black Guard, whose name and black armor create an unambiguous sign as an evil horde-like danger. As such, *Outcast* repurposes the two common iterations of the yellow peril threat.

Even while relying on the stereotype in unproblematic ways, Shing's mastery in combat produces counterhegemonic meanings. In his final showdown against Jacob, he uses a double sword technique that is not predicated on the acrobatics often seen in wushu films, but it is presented as a realistic fighting technique. In the fight, Shing initially prevails over Jacob, overpowering and outclassing him in battle. While this is a common trope of action movies to have the hero overcome the odds by defeating the brawnier villain, it is uncommon for Asian/American villains to play the role of the physically dominant threat. This challenges the ideological feminizing of Asian/American masculinity. As such, although *Outcast* relies on the same yellow peril threat as a larger framing mechanism, ambivalence is created in microlevel details through the management of the coproduction.

Reimagining Coproductions

Departing from the previous chapters' transposition of Asian/American characters for the White leads, it is at least as interesting to imagine changed settings in addition to changed characters, so I will both imagine the leads as Asian Americans and then briefly imagine stories of Chinese people entering the premodern United States. To critically reimagine the films, I envision William as played by Will Yun Lee rather than Matt Damon, Jacob played by Daniel Wu rather than Hayden Christensen, and Jack as Harry Shum, Jr., rather than Uriah Shelton. It opens space for counterhegemonic meanings, although it would come at the cost of the films' already questionable verisimilitude, particularly for *Outcast* and *The Great Wall*, that is, Asian Americans would not be fugitives from Europe or have participated in the Crusades. The redemption narrative of the two films would argue that Asian American and Asian European men are redeemable, too, which would work against the structures of the trope. This would advance a poignant argument that the lives of people of color matter, even those who are flawed. Representations like this would symbolically challenge the greater humanity that is imbued in White men and would share that empathy more broadly.

In Jack's coming-of-age story, a Chinese American teenager would be especially groundbreaking. The bullying Jack experiences could be easily read as racist bullying, an experience that is all too common for Asian American boys and girls in U.S. schools (Wang, 2016). It would be easy, then, to read the bullying as allegorical of White racial prejudice. Furthermore, Jack's successful ability to stand up to the bullies at the end of the movie would demonstrate Asian American boys' ability to counter White racism while earning the acceptance and respect of his mainly White peers. The representation would still only be partially subversive, however, because it would advance the postracist narrative that racism is limited to a few "bad apples." In addition, the film would continue the heterosexist and gendered meanings in the original.

A Chinese American Jack would also raise interesting questions of heritage that are rarely depicted outside niche Asian American cinema. By teleporting temporally and spatially to China, the film could act allegorically to describe Chinese Americans' development of ethnic identity during adolescence and the ways part of the process is to affectively and symbolically journey to the homeland to understand their heritage. As China is a faraway land and heritage rooted in the past, the journey would mirror processes of ethnic identity formation in which he immerses but also does not fit in, facilitating his return to the United States, where he learns to live courageously while recognizing his heritage and difference as valued rather than marginal parts of his identity. Thus, the casting choice would have added layers of subtext missing in the banal choice of representing "universal" (White) fantasies of adolescent heroism.

The most obvious counterhegemonic challenge would be to imagine non-White people as heroic figures in Chinese adventures. This includes the displacement of the White romantic lead with a Chinese American one to counter the invisibility of Asian American couples in the United States' racist cinematic imagination. An even less common pairing is Asian American men with White women on the silver screen. This would only happen if coproductions do not imagine White stories in China but Chinese stories in the West. In this case, it would set the Chinese man as a character in need of redemption through his journeys in medieval Europe or the colonial United States. The utter lack of representation about people of color finding identity and meaning through journeys into *premodern* White spaces has prevented challenges to ideologies about whose stories of adventure are important, the colonial logic of Western intervention, and the idea of the West as modern and the global South and East as less civilized, a familiar Orientalist logic (Said, 1978). This story is nearly unimaginable, as there has been almost no filmic space for this reversal. Because it would be read as strange, the reversal itself would act almost as satire to reveal the commonsensical idea of White men's adventures and heroism that subjectifies White men but rarely the reverse.

I want to take care that this is not read as a vilification of real-life relationships with a White man–Asian/American woman pairing but to assert that this particular on-screen coupling has dominated images of Asian/American romance and sexuality. Although it may assuage wounded egos, it would also be problematic to lionize Asian American men and White women's relationships as a racial badge of honor but rather to claim that, on screen, the pairing would have counterhegemonic reverberations as it inverts White men's colonial fantasies of possessing Asian women (Sun, 2003). The reversal would decouple interracial romance from metaphors of colonial possession and instead signify Asia's rising power as a problematic gendered metaphor. It would also move toward symbolically equalizing patterns of interracial romance.

Conclusion

Whitewashing in Western-Chinese coproductions produces ambivalent representations that are invested in White racial hegemony but constrained by appeals to Chinese audiences, censors, and financiers. This means the movies are still framed within the common Western/Eurocentric trope of the White savior, who redeems his self-worth after his acts of heroism, a heavy-handed allusion to Western representational absolution to their historical, colonial sins while also presenting the current Western-centered world order as benevolent. This impulse is strong enough that it seems to overcome the film industry's usual aversion to financial risk, producing movies that continue to "flop" based on the same formula. It is a bit of racial hubris to believe that stories that appeal to White Americans about White adventure would have the same appeal for Chinese audiences. Perhaps the appeal of the Chinese film market, which is poised to overtake the U.S. market as the largest in the world, will eventually motivate U.S. movie producers. After all, in workshops and special lectures I have seen, they nearly uniformly claim that "green is the only color" they see. So far, at least, it seems that their investments in Whiteness as an invisible racial norm means that this statement is not wholly true. They may have been blind to their racial investments but acted on it all the same.

It would, however, be too analytically convenient to ignore the counterrepresentations, ambivalence, and semiotically open possibilities for reading negotiated meanings that emerge through coproduction and, in the case of *The Great Wall*, Chinese direction. Although the scripts for the movies were all written by White men, the films navigate the White savior trope with some ambivalence. It allows space to represent Chinese masculinity, an active Chinese femininity that resists the "lotus blossom" stereotype, and complications to a Chinese yellow peril threat. While these are optimistic signals, however, the films still operate within an obvious White savior trope set in premodern China. Indeed, it is common in the Western imagination to fetishize East Asia for its premodern past, such as with samurai themes, or in a futuristic, dystopian future; it is difficult to recall a U.S. film, particularly in the action genre, about *contemporary* China in which a White protagonist visits and is culturally changed by his interactions with the nation rather than simply changed through his/her self-discovery in an exotic land.

It is also hardly common for films, even Chinese films, to engage in a linguistic suspension of disbelief in which all characters, regardless of origin, speak in Chinese, although this is a conceit for U.S. films and the use of English, including in two of the analyzed coproductions. With *The Great Wall*, there is at least a narrative explanation for two of the characters speaking English, but *Outcast* and *Enter the Warriors Gate* simply borrow from this common U.S. film conceit. The criticisms reinforce Kraidy's (2005) argument about critical transculturalism, arguing that hybridity, while more multinational and complex than ever, still is structured to favor Western, and especially U.S., power. Perhaps as these films continue to fail at the box office, the economic incentives will convince U.S. filmmakers and Chinese studios to more creatively reimagine coproduced cinema to overcome their Western partners' ideological investments in Whiteness.

Conclusion

● ● ● ● ● ● ● ● ● ● ● ● ● ● ● ● ● ● ● ●

Hall (2003) famously referred to culture as an "ideological terrain of struggle" (89). I have often thought of this as similar to the construction of a city space, the streets that guide our steps, the streetlights and crosswalks that organize movement, and the buildings and monuments that draw attention. The terrain structures how we exist within spaces and what we notice. These structures can be marginalizing, but they are not always so. For this conversation about whitewashing, however, there is little that is redemptive about the ways it works; there is little ambivalence, and the lines are clearly drawn. Thus, it is helpful to understand whitewashing by thinking about the metaphor of terrain differently, as more combative.

In the metaphor of a battlefield, the purpose is to take ideological territory. This might happen most of the time with small skirmishes on the front lines. In media representations of race, this includes postracist portrayals of multicultural utopias that still center Whiteness, arguments made on talk shows or podcasts about a comedian's obligation to humor above all else, or news columns that treat the claim of racism as more harmful than the actual racist act. As a strategy of mediated domination, whitewashing is qualitatively different. It is a brazen intrusion behind the front lines to reclaim large swaths of territory. It is the replacement and displacement of people of color in their own stories, including imagining themselves in historically or narratively unrealistic ways as saviors and heroes of people of color, taking stories of people of color and replacing them with White protagonists, and becoming the other through yellowface, redface, brownface, and blackface. These are overtly problematic representations that powerfully assert White supremacy with less nuance than the frontline ideological battles over racial representation. This is not slow, regressive change but a desire for a decisive ideological victory.

With White racial hegemony, there are two routes to securing power. The more common now is for Whiteness to function as an invisible category of racial difference (Dyer, 1997). This has several benefits. First, it allows representational freedom for White people so that they can imagine themselves in any story and so that they can imagine themselves as being more capable than the "natives." Second, it allows White people to be seen as individuals. Because their representations are not restricted to a narrow range or stereotyped widely in the West, the stereotypes they deal with are largely of their own choosing and ones that are not clearly raced, such as a jock, a nerd, a cheerleader, a goth, a businessman, a police officer, a librarian, and so on. It positions White standpoints as normative and universal (Nakayama and Krizek, 1995). The other more overt way is through naked White supremacy, representing White people as more heroic, more sympathetic, and superior, and representing White people as characters of color. These are representational strategies that have been used since the advent of film in the United States, and whitewashing's ideological purpose, whether intentional or subconscious, is to reclaim more of this representational space, pushing the battle lines back.

The desire for ideological control is seen visibly in whitewashing's contemporary economic failures. The only recent example of a whitewashed film that has been a box office success in my memory is *Doctor Strange*; however, this might be explained by the Ancient One, played by Tilda Swinton, being a supporting character rather than the movie's star. Although there may be a few exceptions, the overwhelming pattern has pointed to a lack of economic success (Jasper, 2017). In addition to the films studied in this book, *Gods of Egypt* (2016), *Prince of Persia: The Sands of Time* (2010), *The Last Airbender* (2010), and *The Lone Ranger* (2013) come to mind as whitewashed movies that underperformed at the box office. These decisions would not continue to be made if "green" really was the only color Hollywood sees. Rather, it seems that Hollywood and other Western film centers advance these representational choices intentionally. This is made even more visible when films such as *Crazy Rich Asians* (2018) and *Black Panther* (2018) far outperform box office expectations. In a copycat industry, it is striking that films about people of color are not copied. Whitewashed movie failures are given the benefit of the doubt, but the success of people of color in their own stories is perhaps thought of as a box office aberration.

I do not mean to claim that White people in the film industry are mostly White supremacist in their beliefs and that there is a conspiracy afoot. Indeed, I would imagine that most White media workers, especially in the entertainment industry, consider themselves liberal. Instead, the structures that are in place benefit White people. Most important, White people occupy most of the creative and leadership positions (Smith, Choueiti, and Pieper, 2016; Yuen, 2017), and it is very likely that stories that center White people resonate with them as marketable or as "authentic." To advance White stories, then, does not require a conspiracy but a critical mass of people who share a similar ideological vantage point. Even if I were to believe that the majority are actively opposed to whitewashing, as long as there are sufficient numbers of producers and financiers to greenlight the movies, then these representations will continue to exist. Also, unlike counterrepresentations that necessarily involve the producer taking a high degree of risk in case the movie is unprofitable, there are few people who associate casting famous White actors as the reason for a movie's failure. As long as the demographics of media producers, racialized assumptions about bankability, and a vantage point that favors White racial hegemony is unchanged, then it is likely that whitewashing will continue.

To return to the battlefield metaphor, the way to prevent territory from being taken and regressing toward White supremacist representation is to fend off incursions and to make advances of one's own. Perhaps this is the kind of terrain Hall (2003) had in mind all along when he referred to ideological "struggle" (p. 89). When domination is not contested, it leads to regression toward existing structures. Consider that in 2020, the OscarsSoWhite hashtag has been revived because of the inclusion of only Cynthia Erivo as a best actress nominee for her role in *Harriet* (2019). This is despite notable actors and actresses of color who were nominated by other awards bodies, including Nora Lum (Awkafina) for *The Farewell* (2019), Jennifer Lopez for *Hustlers* (2019), and Lupito Nyong'o for *Us* (2019). Ironically, the Academy of Motion Pictures Arts and Sciences designated 2020 to be the year when it would double its membership of women and people of color (Sinha-Roy, 2020). So resistance is necessary, though easily vilified.

For White people who take advantage of and enjoy White representational privilege, there is limited patience for criticisms by people of color. Eventually, those criticisms are viewed with a jaundiced eye, seeing activists as "social justice warriors" who are never satisfied. To return once more to the battlefield argument, I would consider arguments such as this to be artillery cover fire that allows these incursions. Disingenuous calls to unity and postracism also serve to hide whitewashing's overt ideological work. Regarding Asian media, I have also seen people argue in online spaces that White people do not complain about the lack of White representation in Asian media culture. There are several problems with this discursive position. First, it positions White people as exceptionally generous and unassuming. It attempts to discipline dissent by arguing that being unbothered is a moral virtue, and it claims simultaneously that White people are superior in this attribute. The problems with this argument notwithstanding, it also rests on a faulty assumption that the United States is a White country. Unlike South Korea, for instance, which has a 95 percent ethnically Korean population, the United States is only about 60 percent non-Hispanic White, according to the 2010 Census. Of the five percent non-ethnic Korean population in Korea, the vast majority are from other Asian countries. White residents across Asia are among the smallest minority of the minority, and only a miniscule percentage are citizens.

Even despite their very small relative numbers, it is also not true that White people do not appear in Asian media. Relative to their percentages in the population, they are overrepresented, at least in Korea. Because I am most familiar with Korean media culture, I will restrict my counterexample to this particular case, though I suspect it may be generally true in other liberal-democratic Asian nations. In Korea, there are several variety shows that are dedicated to the concerns of "foreigners," although they ignore the majority of foreign residents who come from the Global South in favor of White people from Western countries. These shows include but are not limited to *Abnormal Summit*, *Global Talk Show*, *Global Family*, *Welcome! First Time in Korea?*, and *Where Is My Friend's Home*. The participants on these shows have parlayed their fame into roles on other variety shows and occasionally on serialized television. Because of the United States' more powerful role in global media circuits, U.S. actors and musicians also receive favored status, selling out concerts and dominating box offices. As such, the cover fire of these excuses is not true, but it does not need to be. They just need to distract and momentarily weaken resistance to allow the incursion.

Counterstrikes for Social Justice

I differ somewhat from some peer colleagues and activists who decry whitewashing on the grounds that it is racially inauthentic. While I understand the reflexive position as a way of defending the little representational power we are given and as a way of fighting back against visceral racist harms, it nevertheless leans toward racial essentialism. Racial essentialism itself is a means of reifying White racial hegemony. A necessity of racism is to clearly define race as composed of discrete categories of difference that become a commonsense social reality. Without these clear definitions, it becomes impossible to sustain a system of oppression based on it. The rejection of racial essentialism, on the other hand, challenges the fixity of race (Bhabha, 1996). As such, it challenges the system of racism itself.

The problem, however, is that this argument has been co-opted by White racial hegemony. Arguing for race as a fiction and color blindness as a solution without actually practicing it has been a strategy of postracism or colorblind racism (Bonilla-Silva, 2006). In addition, being color blind, or race-oblivious, means ignoring a practical social reality in which systemic racism does, in fact, structure the life opportunities of people of color in restrictive, marginalizing, and oppressive ways. It would mean being unable to organize in solidarity against structural racism. As such, color consciousness is taken up as a politically meaningful cause in antiracism. As long as people view others in a categorical fashion and oppress them based on that believed difference, people who are oppressed will organize to resist their oppression. This perpetuates a system of race even while fighting structural racism. Therefore, as a practical matter, color blindness can only really emerge as a progressive formation once racial inequality no longer exists. The logic, then, is if racism must exist, then it is better to find affirmative meaning in an ascribed racial identity. This is a practical solution given the problem of structural racism, but it does not deconstruct the fixity of race as a social construct. On the contrary, it inadvertently strengthens it. A tactic of resistance that should be pursued, then, could be one that moves toward racial equality while also challenging notions of racial fixity.

As the examples in the chapters have pointed out, simply casting Asian and Asian American characters in stories set in Asian worlds produces different, more progressive connotations even if the script remains the same. The ideological meanings are not purely counterhegemonic as they carry quite a bit of ambivalence, but it would be a productive step, as William Yu imagined in his StarringJohnCho viral hashtag. This should be the easiest step, but it is one that, if taken alone, would reify racial essentialism with notions of authenticity. This is surely better than the status quo, but it is not enough if race itself is meant to be deconstructed. What I would propose instead is casting that intentionally resists White racial hegemony to symbolically deconstruct racial fixity. Unlike calls for color-blind casting that conveniently reinforce White-privileged casting, there should be intentional race-conscious casting that runs counter to racial type.

Recent examples of Asian Americans, who have played roles that might conventionally be understood as White include Gemma Chan as Bess of Hardwick in *Mary Queen of Scots* (2018), Priyanka Chopra as Alex Parrish in the television series *Quantico*, and Henry Golding as Tom Webster in *Last Christmas* (2019). The example of Gemma Chan is especially exceptional because it represents a historically real, White woman as Asian. By having representations like this consistently and in leading roles, it changes the symbolic realm in which White people can be anything while people of color can only be a specific thing. It pushes forward a bold, ideological counterattack that says people of color can be anything, too.

This can be artistically liberating as well, as it frees artists and creators to explore their imaginations in ways that are constricted less by the demands of racial authenticity and, indeed, to deconstruct ideas of racial essentialism. In addition to casting choices, creative choices can be made to tell White stories in racially bent ways, to use Lopez's (2011) conceptualization of the term. Musicals such as *Hamilton* imagine the White Founding Fathers in a refreshing way that symbolically places Black people in the center of the creation of the union, and David Henry Hwang's musical *Soft Power* satirically reimagines *The King and I* as a story about a benevolent Chinese man, who teaches Hillary Clinton important lessons about politics and life. Both of these plays are, however, read as fantasies. In the case of *Soft Power*, it is narratively written into the script as the lead's imagination while in a coma. Stories like these resonate as valuable precisely because they subvert racial essentialism and the power of White people's stories told through White vantage points.

At this point, I should return to the question of what is wrong about whitewashing, particularly if it is not because of its racial inauthenticity. My argument is that it is fundamentally about power inequalities. This is to say that the direction of racial crossing and from whose artistic and narrative standpoint the crossings happen disproportionately favor White racial hegemony. There is roughly a century of film in which this has happened, and centuries of stories about White people's adventures in distant lands. Because of this, the power equation is tilted heavily toward White racial hegemony. What needs to be corrected is not authenticity but the imbalance. There need to be more stories about heroes of color in Europe, a Chinese British King Arthur, a Chicanx American, who is the "last patriot." The modifier "last" should not just belong to White people in movies such as *The Last of the Mohicans* (1992), *The Last Samurai* (2003), and *the Last Airbender* (2010). Counterrepresentations and counternarratives would challenge structures that favor White racial hegemony.

Until there are so many such counterrepresentations that they become banal and the scales reach a balance point, White racial crossings should be minimized. Not only is there less arguable artistic merit to such a common trope, a little bit of counterrepresentation will not effectively counter a preponderance of whitewashed representations. After structures are newly formed that imagine equal crossings in multiple directions, whitewashed representations will lose their ideological vigor because they would have lost the taint of symbolic erasure. That is, if Asian Americans play historically White characters in great numbers, then what does it matter if White Americans play Asian characters? It will have lost its oppressive power. Opposing cross-racial casting matters, however, when the crossings are mostly unidirectional. Just as whitewashing aims to take large ideological territory in favor of White racial hegemony, parallel counternarratives would claim a large swath of resistive ideological ground in favor of representational equality and the dissolving of racial essentialism. With a better understanding of the strategy of whitewashing, it creates a much better chance of dismantling it.

Acknowledgments

As any author knows, it is impossible to write a book without professional and personal support. This project began in 2018 and has taken two years to complete. Over that time, people and institutions have helped make it possible. Beginning with the professional, I would like to thank Ramapo College of New Jersey, my home institution, for its Faculty Development Fund summer grant. This was important time to allow ideas to ferment and to begin the important work of starting to craft the project. As the Korean proverb states, "starting is half the work."

I would also like to express gratitude for the Fulbright program and my host institution in Seoul, South Korea, Hankuk University of Foreign Studies. Although the Fulbright was a teaching grant and did not lead to data collection or analysis, it provided time and space to be away from the requirements of daily service. It allowed space to focus on teaching and scholarship, and this was the first time in my career where I have benefited from a two-course teaching load. It was a luxury that helped facilitate the writing of the book. During my Fulbright, I also gave talks about this project at the University of Macau, Universitas Nasional in Jakarta, Indonesia, and Yonsei University in Seoul. These were productive opportunities to talk with graduate students and colleagues, allowing ideas to take further form. Being outside of the United States and looking in was itself productive, as it allows me to shift my habitus and my vantage point. As I thought about cinema that is not whitewashed, seeing a real and mediated world that reflects Asian subjectivity was liberating.

I also had the opportunity to present chapters at various conferences, including at the Race and Media Conference at the University of Washington, at the National Communication Association's annual convention in 2018 and 2020, the World Congress of Korean Studies in Seoul, the annual conference for the Organization for the Study of Communication, Gender, and Language, and the Association for Asian American Studies. I am grateful for the reviewers' insights, respondents' comments, and colleagues' conversations. These were stimulating and affirmative interactions that helped to advance the project. While I will not have a chance to meet them, I would also like to thank the reviewers of this book. Reviewing is often thankless work, and I want to recognize their labor.

Furthermore, I would like to thank Lisa Banning at Rutgers University Press for seeing the merit in the project and signing it to an advance contract. Her editing advice also helped to sharpen my writing. Of course, I would also like to thank Jasper Chang, who took the reins of the book midway through the project. His enthusiasm has been infectious, his editing has been fair and insightful, and his replies are swift. Working with other editors in the past, I understand how rare this combination of qualities is.

Shifting to the personal, I would like to thank Asian American actors, writers, directors, behind-the-camera workers, and activists who shined a spotlight on practices of whitewashing. Their efforts in combination with Black American activists, including most prominently April Reign, who began the #OscarsSoWhite hashtag, raised necessary awareness. Some advocates are well known, but many are unsung heroes, who toil everyday toward representational justice. Without them, I would have been less aware and less energized to begin this project. Particularly noteworthy is William Yu, the creator of the photoshopped posters and hashtag #StarringJohnCho. His work demonstrates how actualized representation can powerfully shape new possibilities about the future. It is because of his creative imagination that I was motivated to engage my own scholarly one.

Finally, I would be remiss if I did not thank my spouse, Eunyoung, and my two children, Noah and Aaron. They gave me the emotional support I needed during this time, and they provided laughter and joy as I pushed through with the project. They are a source of strength that has helped to make this book possible.

Notes

Introduction

1   When referring to "White" as a racial identity, I capitalize it to more consistently represent racial difference, e.g., Asian, Black, Latinx, White. When referencing the strategies of Whiteness, however, I do not capitalize them to consistently link various strategic discourses, e.g., whitewashing, racism, privilege.

2   Asian/American is a construction that David Palombu-Liu (1999) had formulated to indicate the conflation of Asian and Asian American in the U.S. racial imagination.

3   I use the term "mixed race" instead of multiracial, biracial, or multicultural to be consistent with critical mixed-race studies. I realize the term is controversial, so I am relying on the judgment of scholars in critical mixed-race studies whose expertise in the subject far exceeds my own.

4   I wish to emphasize that whitewashing is not specific to White erasure of Asian/American subjectivities alone but that this is the specific focus of this book.

5   Tuchman (1978) coined the term as she described the trivialization and underrepresentation of marginalized groups.

6   The project was started in 2018; thus, 2008 marked a decade from the start of the book.

Chapter 1   Whitewashing Romance in Hawai'i

1   It should be noted that the film positions the Chinese as a yellow peril threat, which not only is a geopolitical rival but also one that engages in sneaky, under-handed means. This is consistent with yellow peril representations, one of the most enduring stereotypes of Asian/Americans (Ono and Pham, 2009).

Chapter 3   White Grievance, Heroism, and Postracist, Mixed-Race Inclusion in *47 Ronin*

1   This has resonance to contemporary Japanese culture in which mixed-race Japanese are referred to as *hafu*, the Japanese transliteration for "half." The term is problematic

and does carry ambivalent connotations, but it is not as uniformly hostile as represented in the movie.

2 The film romanticizes the *ronin* as samurai without a leader and claims that this is the greatest dishonor for a samurai.

Chapter 4   Satire and the Villainy of Kim Jong-un

1 Korean names are written with the family name first followed by the given name. Because individuals do not follow consistent standards for transliteration, the names may appear differently; however, readers should generally understand that Korean names include a monosyllabic surname followed by a given name of two syllables that are sometimes written with a space, written together, or connected with a hyphen, e.g., North Korean leader Kim Jong-un.

2 Throughout the book, I have used first names to refer to movie characters when first names are given, but because Kim is a real-life figure and is the head of state, I have used his surname instead. Referring to him simply as Jong-un reads as intentionally mocking, which would ironically replicate the standpoint of the movie.

3 The term "honeydick" is a reference to "honeypot," which was used earlier in the film to refer to a woman's seduction and entrapment of a man. Although Kim and Dave do not have a sexual relationship, Kim has "seduced" Dave to believe that he is a good leader by befriending him.

Chapter 6   Whitewashing Anime Remakes

1 It is noteworthy that Chow Yun-Fat, a prominent leading man in Hong King cinema, was subjected to a similar marginalizing role in *Bulletproof Monk* (2003) in which he trains a young White protégé with superhuman powers. His leading man quality was subordinated to relatively obscure White American actors, James Marsters and Seann William Scott.

Chapter 7   Transnational Coproduction and the Ambivalence of White Masculine Heroism

1 Chinese actors' names are written with the surname first unless they have an Anglicized first name, such as Bill.

2 Two characters are named Zhao. In *Outcast*, it is the prince; in *Enter the Warriors Gate*, it is a warrior and bodyguard to the princess.

References

Ahn, J.-H. (2015). Desiring biracial whites: Cultural consumption of white mixed-race celebrities in South Korean popular media. *Media, Culture & Society, 37*(6), 937–947. doi:10.1177/0163443715593050

Alcoff, L. M. (1998). What should White people do? *Hypatia, 13*(3), 6–26. doi:10.1111/j.1527-2001.1998.tb01367.x

Alvaray, L. (2013). Hybridity and genre in transnational Latin American cinemas *Transnational Cinemas, 4*(1), 67–87. doi:10.1386/trac.4.167_1

Ames, C. (1992). Restoring the black man's lethal weapon. *Journal of Popular Film & Television, 20*(3), 52–60. doi:10.1080/01956051.1992.9944228

Andersen, H. C., & Burton, V. L. (1949). *The emperor's new clothes.* Boston: Houghton Mifflin Co.

Anderson, C. S. (2007). The Afro-Asiatic floating world: Post-soul implications of the art of Iona Rozeal Brown. *African American Review, 41*(4), 655–665. Retrieved from http://aar.slu.edu/

Artz, L. (1998). Hegemony in Black and White: Interracial buddy films and the new racism. In Y. R. Kamalipour & T. Carilli (Eds.), *Cultural diversity and the U.S. media* (pp. 67–78). Albany: State University of New York Press.

Artz, L., & Murphy, B. O. (2000). *Cultural hegemony in the United States.* Thousand Oaks, CA: Sage.

Arvin, M. (2018). Polynesia is a project, not a place: Polynesian proximities to Whiteness in *Cloud Atlas* and beyond. In C. Fojas, R. P. Guevarra, & N. T. Sharma (Eds.), *Beyond ethnicity: New politics of race in Hawai'i* (pp. 21–47). Honolulu: University of Hawai'i Press.

Balaji, M. (2011). Racializing pity: The Haiti earthquake and the plight of "others." *Critical Studies in Media Communication, 28*(1), 50–67. doi:10.1080/15295036.2010.545703

Balmain, C. (2009). Oriental nightmares: The "demonic" other in contemporary American adaptations of Japanese horror film. *At the Interface / Probing the Boundaries, 57*, 25–38. doi: 10.1163/9789042028791_004

Ban, Z., Sastry, S., & Dutta, M. J. (2013). "Shoppers' Republic of China": Orientalism in neoliberal U.S. news discourse. *Journal of International and Intercultural Communication, 6*(4), 280–297. doi:10.1080/17513057.2013.792941

Banjo, O. O., & Jennings, N. A. (2016). Content analysis of the portrayal of white characters in Black films across two decades. *Mass Communication & Society*, 1–29. doi:10.1080/15205436.2016.1230220

Barnes, B., & Cieply, M. (2014). Sony drops "Interview" following threats. *The New York Times*, p. B1.

Beltrán, M. (2008). Mixed race in Latinowood: Latino stardom and ethnic ambiguity in the era of *Dark Angels*. In M. Beltrán & C. Fojas (Eds.), *Mixed race Hollywood* (pp. 248–268). New York: New York University Press.

Beltrán, M., & Fojas, C. (2008). Introduction: Mixed race in Hollywood film and media culture. In M. Beltrán & C. Fojas (Eds.), *Mixed race Hollywood* (pp. 1–22). New York: New York University Press.

Ben-Porath, E. N., & Shaker, L. K. (2012). News images, race, and attribution in the wake of Hurricane Katrina. *Journal of Communication, 60*(3), 466–490. doi:10.1111/j.1460-2466.2010.01493.x

Benshoff, H. M., & Griffin, S. (2004). *America on film: Representing race, class, gender, and sexuality at the movies*. Malden, MA: Blackwell.

Berger, A. A. (2016). *Media and communication research: An introduction to qualitative and quantitative approaches* (4th ed.). Washington, DC: Sage.

Berman, E. (2017). A comprehensive guide to the *Ghost in the Shell* controversy. *Time*. Retrieved from http://time.com/4714367/ghost-in-the-shell-controversy-scarlett-johansson/

Bhabha, H. K. (1996). Culture's in-between. In S. Hall & P. Du Gay (Eds.), *Questions of cultural identity* (pp. 53–60). Thousand Oaks, CA: Sage.

Billig, M. (2001). Humour and hatred: The racist jokes of the Ku Klux Klan. *Discourse & Society, 12*(3), 267–289. doi:10.1177/0957926501012003001

Bineham, J. L. (2015). How *The Blind Side* blinds us: Postracism and the American Dream. *Southern Communication Journal, 80*(3), 230–245. doi:10.1080/10417 94X.2015.1030084

Blouin, M. (2011). A Western wake: Difference and doubt in Christopher Nolan's *Inception. Extrapolation, 52*(3), 318–337. doi:10.3828/extr.2011.52.3.4

Bogarosh, N. A. (2013). *The princess, the damsel, and the sidekick: Women as the "other" in popular films (2000–2011)* (Doctoral dissertation, Washington State University). (UMI No. 3598040)

Bonilla-Silva, E. (2006). *Racism without racists: Color-blind racism and racial inequality in contemporary America*. Lanham, MD: Rowman & Littlefield.

Bosanquet, T. (2018). Picture partnership: Co-productions and the Australian screen industries. *Metro Magazine, 195*, 120–123.

Boskin, J., & Dorinson, J. (1985). Ethnic humor: Subversion and survival. *American Quarterly, 37*(1), 81–97. Retrieved from http://www.americanquarterly.org/index.html

Brodkin, K. (2004). How Jews became White folks and what that says about race in America. In P. S. Rothenberg (Ed.), *Race, class, and gender in the United States: An integrated study* (pp. 39–53). New York: Worth.

Brown, H. (2019). Postfeminist re-essentialism in *The Hunger Games* and *The Selection* trilogies. *Women's Studies: An Interdisciplinary Journal, 48*(7), 735–754. doi:10.1080/00497878.2019.1665044

Brown, M. A. (2014). Mourning the land: Kanikau in *Noho Hewa: The Wrongful*

Occupation of Hawai'i. The American Indian Quarterly, 38(3), 374–395. Retrieved from https://muse.jhu.edu/journal/2

Brownstein, B. (2015, January 2). Political farce gets hacky; Much-publicized film goes for adolescent humour rather than smart satire. *The Vancouver Sun*, p. D1.

Bui, L. (2020). Asian roboticism: Connecting mechanized labor to the automation of work. *Perspectives on Global Development and Technology, 19*, 110–126. doi:10.1163 /15691497-12341544

Builder, M. (2014). The real problem with "The Interview" is its racism, not its satire. *Medium*. Retrieved from https://medium.com/@maxine_builder/the-real -problem-with-the-interview-is-its-racism-not-its-satire-4d0cd30d5f0d

Butterworth, M. L. (2007). Race in "the race": Mark McGwire, Sammy Sosa, and the heroic constructions of Whiteness. *Critical Studies in Media Communication, 24*(3), 228–244. doi:10.1080/07393180701520926

Catsoulis, J. (2015). An heir finds trouble on his way to the throne. *The New York Times*. Retrieved from https://www.nytimes.com/2015/02/06/movies/outcast-with -nicolas-cage-and-hayden-christensen.

Chan, K. (2009). *Remade in Hollywood: The global Chinese presence in transnational cinemas*. Hong Kong: Hong Kong University Press.

Chang, I. (2003). *The Chinese in America: A narrative history*. New York: Viking.

Chapman, D. (2006). Discourses of multicultural coexistence (Tabunka Kyōsei) and the "old-comer" Korean residents of Japan. *Asian Ethnicity, 7*(1), 89–102. doi:10.1080 /14631360500498593

Chapman, D. (2007). *Zainichi Korean identity and ethnicity*. New York: Routledge.

Chidester, P. (2008). May the circle stay unbroken: *Friends*, the presence of absence, and the rhetorical reinforcement of Whiteness. *Critical Studies in Media Communication, 25*(2), 157–174. doi:10.1080/15295030802031772

Cho, J. S. P. (2012). Global fatigue: Transnational markets, linguistic capital, and Korean-American male English teachers in South Korea. *Journal of Sociolinguistics, 16*(2), 218–237. doi:10.1111/j.1467-9841.2011.00526.x

Clifford, N. (2001). *"A truthful impression of the country": British and American travel writing in China, 1880–1949*. Ann Arbor: University of Michigan Press.

Cobb, J. N. (2011). No we can't!: Postracialism and the popular appearance of a rhetorical fiction. *Communication Studies, 62*(4), 406–421. doi:10.1080/10510974.2 011.588075

Coloma, R. S. (2012). White gazes, brown beasts: Imperial feminism and disciplining desires and bodies in colonial encounters. *Paedagogica Historica, 48*(2), 243–261. doi:10.1080/00309230.2010.547511

Couch, A. (2019). Taika Waititi's "Akira" sets 2021 release date. *The Hollywood Reporter*. Retrieved from https://www.hollywoodreporter.com/heat-vision/akira -movie-release-date-set-sets-may-2021-1213499

Cox, D. (2013). Attempting the impossible: Why does Western cinema whitewash Asian stories? *Guardian*. Retrieved from https://www.theguardian.com/film /filmblog/2013/jan/02/attempting-the-impossible-asian-roles

Cramer, L. M. (2016). The whitening of *Grey's Anatomy. Communication Studies, 67*(4), 474–487. doi:10.1080/10510974.2016.1205640

Crofts Wiley, S. B. (2004). Rethinking nationality in the context of globalization. *Communication Theory, 14*(1), 78–96. doi:10.1111/j.1468-2885.2004.tb00304.x

Croteau, D. R., Hoynes, W., & Milan, S. (2012). *Media/Society: Industries, images, and audiences*. Thousand Oaks, CA: Sage.

Croteau, D., & Hoynes, W. (2014). *Media/Society: Industries, images, and audiences* (5th ed.). New York, NY: Sage.

Croucher, S. (2009). Migrants of privilege: The political transnationalism of Americans in Mexico. *Identities: Global Studies in Culture and Power, 16*(4), 463–491. doi:10.1080/10702890903020984

Crowe, C. (2015a). A comment on Allison Ng. Retrieved from http://www.theuncool .com/2015/06/02/a-comment-on-allison-ng/

Darling-Wolf, F., & Mendelson, A. L. (2008). Seeing themselves through the lens of the Other: An analysis of the cross-cultural production and negotation of *National Geographic*'s "The Samurai Way" story. *Journalism and Communication Monographs, 10*(3), 285–322. doi:10.1177/152263790801000303

DeBoer, S. (2014). *Co-producing Asia: Locating Japanese-Chinese regional film and media*. Minneapolis: University of Minnesota Press.

de Certeau, M. (1984|2011). *The practice of everyday life* (S. Rendall, Trans. 3rd ed.). Los Angeles: University of California Press.

Dennis, C. (2017). "Dragonball Evolution" writer pens an apology to fans 7 years later. Retrieved from www.inverse.com/article/15172-dragonball-evolution-writer-pens -an-apology-to-fans-7-years-later

Dew, O. (2016). *Zainichi cinema: Korean-in-Japan film culture*. London: Palgrave Macmillan.

DiAngelo, R. (2011). White fragility. *International Journal of Critical Pedagogy, 3*(3), 54–70. Retrieved from http://libjournal.uncg.edu/ijcp

Dixon, T. L., & Linz, D. (2000). Race and the misrepresentation of victimization on local television news. *Communication Research, 27*(5), 547–573. doi:10.1177/009365000027005001

Drew, E. M. (2011). Pretending to be "postracial": The spectacularization of race in reality TV's survivor. *Television & New Media, 12*(4), 326–346. doi:10.1177 /1527476410385474

Dubrofsky, R. E. (2013). Jewishness, Whiteness, and Blackness on *Glee*: Singing to the tune of postracism. *Communication, Culture, & Critique, 6*(1), 82–102. doi:10.1111/ cccr.12002

Dubrofsky, R. E., & Ryalls, E. D. (2014). *The Hunger Games*: Performing not-performing to authenticate femininity and whiteness. *Critical Studies in Media Communication, 31*(5), 395-409. doi:10.1080/15295036.2013.874038

Dubrofsky, R. E., & Wood, M. M. (2014). Posting racism and sexism: Authenticity, agency and self-reflexivity in social media. *Communication and Critical/Cultural Studies, 11*(3), 282–287. doi:10.1080/1479120.2014.926247

Ducat, S. J. (2004). *The wimp factor: Gender gaps, holy wars, and the politics of anxious masculinity*. Boston: Beacon Press.

Dyer, R. (1988). White. *Screen, 29*(4), 44–64. doi:10.1093/screen/29.4.44

Dyer, R. (1997). *White*. New York: Routledge.

Egan, T. (2017). The whitewashing in "Ghost in the Shell" is even worse than we thought. *Complex*. Retrieved from https://www.complex.com/pop-culture/2017 /03/ghost-in-the-shell-whitewashing-worse-than-thought-possible

Eguchi, S. (2015). Queer intercultural relationality: An autoethnography of Asian-Black (dis)connections in White gay America. *Journal of International and Intercultural Communication, 8*(1), 27–43. doi:10.1080/17513057.2015 .991077

Ehrlich, R. (2015). Opinion: Why "No Escape" is the worst movie to see before traveling to Asia. Retrieved from CNN website: https://www.cnn.com/travel/article/movie-no-escape-opinion/index.html

Enck-Wanzer, D. (2011). Barack Obama, the tea party, and the threat of race: On racial neoliberalism and born again racism. *Communication, Culture & Critique, 4*(1), 23–30. doi:10.1111/j.1753-9137.2010.01090.x

Entman, R. M., & Rojecki, A. (2000). *The Black image in the White mind: Media and race in America*. Chicago: University of Chicago Press.

Eshun, K. (2003). Further considerations of Afrofuturism. *The New Centennial Review, 3*(2), 287–302. doi:10.1353/ncr.2003.0021

Espiritu, Y. L. (2004). Ideological racism and cultural resistance: Constructing our own images. In M. L. Andersen & P. Hill Collins (Eds.), *Race, Class, and Gender: An Anthology* (5th ed., pp. 175–184). Belmont, CA: Wadsworth.

Esposito, J. (2009). What does race have to do with Ugly Betty? An analysis of privilege and postracial(?) representations on a television sitcom. *Television & New Media, 10*(6), 521–535. doi:10.117/1527476409340906

Feng, P. X. (2002). *Identities in motion: Asian American film and video*. Durham, NC: Duke University Press.

Fitzgerald, M. R. (2013). The White savior and his junior partner: The Lone Ranger and Tonto on Cold War television (1949–1957). *Journal of Popular Culture, 46*(1), 79–108. doi:10.1111/jpcu.12017

Fojas, C. (2014). *Islands of empire: Pop culture and U.S. power*. Austin: University of Texas Press.

Fojas, C. (2018). Mixed-race Hollywood, Hawaiian style. In C. Fojas, R. P. Guevarra, & N. T. Sharma (Eds.), *Beyond ethnicity: New politics of race in Hawai'i* (pp. 48–60). Honolulu: University of Hawai'i Press.

Fong, T. P. (2008). *The contemporary Asian American experience: Beyond the model minority* (3rd ed.). Upper Saddle River, NJ: Pearson Prentice Hall.

Frank, A. (2017). Hollywood's whitewashed version of anime never sells. *Polygon*. Retrieved from https://www.polygon.com/2017/4/3/15142608/hollywood-anime-live-action-adaptations-ghost-in-the-shell

Frankenberg, R. (1993). *White women, race matters: The social construction of whiteness*. Minneapolis: University of Minnesota Press.

Frizell, S. (2014). Kim Jong Un swears "merciless" retaliation if new Seth Rogen film released. *Time*. Retrieved from https://time.com/2921071/kim-jong-un-seth-rogen-the-interview-james-franco/

Fulop, R. N. (2012). *Heroes, dames, and damsels in distress: Constructing gender types in classical Hollywood film music* (Doctoral dissertation, University of Michigan).

Gabriel, J. (1998). *Whitewash: Racialized politics and the media*. New York: Routledge.

Gandy, O. H. (1998). *Communication and race: A structural perspective*. London: Arnold.

Gates, P. (2004). Always a partner in crime: Black masculinity in the Hollywood detective film. *Journal of Popular Film and Television, 32*(1), 20–29. doi:10.3200/JPFT.32.1.20-30

Ghabra, H. S. (2018). *Muslim women and white femininity: Reenactment and resistance*. New York: Peter Lang.

Gilbert, W. S., & Sullivan, A. (1885). *The Mikado*. New York: Kalmus.

Gilroy, P. (2012). "My Britain is fuck all" zombie multiculturalism and the race politics of citizenship. *Identities: Global Studies in Culture and Power, 19*(4), 380–397. doi:10.1080/1070289X.2012.725512

Giresunhu, L. (2009). Cyborg goddesses: The mainframe revisited. *At the Interface /
Probing the Boundaries, 56,* 157–187. doi:10.1163/9789401206747_008

Giroux, H. A. (1997). Race, pedagogy, and whiteness in *Dangerous Minds. Cineaste,
22*(4), 46–49.

Giroux, H. A. (2003). Spectacles of race and pedagogies of denial: Anti-Black racist
pedagogy under the reign of neoliberalism. *Communication Education, 52*(2),
191–211. doi:10.1080/0363452032000156190

Goldberg, M. (2017). "Ghost in the Shell" is racist in unexpected ways. *Collider.*
Retrieved from https://www.businessinsider.com/ghost-in-the-shell-is-racist-in
-unexpected-ways-2017-3

Goodyear-Ka'ōpua, N., & Kuwada, B. K. (2018). Making 'Aha: Independent Hawaiian
pasts, presents, & futures. *Daedalus, 147*(2), 49–59. doi:10.1162/DAED_a_00489

Gries, P. H. (2014). "Red China" and the "Yellow Peril": How ideology divides
Americans over China. *Journal of East Asian Studies, 14,* 317–346. doi:10.1017/
S1598240800005518

Griffin, R. A. (2015). Problematic representations of strategic whiteness and "postracial" pedagogy: A critical intercultural reading of *The Help. Journal of International and Intercultural Communication, 8*(2), 147–166. doi:10.1080/17513057.2015
.1025330

Gring-Pemble, L., & Watson, M. S. (2003). The rhetorical limits of satire: An analysis
of James Finn Garner's *Politically Correct Bedtime Stories. Quarterly Journal of
Speech, 89*(2), 132–153. doi:10.1080/0033563032000102543

Guillem, S. M., & Barnes, C. C. (2018). "Am I a good [white] mother?": Mad men, bad
mothers, and post(racial)feminism. *Critical Studies in Media Communication, 35*(3),
286–299. doi:10.1080/15295036.2017.1416419

Guo, L., & Lee, L. (2013). The critique of YouTube-based vernacular discourse: A case
study of YouTube's Asian community. *Critical Studies in Media Communication,
30*(5), 391–406. doi:10.1080/15295036.2012.755048

Hall, S. (1997). Work of representation. In S. Hall (Ed.), *Representation: Cultural
representations and signifying practices* (pp. 15–30). Thousand Oaks, CA: Sage.

Hall, S. (2003). The whites of their eyes: Racist ideologies and the media. In G. Dines &
J. M. Humez (Eds.), *Gender, race, and class in media: A text-reader* (2nd ed.,
pp. 89–93). Thousand Oaks, CA: Sage.

Hamad, R. (2013). Whitewashing *The Impossible. The Sydney Morning Herald.*
Retrieved from https://www.smh.com.au/lifestyle/whitewashing-ithe-impossiblei
-20130131-2dmes.html

Hamamoto, D. Y. (1994). *Monitored peril: Asian Americans and the politics of
representation.* Minneapolis: University of Minnesota Press.

Hamamoto, D. Y. (2000a). Introduction: On Asian American film and criticism.
In D. Y. Hamamoto & S. Liu (Eds.), *Countervisions: Asian American film criticism*
(pp. 1–20). Philadelphia, PA: Temple University Press.

Hamamoto, D. Y. (2000b). The Joy Fuck Club: Prolegomenon to an Asian American
porno practice. In D. Y. Hamamoto & S. Liu (Eds.), *Countervisions: Asian
American Film Criticism* (pp. 59–89). Philadelphia: Temple University Press.

Harris, A. (2017, February 20). #OscarsSoWhite Creator April Reign on Hollywood's
Progress and What Work Still Needs to Be Done. *Slate.* Retrieved from http://
www.slate.com/blogs/browbeat/2017/02/20/the_creator_of_oscarssowhite_on
_the_success_of_the_hashtag_and_the_work.html

Hasinoff, A. A. (2008). Fashioning race for the free market on *America's Next Top*

Model. Critical Studies in Media Communication, 25(3), 323–343. doi:10.1080/15295030802192012

Hatfield, E. F. (2010). "What it means to be a man": Examining hegemonic masculinity in *Two and a Half Men. Communication, Culture, & Critique, 3*(4), 526–548. doi:10.1111/j.1753-9137.2010.01084.x

Headley, C. (2010, July 2). The whitewashing of Hollywood. *WNYC*. Retrieved from https://www.wnyc.org/story/69861-whitewashing-hollywood/

Hellenbrand, M. (2008). Of myths and men: *Better Luck Tomorrow* and the mainstreaming of Asian American cinema. *Cinema Journal, 47*(4), 50–75. Retrieved from https://www.cmstudies.org/page/JCMS

Hesmondhalgh, D. (2007). *The cultural industries* (2nd ed.). Thousand Oaks, CA: Sage.

Hess, A. (2016, May 25). Asian-American actors are fighting for visibility. They will not be ignored. *The New York Times*. Retrieved from https://www.nytimes.com/2016/05/29/movies/asian-american-actors-are-fighting-for-visibility-they-will-not-be-ignored.html

Higate, P., & Hopton, J. (2005). War, Militarism and Masculinities. In M. S. Kimmel, J. Hearn, & R. Connell (Eds.), *Handbook of studies on men and masculinities* (pp. 432–447). Thousand Oaks, CA: Sage

Hoerl, K. (2009). Burning Mississippi into memory? Cinematic amnesia as a resource for remembering civil rights. *Critical Studies in Media Communication, 26*(1), 54–79. doi:10.1080/15295030802684059

Holland, J. J. (2016, June 23). Census: Asians remain fastest-growing racial group in US: New data from the Census Bureau shows that Asians remain the fastest-growing racial group in the United States. *U.S. News & World Report*. Retrieved from https://www.usnews.com/news/politics/articles/2016-06-23/census-asians-remain-fastest-growing-racial-group-in-us

hooks, b. (1992). *Black looks: Race and representation*. Boston: South End Press.

Horiguchi, S., & Imoto, Y. (2016). Historicizing mixed-race representations in Japan: From politicization to identity formation. In K. Iwabuchi, H. M. Kim, & H.-C. Hsia (Eds.), *Multiculturalism in East Asia: A transnational exploration of Japan, South Korea, and Taiwan* (pp. 163–184). New York: Rowman & Littlefield.

Hornaday, A. (2014, December 25). "The Interview" isn't that edgy. *The Washington Post*, p. C01.

Htun, T. T. (2012). Social identities of minority others in Japan: Listening to the narratives of Ainu, Buraku, and Zainichi Koreans. *Japan Forum, 24*(1), 1–22. doi:10.1080/09555803.2011.637635

Hu, B. (2017). The coin of the realm: Valuing the Asian American feature-length film. In L. K. Lopez & V. N. Pham (Eds.), *The Routledge companion to Asian American media* (pp. 63–73). New York: Routledge.

Hu, B., & Pham, V. N. (2017). In focus: Asian American film and media. *Cinema Journal, 56*(3), 115–118. doi:10.1353/cj.2017.0025

Hughey, M. W. (2010). The white savior film and reviewers' reception. *Symbolic Interaction, 33*(3), 475–496. doi:10.1525/si.2010.33.3.475

Hui, L. F. (2012). Interview: Filmmaker Daniel Hsia plays with cultural assumptions in "Shanghai Calling." Retrieved from https://asiasociety.org/blog/asia/interview-filmmaker-daniel-hsia-plays-cultural-assumptions-shanghai-calling

Hwang, D. H. (Writer), Tesori, J. (Composer), & Pinkleton, S. (Director). (2018, May 11). *Soft Power*. Live performance at the Ahmanson Theatre.

Itagaki, R. (2015). The anatomy of Korea-phobia in Japan. *Japanese Studies, 35*(1), 49–66. doi:10.1080/10371397.2015.1007496

Iwabuchi, K. (2004). How "Japanese" is Pokemon? In J. Tobin (Ed.), *Pikachu's global adventure: The rise and fall of Pokemon* (pp. 53–79). Durham, NC: Duke University Press.

Iwabuchi, K. (2017). In search of proximate enemies. *Japan Forum, 29*(4), 437–449. doi:10.1080/09555803.2017.1378704

Iwabuchi, K., Kim, H. M., & Hsia, H.-C. (2016). Rethinking multiculturalism from a trans-East-Asian perspective. In K. Iwabuchi, H. M. Kim, & H.-C. Hsia (Eds.), *Multiculturalism in East Asia: A transnational exploration of Japan, South Korea and Taiwan* (pp. 1–18). New York: Rowman & Littlefield.

Jasper, M. (2017). After *Ghost in the Shell* and *The Great Wall*, can we admit that whitewashing bombs at the box office? Retrieved from *The Mary Sue* website: https://www.themarysue.com/ghost-in-the-shell-box-office/

Jayakumar, U. M., & Adamian, A. S. (2017). The fifth frame of colorblind ideology: Maintaining the comforts of colorblindness in the context of white fragility. *Sociological Perspectives, 60*(5), 912–936. doi:10.1177/0731121147721910

Jenkins, H. (1992). *Textual poachers: Television fans & participatory culture*. New York: Routledge.

Johnson, J. R., Rich, M., & Cargile, A. C. (2008). "Why are you shoving this stuff down our throats?": Preparing intercultural educators to challenge performances of White racism. *Journal of International and Intercultural Communication, 1*(2), 113–135. doi:10.1080/17513050801891952

Johnson, P. E. (2017). Walter White(ness) lashes out: *Breaking Bad* and male victim-age. *Critical Studies in Media Communication, 34*(1), 14–28. doi:10.1080/15295036.2016.1238101

Jones, B., & Mukherjee, R. (2010). From California to Michigan: Race, rationality, and neoliberal governmentality. *Communication and Critical/Cultural Studies, 7*(4), 401–422. doi:10.1080/14791420.2010.523431

Jones, M. (2015, January 3). *No Escape* and erasure films: Hollywood's version of #AllLivesMatter.

Jung, S. (2006). Bae Yong-Joon, hybrid masculinity & the counter-coeval desire of Japanese female stars. *Particip@tions, 3*(2). https://www.participations.org/index.htm

Kakoudaki, D. (2011). Representing politics in disaster films. *International Journal of Media & Cultural Politics, 7*(3), 349–356. doi:10.1386/macp.7.3.349_3

Kang, L. H.-Y. (2002). The desiring of Asian female bodies: Interracial romance and cinematic subjection. In P. X. Feng (Ed.), *Screening Asian Americans* (pp. 71–98). New Brunswick, NJ: Rutgers University Press.

Kawai, Y. (2005). Stereotyping Asian Americans: The dialectic of the model minority and the yellow peril. *Howard Journal of Communications, 16*(2), 109–130. doi:10.1080/10646170590948974

Keane, S. (2006). *Disaster movies: The cinema of catastrophe* (2nd ed.). New York: Wallflower Press.

Kellner, D. (1995). *Media culture: Cultural studies, identity, and politics between the modern and the postmodern*. New York: Routledge.

Kelly, C. R. (2018). The wounded man: *Foxcatcher* and the incoherence of white masculine victimhood. *Communication and Critical/Cultural Studies, 15*(2), 161–178. doi:10.1080/14791420.2018.1456669

Kelly, C. R. (2020). *Apocalypse man: The death drive and the rhetoric of White masculine victimhood*. Columbus: Ohio State University Press.

Kennedy, L. (1996). Alien nation: White male paranoia and imperial culture in the United States. *Journal of American Studies, 30*(1), 87–100.

Kilday, G. (2017). "Ghost in the Shell": How a complex concept, "whitewashing" and critics kept crowds away. *The Hollywood Reporter*. Retrieved from https://www .hollywoodreporter.com/heat-vision/ghost-shell-how-a-complex-concept-white washing-critics-kept-crowds-away-990661

Kim, B. (2006). From exclusion to inclusion? The legal treatment of "foreigners" in contemporary Japan. *Immigration & Minorities, 24*(1), 51–73. doi:10.1080 /02619280600590225

Kim, B. (2008). Bringing class back in: The changing basis of inequality and the Korean minority in Japan. *Ethnic and Racial Studies, 31*(5), 871–898. doi:10 .1080/01419870701682279

Kim, J. (2015). From Cold Wars to the War on Terror: North Korea, racial morphing, and gendered parodies in *Die Another Day* and *Team America: World Police*. The *Journal of Popular Culture, 48*(1), 124–138.

Kim, J. K. (2015). Yellow over black: History of race in Korea and the new study of race and empire. *Critical Sociology, 41*(2), 205–217. doi:10.1177/0896920513507787

Kim, N. Y. (2006). "Patriarchy is so third world": Korean immigrant women and "migrating" White Western masculinity. *Social Problems, 53*(4), 519–536. doi:10 .1525/sp.2006.53.4.519

Kimmel, M. S. (2006). *Manhood in America: A cultural history*. New York: Oxford University Press.

Klein, H., & Shiffman, K. S. (2009). Underrepresentation and symbolic annihilation of socially disenfranchised groups ("out groups") in animated cartoons. *The Howard Journal of Communications, 20*(1), 55–72. doi:10.1080/10646170802665208

Kogan, L. R., Hoyt, W. D., Rickard, K. M., & Kellaway, J. A. (2004). Power in Black and White: The representation of power in women's magazines. *Media Report to Women, 32*(2), 13–18.

Kollin, S. (2010). "Remember, you're the good guy": *Hidalgo*, American identity, and histories of the Western. *American Studies, 51*(1/2), 5–25. Retrieved from https:// journals.ku.edu/amerstud/index

Konzett, D. C. (2017). *Hollywood's Hawaii: Race, nation, and war*. New Brunswick, NJ: Rutgers University Press.

Kornfield, S. (2012). The e-man-ci-pation of Jeannie: Feminist doppelgangers on U.S. television. *Communication, Culture, & Critique, 5*(3), 445–462. doi:10.1111/j.1753 -9137.2012.01136.x

Kraidy, M. (2005). *Hybridity, or the cultural logic of globalization*. Philadelphia: Temple University.

Lacroix, C. C. (2011). High stakes stereotypes: The emergence of the "Casino Indian" trope in television depictions of contemporary Native Americans. *Howard Journal of Communications, 22*(1), 1–23. doi:10.1080/10646175.2011.546738

Larabee, A. (2013). Editorial: The new television anti-hero. *The Journal of Popular Culture, 46*(6), 1131–1132. doi:10.1111/jpcu.12080

Lawler, K. (2016, November 7). Whitewashing controversy still haunts "Doctor Strange." *USA Today*. Retrieved from https://www.usatoday.com/story/life /entertainthis/2016/11/07/doctor-strange-whitewashing-ancient-one-tilda-swinton -fan-critical-reaction/93416130/

LeBlanc, A. K. (2018). "There's nothing I hate more than a racist": (Re)centering whiteness in *American Horror Story: Coven. Critical Studies in Media Communication, 35*(3), 273–285. doi:10.1080/15295036.2017.1416418

Lee, J. (2010). *The Japan of pure invention: Gilbert & Sullivan's* The Mikado. Minneapolis: University of Minnesota Press.

Lee, M. (2013). "47 Ronin" and the Hollywood outcast. Retrieved from http://www.racebending.com/v4/featured/47-ronin-hollywood-outcast/

Lee, M. (2016). Film review: Matt Damon in "The Great Wall." *Variety*. Retrieved from https://variety.com/2016/film/reviews/the-great-wall-review-chang-cheng-matt-damon-1201942358/

Lee, R. G. (1999). *Orientals: Asian Americans in popular culture*. Philadelphia: Temple University Press.

Lester, N. A., & Goggin, M. Daly. (2005). In living color: Politics of desire in heterosexual interracial Black/White personal ads. *Communication and Critical/Cultural Studies, 2*(2), 130–162. doi:10.1080/14791420500082668

Lippmann, W. (1927). *Public Opinion*. New York: Macmillan.

Lipsitz, G. (1998). *The possessive investment in Whiteness: How White people profit from identity politics*. Philadelphia: Temple University Press.

Locke, B. (2003). Here comes the judge: The dancing Itos and the televisual construction of the enemy Asian male. In G. Dines & J. M. Humez (Eds.), *Gender, race, and class in media: A text-reader* (2nd ed., pp. 651–655). Thousand Oaks, CA: Sage.

Locke, B. (2009). *Racial stigma on the Hollywood screen from World War II to the present: The Orientalist buddy film*. New York: Palgrave Macmillan.

Lopez, L. K. (2011). Fan activists and the politics of race in *The Last Airbender. International Journal of Cultural Studies, 15*(5), 431–445. doi:10.1177/1367877911422862

Lopez, L. K., & Pham, V. N. (2017). Introduction: Why Asian American media matters. In L. K. Lopez & V. N. Pham (Eds.), *The Routledge Companion to Asian American Media* (pp. 1–8). New York: Routledge.

Loughrey, C. (2017). *Ghost in the Shell*: Studio admits whitewashing controversy hurt film at the box office. *Independent*. Retrieved from https://www.independent.co.uk/arts-entertainment/films/news/ghost-in-the-shell-box-office-paramount-white washing-japanese-scarlett-johansson-a7669591.html

Lusksza, A. (2015). Sleeping with a vampire: Empowerment, submission, and female desire in contemporary vampire fiction. *Feminist Media Studies, 15*(3), 429–443. doi:10.1080/14680777.2014.945607

Madison, K. J. (1999). Legitimation crisis and containment: The "anti-racist-White-hero" film. *Critical Studies in Mass Communication, 16*(4), 399–416. doi:10.1080/15295039909367108

Maeseele, P., & van der Steen, L. (2016). Three twenty-first-century disaster films, the ideology of science and the future of the democratic debate. *Catalan Journal of Communication & Cultural Studies, 8*(2), 189–205. doi:10.1386/cjcs.8.2.189_1

Magnan-Park, A. H. (2018). Leukocentric Hollywood: Whitewashing, Alohagate, and the dawn of Hollywood with Chinese characteristics. *Asian Cinema, 29*(1), 133–162. doi:10.1386/ac.29.1.133_1

Marchetti, G. (1993). *Romance and the "yellow peril": Race, sex, and discursive strategies in Hollywood fiction*. Los Angeles: University of California Press.

Marston, K. (2016). The world is her oyster: Negotiating contemporary White womanhood in Hollywood's tourist spaces. *Cinema Journal, 55*(4), 3–27. doi:10.1353/cj.2016.0045

Matlow, R. (2007). *Love. Appropriation. Music. Baby: Gwen Stefani and her Harajuku girls* (Master's thesis, Concordia University).

Matsunaga, M., & Torigoe, C. (2008). Looking at the Japan-residing Korean identities through the eyes of the "outsiders within": Application and extension of co-cultural theory. *Western Journal of Communication, 72*(4), 349–373. doi:10.1080/10570310802446007

McFarlane, M. D. (2015). Anti-racist White hero, the sequel: Intersections of race(ism), gender, and social justice. *Critical Studies in Media Communication, 32*(2), 81–95. doi:10.1080/15295036.2014.1000350

McHenry, J. (2016). *Ghost in the Shell* casts Rila Fukushima, but not to replace Scarlett Johansson. *Vulture*. Retrieved from https://www.vulture.com/2016/05/rila-fukushima-joins-ghost-in-the-shell.html

McIntosh, P. (1988|2004). White privilege: Unpacking the invisible knapsack. In M. L. Andersen & P. Hill Collins (Eds.), *Race, class, and gender: An anthology* (5th ed., pp. 103–107). Belmont, CA: Thomson Wadsworth.

McRobbie, A. (2006). Post-feminism and popular culture: Bridget Jones and the new gender regime. In J. Curran & D. Morley (Eds.), *Media and cultural theory* (pp. 59–69). New York: Routledge.

Mendelson, S. (2017). Box office: "The Great Wall" targeted American and Chinese audiences but pleased neither. *Forbes*. Retrieved from https://www.forbes.com/sites/scottmendelson/2017/02/23/box-office-the-great-wall-targeted-american-and-chinese-audiences-but-pleased-neither/#51f7da902e23

Milazzo, M. (2015). The rhetorics of racial power: Enforcing colorblindness in post-Apartheid scholarship on race. *Journal of International and Intercultural Communication, 8*(1), 7–26. doi:10.1080/17513057.2015.991075

Miller, G. (1996). The death of the western hero: Martin Ritt's *Hud* and *Hombre*. *Film Criticism, 20*(3), 34–51. Retrieved from http://www.jstor.org/stable/44018853

Miranda, L. (2016). *Hamilton: An American musical*. New York: Grand Central Publishing.

Mittell, J. (2015). *Complex TV: The poetics of contemporary storytelling*. New York: New York University Press.

Morley, D., & Robins, K. (1995). *Spaces of identity: Global media, electronic landscapes and cultural boundaries*. New York: Routledge.

Mueller, J. C. (2017). Producing colorblindness: Everyday mechanisms of White ignorance. *Social Problems, 64*(2), 219–238. doi:10.1093/socpro/spw061

Mukherjee, R. (2006). *The racial order of things: Cultural imaginaries of the post-soul era*. Minneapolis: University of Minnesota Press.

Murphy, M. K., & Harris, T. M. (2018). White innocence and Black subservience: The rhetoric of White heroism in *The Help*. *Howard Journal of Communications, 29*(1), 49–62. doi:10.1080/10646175.2017.1327378

Nakayama, T. K. (1988). "Model minority" and the media: Discourse on Asian America. *Journal of Communication Inquiry, 12*(1), 65–73. doi:10.1177/019685998801200106

Nakayama, T. K. (1994). Show/down time: "Race," gender, sexuality, and popular culture. *Critical Studies in Mass Communication, 11*(2), 162–179. doi:10.1080/15295039409366893

Nakayama, T. K. (2017). What's next for whiteness and the Internet. *Critical Studies in Media Communication, 34*(1), 68–72. doi:10.1080/15295036.2016.1266684

Nakayama, T. K., & Krizek, R. L. (1995). Whiteness: A strategic rhetoric. *Quarterly Journal of Speech, 81*(3), 291–309. doi:10.1080/00335639509384117

Nelson, A. (2002). Introduction: Future texts. *Social Text, 71*(2), 1–15. doi:10.1215/01642472-20-2_71-1

Nishime, L. (2014). *Undercover Asian: Multiracial Asian Americans in visual culture.* Urbana: University of Illinois Press.

Nishime, L. (2017a). Mixed race matters: What Emma Stone and Bruno Mars can tell us about the future of Asian American media. *Cinema Journal, 56*(3), 148–152. doi:10.1353/cj.2017.0031

Nishime, L. (2017b). Whitewashing yellow futures in *Ex Machina, Cloud Atlas*, and *Advantageous. Journal of Asian American Studies, 20*(1), 29–49. doi:10.1353/jaas.2017.0003

North Korea continues protest on "kill Kim" film. (2014). *Korea Times*. Retrieved from http://www.koreatimes.co.kr/www/nation/2018/05/103_160718.html

No whitewashing: Zhang Yimou on the controversy about his new film. (2016). *Shenzhen Daily*. Retrieved from http://www.szdaily.com/content/2016-12/09/content_1447156 5.htm

Oehling, R. (1980). The yellow menace: Asian images in American film. In R. M. Miller (Ed.), *The kaleidoscopic lens: How Hollywood views ethnic groups* (pp. 182–206). Englewood, NJ: Jerome S. Ozer.

Oh, D. C. (2012). Black-Yellow fences: Multicultural boundaries and Whiteness in the *Rush Hour* franchise. *Critical Studies in Media Communication, 29*(5), 349–366. doi:10.1080/15295036.2012.697634

Oh, D. C. (2016). Techno-Orientalism and the yellow peril in the Wolverine movies. In C. Bucciferro (Ed.), *The X-Men films: A cultural analysis* (pp. 151–164). Landham, MD: Rowman & Littlefield.

Oh, D. C. (2017). "Turning Japanese": Deconstructive criticism of White women, the Western imagination, and popular music. *Communication, Culture, & Critique, 10*(2), 365–381. doi:10.1111/cccr.12153

Oh, D. C. (2018a). Elder men's bromance in Asian lands: Normative Western masculinity in *Better Late Than Never. Critical Studies in Media Communication, 35*(4), 350–362. doi:10.1080/15295036.2018.1463102

Oh, D. C. (2018b). Seeing myself through film: Diasporic belongings and racial identifications. *Cultural Studies <-> Critical Methodologies, 18*(2), 107–115. doi:10.1177/1532708617742045

Oh, D. C., & Banjo, O. O. (2012). Outsourcing postracialism: Voicing neoliberal multiculturalism in *Outsourced. Communication Theory, 22*(4), 449–470. doi:10.1111/j.1468-2885.2012.01414.x

Oh, D. C., & Kutufam, D. V. (2014). The Orientalized "other" and corrosive femininity: Threats to White masculinity in *300. Journal of Communication Inquiry, 38*(2), 149–165. doi:10.1177/0196859914523983

Oh, D. C., & Nishime, L. (2019). Imag(in)ing the post-national television fan: Counterflows and hybrid ambivalence in Dramaworld. *International Communication Gazette, 81*(2), 121–138. doi:10.1177/1748048518802913

Oh, D. C., & Wong Lowe, A. (2016). Spectacles in hybrid Japan: Deconstruction, semiotic excess, and obtuse meanings in *Lost in Translation. Journal of*

International and Intercultural Communication, 10(2), 153–167. doi:10.1080/1751305 .2016.1231335

Okada, J. (2015). *Making Asian American film and video: Histories, institutions, and movements*. New Brunswick, NJ: Rutgers University Press.

Omi, M., & Winant, H. (1994). *Racial formations in the United States: From the 1960s to the 1990s* (2nd ed.). New York: Routledge.

Ono, K. A. (2010). Postracism: A theory of the "post"-as political strategy. *Journal of Communication Inquiry, 34*(3), 227–233. doi:10.1177/0196859910371375

Ono, K. A., & Jiao, J. Y. (2008). China in the US imaginary: Tibet, the Olympics, and the 2008 earthquake. *Communication and Critical/Cultural Studies, 5*(4), 406–410. doi:10.1080/14791420802416168

Ono, K. A., & Pham, V. N. (2009). *Asian Americans and the media*. Malden, MA: Polity.

Ono, K. A., & Sloop, J. M. (1995). The critique of vernacular discourse. *Communication Monographs, 62*(1), 19–46. doi:10.1080/03637759509376346

Oshima, K. (2014). Perception of *hafu* or mixed-race people in Japan: Group-session studies among *hafu* students at a Japanese university. *Intercultural Communication Studies, 33*(3), 22–34.

Palencia, C. S. (2015). "The tropics make it difficult to mope": The imaginative geography of Alexander Payne's *The Descendants* (2011). *International Journal of English Studies, 15*(2), 81–95. doi:10.6018/ijes/2015/2/222671

Palumbo-Liu, D. (1999). *Asian/American: Historical crossings of a racial frontier*. Palo Alto, CA: Stanford University Press.

Park, J. (2008). Virtual race: The racially ambiguous action hero in *The Matrix* and *Pitch Black*. In M. Beltrán & C. Fojas (Eds.), *Mixed race Hollywood* (pp. 182–202). New York: New York University Press.

Park, S. (2017). Inventing aliens: Immigration control, "xenophobia" and racism in Japan. *Race & Class, 58*(3), 64–80. doi:10.1177/0306396816657719

Paulk, C. (2011). Post-national cool: William Gibson's Japan. *Science Fiction Studies, 38*(3), 478–500. doi:10.5621/sciefictstud.38.3.0478

Peng, W. (2016). Chasing the dragon's tail: Sino-Australian film co-productions. *Media International Australia, 159*(1), 73–82. doi:10.1177/1329878X16638939

Pérez, E. (2009). *Forgetting the Alamo, or, Blood Memory*. Austin: University of Texas Press.

Perez, R. (2013). Learning to make racism funny in the "color-blind" era: Stand-up comedy students, performance strategies, and the (re)production of racist jokes in public. *Discourse & Society, 24*(4), 478–503. doi:10.1177/0957926513482066

Perks, L. G. (2010). Polysemic scaffolding: Explicating discursive clashes in *Chappelle's Show*. *Communication, Culture & Critique, 3*(2), 270–289. doi:10.1111 /j.1753-9137.2010.01070.x

Pham, M.-H. T. (2004). The Asian invasion (of multiculturalism) in Hollywood. *Journal of Popular Film & Television, 32*(3), 121–131. doi:10.1080/01956051.2004 .10662057

Phillips, J. (1999). Lagging behind: Bhabha, post-colonial theory and the future. In S. Clark (Ed.), *Travel writing and empire: Postcolonial theory in transit* (pp. 63–80). New York: Zed Books.

Pieterse, J. N. (1992). *White on Black: Images of Africa and Blacks in Western popular culture* (J. N. Pieterse, Trans.). New Haven, CT: Yale University Press.

Pollard, T. (2017). Hollywood's Asian-Pacific pivot: Stereotypes, xenophobia, and racism. *Perspectives on Global Development and Technology, 16*(1–3), 131–144. doi:10.1163/15691497-12341424

Prashad, V. (2001). *Everybody was kung fu fighting: Afro-Asian connections and the myth of cultural purity.* Boston: Beacon Press.

Prendergast, C. (2007). Asians: The present absence in *Crash. College English, 69*(4), 347–348.

Projansky, S., & Ono, K. A. (1999). Strategic whiteness as cinematic racial politics. In T. K. Nakayama & J. N. Martin (Eds.), *Whiteness: The communication of social identity* (pp. 149–174). Thousand Oaks, CA: Sage.

Puccini, G. (1986) *Madama Butterfly: Libretto.* New York: G. Schirmer, Inc. (Original work published 1898).

Rabin, N. M. (2012). Picturing the mix: Visual and linguistic representations in Kip Fulbeck's *Part Asian·100% Hapa. Critical Studies in Media Communication, 29*(5), 387–402. doi:10.1080/15295036.2012.691610

Rada, J. A., & Wulfemeyer, K. T. (2004). Calling class: Sports announcers and the culture of poverty. In D. Heider (Ed.), *Class and News* (pp. 150–164). New York: Rowman & Littlefield.

Rich, K. (2013). What went wrong with *47 Ronin*? Oh, pretty much everything. *Vanity Fair.* Retrieved from https://www.vanityfair.com/news/2013/12/47-ronin-what -went-wrong

Richards, J. (1999). From Christianity to paganism: The new "Middle Ages" and the values of "Medieval" masculinity. *Cultural Values, 3*(2), 213–234. doi: 10.1080 /14797589909367162

Rivas, Z. M. (2015). Mistura for the fans: Performing mixed-race Japanese Brazilian-ness in Japan. *Journal of Intercultural Studies, 36*(6), 710–728. doi:10.1080/0725686 8.2015.1095714

Rodgers, R., & Hammerstein, O. (1951). *The King and I.* New York: Williamson Music.

Rogers, K. (2016, May 10). John Cho, starring in every movie ever made? A diversity hashtag is born. *The New York Times.* Retrieved from https://www.nytimes.com /2016/05/11/movies/john-cho-starring-in-every-movie-ever-made-a-diversity -hashtag-is-born.html

Rose, S. (2017). *Ghost in the Shell*'s whitewashing: Does Hollywood have an Asian problem. *The Guardian.* Retrieved from https://www.theguardian.com/film/2017 /mar/31/ghost-in-the-shells-whitewashing-does-hollywood-have-an-asian-problem

Ruthven, A. (2017). The contemporary postfeminist dystopia: Disruptions and hopeful gestures in Suzanne Collins' *The Hunger Games. Feminist Review, 116*(1), 47–62. doi: 10.1057/s41305-017-0064-9

Ryang, S. (2014). Space and time: The experience of the Zainichi, the ethnic Korean population of Japan. *Urban Anthropology and Studies of Cultural Systems and World Economic Development, 43*(4), 519–550. Retrieved from https://www.jstor .org/journal/urbaanthstudcult?refreqid=excelsior%3Ad168fc7e1836188928 1a8e066 8911652

Said, E. W. (1978). *Orientalism.* New York: Vintage Books.

Sampson, M. (2016). Exclusive: "Ghost in the Shell" producers reportedly tested visual effects that would make actors appear Asian. *Screen Crush.* Retrieved from https://screencrush.com/ghost-in-the-shell-whitewashing-scarlett-johnasson-vfx/

Sánchez-Escalonilla, A. (2010). Hollywood and the rhetoric of panic: The popular genres of action and fantasy in the wake of the 9/11 attacks. *Journal of Popular Film & Television, 38*(1), 10–20. doi:10.1080/01956050903449640

Sandoval, A. M. (2008). *Toward a Latina feminism of the Americas: Repression and resistance in Chicana and Mexicana literature.* Austin: University of Texas Press.

Saul, R. (2010). KevJumba and the adolescence of YouTube. *Educational Studies, 46*(5), 457–477. doi:10.1080/00131946.2010.510404

Schaub, J. C. (2001). Kusanagi's body: Gender and technology in mecha-anime. *Asian Journal of Communication, 11*(2), 79–100. doi:10.1080/01292980109364805

Schiller, D. (2008). China in the United States. *Communication and Critical/Cultural Studies, 5*(4), 411–415. doi: 10.1080/14791420802416176

Schulman, N. M. (1992). Laughing across the color barrier: *In Living Color. Journal of Popular Film & Television, 20*(1), 2–7. doi: 10.1080/01956051.1992.9943957

Schultz, J. (2014). *Glory Road* (2006) and the White savior historical sport film. *Journal of Popular Film & Television, 42*(4), 205–213. doi:10.1080/01956051.2014.913001

Seo, H. (2009). International media coverage of North Korea: Study of journalists and news reports on the six-party nuclear talks. *Asian Journal of Communication, 19*(1), 1–17. doi:10.1080/01292980802618056

Sharf, Z. (n.d.). 25 worst cases of Hollywood whitewashing since 2000. *IndieWire.* Retrieved from http://www.indiewire.com/gallery/hollywood-whitewashing-25-roles-emma-stone-jake-gyllenhaal-scarlett-johansson/

Shaw, L., & Waxman, S. (2012). Universal pulls *47 Ronin* from director as budget swells to $225M. *The Wrap.* Retrieved from https://www.thewrap.com/universal-pulls-47-ronin-director-budget-swells-225m-exclusive-57111/

Shim, D. (1998). From yellow peril through model minority to renewed yellow peril. *Journal of Communication Inquiry, 22*(4), 385–409. doi:10.1177/0196859998022004004

Shimizu, C. P. (2007). *The Hypersexuality of Race: Performing Asian/American Women on Screen and Scene.* Durham, NC: Duke University Press.

Shimizu, C. P. (2017). Gnawing at the whiteness of cinema studies: On Asian American media now. *Cinema Journal, 56*(3), 119–124. doi:10.1353.cj.2017.0026

Shipper, A. W. (2010). Nationalisms of and against Zainichi Koreans in Japan. *Asian Politics & Policy, 2*(1), 55–75. doi:10.1111/j.1943-0787.2009.01167.x

Shohat, E., & Stam, R. (1994). *Unthinking Eurocentrism: Multiculturalism and the media.* New York: Routledge.

Shome, R. (1996). Race and popular cinema: The rhetorical strategies of whiteness in *City of Joy. Communication Quarterly, 44*(4), 502–518. doi:10.1080/10646170500207899

Shome, R. (2014). *Diana and beyond: White femininity, national identity, and contemporary media culture.* Urbana: University of Illinois Press.

Shugart, H. A. (2001). Parody as subversive performance: Denaturalizing gender and reconstituting desire in *Ellen. Text and Performance Quarterly, 21*(2), 95–113. doi:10.1080/10462930128124

Sienkiewicz, M., & Marx, N. (2009). Beyond a cutout world: Ethnic humor and discursive integration in *South Park. Journal of Film and Video, 61*(2), 5–18. Retrieved from http://www.press.uillinois.edu/journals/jfv.html

Sinha-Roy, P. (2020). Oscars: From "Joker" to "The Irishman," white male stories dominate nominations. *The Hollywood Reporter.* Retrieved from https://www

.hollywoodreporter.com/news/joker-irishman-white-male-stories-dominate-oscar
-nominees-1269170

Smith, N. M. (2015). Emma Stone says *Aloha* casting taught her about whitewashing in
Hollywood. *The Guardian*. Retrieved from https://www.theguardian.com/film
/2015/jul/17/emma-stone-admits-her-casting-in-aloha-was-misguided

Smith, S. L., Choueiti, M., & Pieper, K. (2016). *Inclusion or invisibility? Comprehensive
Annenberg report on diversity in entertainment*. Retrieved from https://annenberg
.usc.edu/sites/default/files/2017/04/07/MDSCI_CARD_Report_FINAL_Exec
_Summary.pdf

Sony backtracks on yanking *The Interview*. (2014). *The Toronto Star*, p. E2.

Su, W. (2017). A brave new world? Understanding U.S.-China coproductions:
Collaboration, conflicts, and obstacles. *Critical Studies in Media Communication,
34*(5), 480–494. doi:10.1080/15295036.2017.1349326

Sullivan, S. (2006). *Revealing whiteness: The unconscious habits of racial privilege*.
Bloomington: Indiana University Press.

Sun, C. F. (2003). Ling Woo in historical context: The new face of Asian American
stereotypes on television. In G. Dines & J. M. Humez (Eds.), *Gender, race, and class
in media: A text-reader* (2nd ed., pp. 656–664). Thousand Oaks, CA: Sage.

Supriya, K. E. (1999). White difference: Cultural constructions of white identity.
In T. K. Nakayama & J. N. Martin (Eds.), *Whiteness: The communication of social
identity* (pp. 129–148). Thousand Oaks, CA: Sage.

Syed, J., & Ali, F. (2011). The White woman's burden: From colonial *civilisation* to
Third World *development*. *Third World Quarterly, 32*(2), 349–365. doi:10.1080/0143
6597.2011.560473

Tai, E. (2004). "Korean Japanese": A new identity option for resident Koreans in
Japan. *Critical Asian Studies, 36*(3), 355–382. doi:10.1080/1467271042000241586

Tan, K. (2018). Interview: Daniel Hsia, writer and director of *Shanghai Calling*.
Retrieved from http://shanghaiist.com/2012/09/27/interview_daniel_hsia
_shanghai_calling/

Taylor, J. T. (2015). "You can't spend your whole life on a surfboard": Elvis Presley,
exotic Whiteness, and native performance in *Blue Hawaii* and *Girls! Girls!
Girls! Quarterly Journal of Film and Video, 32*(1), 21–37. doi:10.1080/10509208
.2012.757532

Thompson, E. (2009). "I am not down with that": *King of the Hill* and sitcom satire.
Journal of Film and Video, 61(2), 38–51. doi:10.1353/jfv.0.0029

Thornton, D. J. (2011). Psych's comedic tale of Black-White friendship and the
lighthearted affect of "post-race" America. *Critical Studies in Media Communication, 28*(5), 424–449. doi:10.1080/15295036.2010.518621

Thussu, D. K. (2007). Mapping global media flow and contra-flow. In D. K. Thussu (Ed.),
Media on the move: Global flow and contra-flow (pp. 11–32). New York: Routledge.

Tierney, S. M. (2006). Themes of Whiteness in *Bulletproof Monk, Kill Bill*, and *The
Last Samurai. Journal of Communication, 56*(3), 607–624. doi:10.1111/j.1460
-2466.2006.00303.x

Törngren, S. O. (2018). Ethnic options, covering and passing: Multiracial and
multiethnic identities in Japan. *Asian Journal of Social Science, 46*(6), 748–773.
Retrieved from https://brill.com/view/journals/ajss/ajss-overview.xml

Triana, B. (2018). Deadpool: When our (anti)heroes do less and we reward them more.
The Journal of Popular Culture, 51(4), 1016–1035. doi:10.1111/jpcu.12712

Tsukawaki, R. (2017). So you want to talk about Ghost in the Shell: The whitewashed edition? *HuffPost*. Retrieved from https://www.huffpost.com/entry/so-you-want -to-talk-about-ghost-in-the-shell-the-whitewashed_b_58f90f6ee4b0f02c3870e803

Tuchman, G. (1978). *Making news: A study in the construction of reality*. New York: The Free Press.

Tuck, E., & Yang, K. W. (2012). Decolonization is not a metaphor. *Decolonization: Indigeneity, Education, & Society, 1*(1), 1–40. Retrieved from https://jps.library .utoronto.ca/index.php/des/index

Turner, K. S. H. (1999). From classical to imperial: Changing visions of Turkey in the Eighteenth Century. In S. Clark (Ed.), *Travel writing and empire: Postcolonial theory in transit* (pp. 113–128). New York: Zed Books.

Vaage, M. B. (2015). *The antihero in American television*. New York: Routledge.

Visočnik, N. (2014). Living on the edge: Buraku in Kyoto, Japan. *Anthropological Notebooks, 20*(2), 127–143. Retrieved from http://www.drustvo-antropologov.si /anthropological_notebooks_eng.html

von Tunzelmann, A. (2013). The Impossible submerges the true impact of the tsunami. *The Guardian*. Retrieved from https://www.theguardian.com/film/filmblog/2013 /jan/03/reel-history-the-impossible

von Tunzelmann, A. (2014). *47 Ronin*: fighting? Yes. To stay awake. *The Guardian*. Retrieved from https://www.theguardian.com/film/filmblog/2014/may/29/47 -ronin-reel-history-fighting-to-stay-awake

Wald, G. (2009). Same difference: Racial masculinity in Hong Kong and cop-buddy "hybrids." In S.-K. Tan, P. X. Feng, & G. Marchetti (Eds.), *Chinese connections: Critical perspectives on film, identity, and diaspora* (pp. 68–81). Philadelphia, PA: Temple University Press.

Wang, F. K.-H. (2016). Asian-American students targets of bullying: Federal report. *NBC News*. Retrieved from https://www.nbcnews.com/news/asian-america/asian -american-students-targets-bullying-federal-report-n633566

Watts, E. K. (2005). Border patrolling and "passing" in Eminem's *8 Mile*. *Critical Studies in Media Communication, 22*(3), 187–206. doi:10.1080/07393180500201686

Watts, E. K. (2010). The (nearly) apocalyptic politics of "postracial" America: Or "This is now the United States of Zombieland." *Journal of Communication Inquiry, 34*(3), 214–222. doi:10.1177/0196859910371375

Watts, E. K. (2017). Postracial fantasies, blackness, and zombies. *Communication and Critical/Cultural Studies, 14*(4), 317–333. doi:10.1080/14791420.2017.1338742

Wayne, M. L. (2014). Mitigating colorblind racism in the postnetwork era: Class-inflected masculinities in *The Shield, Sons of Anarchy,* and *Justified*. *The Communication Review, 17*(3), 183–201. doi:10.1080/10714421.2014.930271

Whitewashing, a long history. (2016). *The New York Times*. Retrieved from https:// www.nytimes.com/slideshow/2016/04/22/opinion/whitewashing-a-long-history/s /chow-ss-slide-HTTQ.html

Wilkins, K., & Downing, J. (2002). Mediating terrorism: Text and protest in interpretations of *The Siege*. *Critical Studies in Media Communication, 19*(4), 419–437. doi:10.1080/07393180216571

Winn, P. (n.d.). Hollywood made a zombie movie but replaced the zombies with Asians. *PRI*. Retrieved from https://www.pri.org/stories/hollywood-made-zombie -movie-replaced-zombies-asians#:~:text=Hollywood%20made%20a%20 zombie%20movie%20but%20replaced%20the%20zombies%20with%20Asians,

-GlobalPost&text=BANGKOK%20%E2%80%94%20Behold%20the%20
trailer%20for,against%20faceless%20Southeast%20Asian%20hordes.

Womack, Y. L. (2013). *Afrofuturism*. Chicago: Lawrence Hill Books.

Wong, C. (n.d.). *Already Tomorrow in Hong Kong.* Q&A with Director Emily Ting. *Borrowing Tape.* Retrieved from https://borrowingtape.com/interviews/already-tomorrow-hong-kong-qa-director-emily-ting

Wong, D. (2012). The remake as translation: Localism, globalism and the afterlife of horror films. *Translation Quarterly, 66,* 21–30. Retrieved from https://cup.cuhk.edu.hk/index.php?route=product/product&product_id=3072

Wu, F. H. (2002). *Yellow: Race in America beyond Black and White*. New York: Basic Books.

Yamaguchi, T. (2013). Xenophobia in action: Ultranationalism, hate speech, and the Internet in Japan. *Radical History Review, 117,* 98–118. doi:10.1215/01636545-2210617

Yamano, S. (2005). *Manga Kenkanryu [Hate Korean Wave Manga]*. Tokyo: Shinyosha.

Yamato, G. (2004). Something about the subject makes it hard to name. In M. L. Andersen & P. Hill Collins (Eds.), *Race, class, and gender: An anthology* (pp. 99–103). Belmont, CA: Thomson Wadsworth.

Yamato, J. (2015). The unbearable whiteness of Cameron Crowe's *Aloha*: A Hawaii-set film starring Asian Emma Stone. *Daily Beast.* Retrieved from https://www.thedailybeast.com/the-unbearable-whiteness-of-cameron-crowes-aloha-a-hawaii-set-film-starring-asian-emma-stone

Yang, J. (2014). The reinvention of Hollywood's classic white saviour tale in contemporary Chinese cinema: *Pavilion of Women* and *The Flowers of War. Critical Arts: A South-North Journal of Cultural & Media Studies, 28*(2), 247–263. doi:10.1080/02560046.2014.906343

Yoshihara, M. (2002). *Embracing the East: White women and American Orientalism*. New York: Oxford University Press.

Yoshihara, M. (2004). The flight of the Japanese butterfly: Orientalism, nationalism, and performances of Japanese womanhood. *American Quarterly, 56*(4), 975–1001. doi:10.1353/aq.2004.0067

Yousman, B. (2003). Blackophilia and Blackophobia: White youth, the consumption of rap music, and White supremacy. *Communication Theory, 13*(4), 366–391. doi:10.1111/j.1468-2885.2003.tb00297.x

Yu, L. (2008). Oriental cities, postmodern futures: *Naked Lunch, Blade Runner,* and *Neuromancer. MELUS, 33*(4), 45–71. doi:10.1093/melus/33.4.45

Yuen, N. W. (2017). *Reel inequality: Hollywood actors and racism*. New Brunswick, NJ: Rutgers University Press.

Multimedia References

Ansari, A., Yang, A., Schur, M., Becky, D., & Miner, D. (Executive Producers). (2015–2021). *Master of None* [TV Series]. Alan Yang Productions.

Avildsen, J. G. (Director). (1984). *The Karate Kid* [Film]. Columbia Pictures.

Ball, W. (Director). (2014). *The Maze Runner* [Film]. Gotham Group.

Ball, W. (Director). (2015). *Maze Runner: Scorch Trials* [Film]. Gotham Group.

Ball, W. (Director). (2018). *Maze Runner: The Death Cure* [Film]. Gotham Group.

Bang, H. (Executive Producer). (2015–2016) *Where is My Friend's Home?* [TV Series]. JTBC.

Bayona, J. A. (Director). (2012a). *The Impossible* [Film]. Mediaset España.

Bayona, J. A. (Director). (2012b). *The Impossible* [Film; Audio commentary with Director J. A. Bayona, Writer Sergio G. Sanchez, Producer Belen Atienza, and Maria Belón on DVD]. Summit Entertainment.

Berg, P. (Director). (2012). *Battleship* [Film]. Bluegrass Films.

Bessho, K., & Masaki, M. (Executive Producers). (1963–1966). *Astro Boy* [TV Series]. Mushi Production.

Besson, L. (Director). (2014). *Lucy* [Film]. EuropaCorp.

Black, S. (Director). (2013). *Iron Man 3* [Film]. Marvel Studios.

Bong, J. H. (Director). (2017). *Okja* [Film]. Kate Street Productions.

Bradley, D. (Director). (2012). *Red Dawn* [Film]. Metro-Goldwyn Mayer.

Brooks, M., & Henry, B. (Creators). (1965–1970). *Get Smart* [TV Series]. CBS Television Network.

Buck, S. (Creator). (2017-2018). *Iron Fist* [TV Series]. Marvel Television.

Burger, N. (Director). (2014). *Divergent* [Film]. Red Wagon Entertainment.

Carpenter, J. (Director). (1978). *Halloween* [Film]. Compass International Pictures.

Chu, J. M. (Director). (2018). *Crazy Rich Asians* [Film]. Warner Bros.

Coogler, R. (Director). (2018). *Black Panther* [Film]. Walt Disney Pictures.

Coppolla, S. (Director). (2003). *Lost in Translation* [Film]. Focus Features.

Cosmatos, G. P. (Director). (1985). *Rambo: First Blood Part II*. Estudios Churubusco Azteca S.A.

Crowe, C. (Director). (2015b). *Aloha* [Film]. Sony Pictures Entertainment.

Crowe, C. (Director). (2015c). *Aloha* [Film; *Making of Aloha* Special Feature on DVD]. Sony Pictures Entertainment.

Cunningham, S. S. (Director). (1980). *Friday the 13th* [Film]. Paramount Pictures.

David, L., & Seinfeld, J. (1989-1998). *Seinfeld* [TV Series]. Castle Rock Entertainment.

DeGroot, N. (Director). (2016–2018). *Better Late Than Never* [TV Series]. National Broadcasting Company.

Derrickson, S. (Director). (2016). *Doctor Strange* [Film]. Marvel Studios.

Dowdle, J. E. (Director). (2015). *No Escape* [Film]. Bold Films.

Dowdle, J. E. (Director). (2015b). *No Escape* [Film; Feature commentary with Writer/Director John Erick Dowdle and Writer/Producer Drew Dowdle on DVD]. Bold Films.

Erickson, D., & Kirkman, R. (Creators). (2015–). *Fear the Walking Dead* [TV Series]. Skybound Entertainment.

Feig, P. (Director). (2019). *Last Christmas* [Film]. Calamity Films

Forster, M. (Director). (2013). *World War Z* [Film]. Plan B Entertainment.

Franklin, S. (Director). (1937). *The Good Earth* [Film]. Metro-Goldwyn-Mayer.

Fuqua, A. (Director). (2013). *Olympus Has Fallen* [Film]. FortyFour Studios.

Gartner, J. (Director). (2006). *Glory Road* [Film]. Walt Disney Pictures.

Goldberg, E., & Rogen, S. (Directors). (2014a). *The Interview* [Film]. Columbia Pictures.

Goldberg, E., & Rogen, S. (Directors). (2014b). *The Interview* [Film; Director's commentary on DVD]. Columbia Pictures

Goldberg, E., & Rogen, S. (Directors). (2014). *This Is the End* [Film]. Point Grey Productions.

Gordon, M., Sertner, R., Pepper, N., Safran, J., Seitzman, M., & Coburn, J. (Executive Producers). (2015–2018) *Quantico* [TV Series]. The Mark Gordon Company.

Green, D. G. (Director). (2008). *Pineapple Express*. Columbia Pictures.

Griffith, D. W. (Director). (1919). *Broken Blossoms* [Film]. D. W. Griffith Productions.

Griffith, D. W. (Director). (1920). *The Idol Dancer* [Film]. D. W. Griffith Productions.

Gunn, J. (Director). (2014). *Guardians of the Galaxy* [Film]. Walt Disney Pictures.

Gunn, J. (Director). (2017). *Guardians of the Galaxy Vol. 2* [Film]. Walt Disney Pictures.

Hancock, J. L. (Director). (2009). *The Blind Side* [Film]. Alcon Entertainment.

Hemingway, A. (Director). (2012). *Red Tails* [Film]. Twentieth Century Fox.

Herek, S. (Director). (1989). *Bill and Ted's Excellent Adventure* [Film]. De Laurentiis Film Partners.

Hoene, M. (Director). (2016a). *Enter the Warriors Gate* [Film]. Fundamental Films.

Hoene, M. (Director). (2016b). *Enter the Warriors Gate* [Film; Beyond the Gate: Making *Enter the Warriors Gate* on DVD]. Fundamental Films.

Hoene, M. (Director). (2016c). *Enter the Warriors Gate* [Film; Audio commentary with Director Matthias Hoene on DVD]. Fundamental Films.

Hsia, D. (Director). (2012a). *Shanghai Calling* [Film]. Americatown.

Hsia, D. (Director). (2012b). *Shanghai Calling* [Film; *Shanghai Calling: Behind the Scenes* Special Feature on DVD]. Americatown.

Hunter, P. (Director). (2003). *Bulletproof Monk* [Film]. Lakeshore Entertainment.

Jackson, P. (Director). *The Lord of the Rings: The Return of the King* [Film]. New Line Cinema.

Jang, J. (Executive Producer). (2017–) *Welcome! First Time in Korea?* [TV Series]. MBC.

Jeong, S. (Producer). (2015–2016). *Global Family Living in Korea* [TV Series]. EBS.

Johnson, S. (Director). (2018). *To All the Boys I've Loved Before* [Film]. Awesomeness Films.

Khan, N. (Director). (2019). *Always Be My Maybe* [Film]. Netflix.

Kim, S. (Producer). (2005). *My Lovely Samsoon* [TV Series]. MBC Production.

King, H. (Director). (1955). *Love Is a Many-Splendored Thing* [Film]. Twentieth Century Fox.

Kishimito, M. (Creator). (2002–2007). *Naruto* [TV Series]. Pierrot.

LaGravenese, R. (Director). (2007). *Freedom Writers* [Film]. Paramount Pictures.

Lawrence, F. (Director). (2013). *The Hunger Games: Catching Fire* [Film]. Lionsgate.

Lawrence, F. (Director). (2014). *The Hunger Games: Mockingjay—Part I* [Film]. Lionsgate.

Lawrence, F. (Director). (2015). *The Hunger Games: Mockingjay—Part 2* [Film]. Lionsgate.

Leiner, D. (Director). (2004). *Harold and Kumar Go to White Castle* [Film]. Endgame Entertainment.

Lemmons, K. (Director). (2019). *Harriet* [Film]. Perfect World Productions.

Lester, M. (Director). (1991). *Showdown in Little Tokyo* [Film]. Little Tokyo Productions.

Lim, J., & Cho, S. (Executive Producers). (2014–). *Abnormal Summit* [TV Series]. JTBC.

Lin, J. (Director). (2002). *Better Luck Tomorrow* [Film]. Cherry Sky Films.

Lin, J. (Director). (2006). *The Fast and the Furious: Tokyo Drift* [Film]. Universal Pictures.

Lin, J. (Director). (2009). *Fast & Furious* [Film]. Universal Pictures.

Lin, J. (Director). (2011). *Fast Five* [Film]. Universal Pictures.

Lin, J. (Director). (2013). *Fast & Furious 6* [Film]. Universal Pictures.

Lin, J. (Director). (2021). *F9* [Film]. Universal Pictures.

Linklater, R. (Director). (1995). *Before Sunrise* [Film]. Castle Rock Entertainment.

Luketic, R. (Director). (2008). *21* [Film]. Columbia Pictures.

Mangold, J. (Director). (2013). *The Wolverine* [Film]. Twentieth Century Fox.

MacFarlane, S., & Zuckerman, D. (Creators). (1999–) *Family Guy* [TV Series]. Fox Television Animation.

Mann, M. (Director). (1992). *The Last of the Mohicans* [Film]. Morgan Creek Entertainment.

Minami, M., & Ikeguchi, K. (Executive Producers). (1998–1999). *Cowboy Bebop* [TV Series]. Bandai Visual Company.

Mottola, G. (Director). (2007). *Superbad* [Film]. Apatow Productions

Newell, M. (Director). (2010). *Prince of Persia: The Sands of Time* [Film]. Walt Disney Pictures.

Oeding, L. (Director). (2018). *Braven* [Film]. Hassell Free Productions.

Otomo, K. (Director). (1988). *Akira* [Film]. Akira Committee Company.

Park, H., & Kim, J. (Executive Producers). (2006–2010). *Global Talk Show* [TV Series]. KBS.

Parker, A. (Director). (1988). *Mississippi Burning* [Film]. Orion Pictures.

Parker, T. (Director). (2004). *Team America: World Police* [Film]. Scott Rudin Productions.

Payne, A. (Director). (2011). *The Descendants* [Film]. Fox Searchlight Pictures.

Peele, J. (Director). (2019). *Us* [Film]. Monkeypaw Productions.

Powell, N. (Director). (2014a). *Outcast* [Film]. Notorious Films.

Powell, N. (Director). (2014b). *Outcast* [Film; Interviews with cast and crew on DVD]. Notorious Films.

Proyas, A. (Director). (2016). *Gods of Egypt* [Film]. Summit Entertainment.

Quine, R. (Director). (1960). *The World of Suzie Wong* [Film]. World Enterprises.

Reitman, I. (Director). (1984). *Ghostbusters* [Film]. Columbia Pictures.

Rinch, C. (Director). (2013). *47 Ronin* [Film]. Bluegrass Films.

Ross, G. (Director). (2012). *The Hunger Games* [Film]. Lionsgate.

Rourke, J. (Director). (2018). *Mary Queen of Scots* [Film]. Focus Features.

Sanders, R. (Director). (2017). *Ghost in the Shell* [Film]. Paramount Pictures.

Scafaria, L. (Director). (2019). *Hustlers* [Film]. Gloria Sanchez Pictures.

Schumacher, J. (Director). (1993). *Falling Down* [Film]. Alcor Films.

Schwentke, R. (Director). (2015). *The Divergent Series: Insurgent* [Film]. Red Wagon Entertainment.

Schwentke, R. (Director). (2016). *Allegiant* [Film]. Red Wagon Entertainment.

Scott, R. (Director). (1982). *Blade Runner* [Film]. The Ladd Company.

Scott, T. (Director). (1986). *Top Gun* [Film]. Paramount Pictures

Sherman-Palladino, A., Palladino, D., Polone, G., & Rosenthal, D. S. (Executive Producers). (2000–2007). *Gilmore Girls* [TV Series]. Dorothy Parker Drank Here Productions.

Shyamalan, M. N. (Director). (2010). *The Last Airbender* [Film]. Paramount Pictures.

Showalter, M. (Director). (2017). *The Big Sick* [Film]. Apatow Productions.

Smith, J. (Director). (1995). *Dangerous Minds* [Film]. Hollywood Pictures.

Snyder, Z. (Director). (2006). *300* [Film]. Warner Bros.

Stallone, S. (Director). (2010). *The Expendables* [Film]. Millennium Films.

Tamahori, L. (Director). (2002). *Die Another Day* [Film]. Metro-Goldwyn-Mayer.

Tarantino, Q. (Director). (2003). *Kill Bill, Vol. 1* [Film]. Miramax.

Taurog, N. (Director). (1961). *Blue Hawaii* [Film]. Hal Wallis Productions.

Taylor, T. (Director). (2011). *The Help* [Film]. DreamWorks.

Thurber, R. M. (Director). (2018). *Skyscraper* [Film]. Legendary PIctures.

Tiernan, G., & Vernon, C. (Directors). (2016). *Sausage Party* [Film]. Annapurna Pictures.

Ting, E. (Director). (2015a). *Already Tomorrow in Hong Kong* [Film]. Unbound Feet Productions.

Ting, E. (Director). (2015b). *Already Tomorrow in Hong Kong* [Film; Audio commentary track with Director/Writer Emily Ting on DVD]. Unbound Feet Productions.

Ting, E. (Director). (2015c). *Already Tomorrow in Hong Kong* [Film; *Behind the Scenes* featurette on DVD]. Unbound Feet Productions.

Tykwer, T. (Director). (2012). *Cloud Atlas* [Film]. Cloud Atlas Productions.

Verbinski, G. (Director). (2013). *The Lone Ranger* [Film]. Blind Wink Productions.

Verbinski, G. (Director). (2002). *The Ring* [Film]. Dreamworks Pictures.

Wachowski, L., & Wachowski, L. (Directors). (2008). *Speed Racer* [Film]. Village Roadshow Pictures.

Wang, L. (Director). (2019). *The Farewell* [Film]. Big Beach Films.

Wang, W. (Director). (1993). *The Joy Luck Club* [Film]. Hollywood Pictures.

Wingard, A. (Director). (2017). *Death Note* [Film]. Netflix.

Wong, J. (Director). (2009). *Dragonball Evolution* [Film]. Twentieth Century Fox.

Yim, H. (Director). (2001). *Pavilion of Women* [Film]. Beijing Film Studio.

Zhang, Y. (Director). (2004). *House of Flying Daggers* [Film]. Beijing New Picture Film Co.

Zhang, Y. (Director). (2011). *The Flowers of War* [Film]. Beijing New Picture Film Co.

Zhang, Y. (Director). (2016). *The Great Wall* [Film]. Legendary East.

Zwick, E. (Director). (2013). *The Last Samurai* [Film]. Warner Bros.

Index

About the Author

DAVID C. OH is an associate professor of communication arts at Ramapo College of New Jersey. He is the author of *Diasporic Identifications: Second-Generation Korean Americans and Transnational Media.*